Dedication

Sari March Terry

In Loving Memory

“ The Real El Dorado Is Still Further On”

From Pecks’ 1837 *New Guide To The West*

Notes on the Second Edition

The response to *Colorful Men and Women of the Motherlode* was overwhelming. The book had been on the market less than a year when it sold out. Hence the second edition. My thanks to all my readers for their support.

A sequel will follow in 2005 or early 2006 *More Colorful Men and Women of the Motherlode.*

Table of Contents

Dedication iii
List of Illustrations viii
Acknowledgments xi
Introduction xix
Dr. Albert Michelson, *First American winner of the Nobel Prize in Physics, 1907, Murphys* 1
Glen Bell, *Taco Bell Founder, Westside and Cherry Valley Railroad Historic Theme Park, Tuolumne* 25
Otheto Weston, *Artist, preservationist, Columbia* 45
Melvin Belli, *Attorney, Sonora* 59
Clarence Ayers, *Architect, Sonora* 71
Annie Kline Rikert, *Founder, The Stockton Tuolumne Railroad, Jamestown* 85
John Studebaker, *Automobile manufacturer, Placerville* 105
Michel Goldwater and Barry Goldwater, *Store Owner, Sonora* 119
William Murphy, *Inventor of the Murphy Bed, Columbia* 137
Sonora's Cleopatra, *Siren, Sonora* 149
Albert Francisco, *Founder of the Union Democrat, Sonora* 155
Captain William Nevills, *Owner of the Rawhide Mine, Hotel builder. Jamestown, Sonora* 171
Hollywood in Tuolumne County, *Sonora* 193
John Curtin, *Senator, Sonora* 209
Dave Brubeck, *Musician, Ione* 221
Business Directory 231
Author's Biography 255

List of Illustrations

Cover Illustration:
Wendell Dowling

Sonora of the 1890's xviii
Courtesy of Tuolumne County Museum
Artist, Archie T. Newsom

Dr. Albert Michelson xxii
Wendell Dowling

Glen Bell 24
Wendell Dowling
Logo Westside Cherry Valley Railroad

Otheto Weston 44
Wendell Dowling

Melvin Belli and Butch Cameron 58
Wendell Dowling

Clarence Ayers and the Red House 70
Wendell Dowling

Annie Kline Rikert 84
Wendell Dowling
The Women's Railroad, Stockton Evening Mail

Mrs. Rikert Plans the Railroad (woodcut) 97
Ralph Yardley

John Studebaker 104
Wendell Dowling

Illustrations, (Cont.)

Studebaker Wagons 109
Wendell Dowling

Barry Goldwater..118
Wendell Dowling

Michel Goldwater 121
Wendell Dowling

William Murphy and Gladys Murphy 136
Wendell Dowling

Sonora's Cleopatra..148
Wendell Dowling

Albert Francisco..154
Wendell Dowling

Captain William Nevills and Delia Nevills 170
Wendell Dowling

The Victoria Inn..176
Painting by Chris Holman

The Jamestown Hotel (photo) 181

Hollywood in Tuolumne County 192
Wendell Dowling

John Curtin..208
Wendell Dowling

Gold Springs, 1850 211
Bruce Bomberger

Dave Brubeck.. 220
Wendell Dowling

Acknowledgments

People invariably ask me where I find my information. Generally, it's just plain simple research. But there are some unusual twists and turns. When one resides in a small town, one does not rely totally on the Internet. Research is carried on at the Bancroft Library in Berkeley, the California State Library in Sacramento and the local library. But a great deal of the research comes from people who have lived in the area a very long time.

Foremost, I want to thank the Tuolumne County Library on Greenley Road in Sonora. They have "put up" with me and my request for material for years. Joan Rutty laughingly told me one day, "with you around Jan, I don't have to worry about job security." Kathy Meyer and Verna Cabral-King handled most of my inter-library loan request and often heaved an exhaustive sigh of despair when they saw me walking through the front door. Keith Behymer has the patience of Job and always took the time to answer my questions. They are an unusual team and the city of Sonora is lucky indeed to have them.

Secondly, my heartfelt thanks to the Tuolumne County Museum and Annex on Bradford Avenue. On Tuesday morning, the Annex is open to the general public and researchers turn up at their doorstep come nine A.M. where Richard Camarena, Museum Supervisor, is always on hand to help. My thanks also to Dr. Pat Rhodes, Leonard Ruff, Mary Farrington and Sharon Marovich, for the dozens of requests made and filled in their very capable hands.

My gratitude goes out to the Tuolumne County Genealogical Society. They hold forth in the museum as well as the historical society on Tuesday, Thursday and Saturday. They are a remarkable group of men and women who really know how to document, record, index and keep excellent, up-to-date files. They are first rate sleuths and attack questions with the persistence of a Sherlock Holmes. Special thanks to Anne Williams and Nell Holloway.

My thanks also to Carlo De Ferrari, who seems to know everyone and everything that ever happened in Tuolumne County. His family has been in the area since the 1850's and Carlo was the county clerk-auditor controller from 1947 to 1978, becoming head of the Department in 1968. He has filled the post of County Historian since 1974. If there is something he does not know, he certainly knows the best path to procure the necessary information. My thanks also to Lyle Scott, historian and local barber. How many times I took my father into the Mother Lode Barber for a haircut, when what I really wanted was information. And finally, my indebtedness to my talented and patient illustrator, Wendell Dowling. He insisted on seeing the material I had written in order to get an idea of the character he asked to illustrate. His work, in my opinion, is brilliant.

For my research on Dr. Michelson, I wish to extend a warm thank you to the Michelson School in Murphys. I spent a delightful morning viewing an excellent film on Dr. Michelson made by Paul Preuss. They also possessed other material on Dr. Michelson which they shared with me. Judith Marvin was invaluable for her help with questions regarding the Michelson Home and Albert's early schooling in Murphys. To Lowell High School in San Francisco and their Alumni Association, my thanks. I am grateful to Mr. Selby Collins at the San Francisco Public Library and his help in locating information for me on Dr. Michelson's early schooling. To the U.S. Naval Academy at Annapolis, Maryland, and James Cheeves who sent me Michelson's academic record. My appreciation to Earl Schmidt and Don Gault who answered so many of my questions regarding Michelson's early career. I also extend a warm thanks to the Chicago Historical Society and Don McAlister at the Naval Air

Weapons Center at China Lake, California.

For my research on Glen Bell, I want to extend my appreciation to Debra Baldwin, whose authorized biography on Glen Bell: *Taco Titan: The Glen Bell Story*, was an invaluable source of information on Bell's formative years. To Mr. and Mrs.Grant, I extend many thanks for the hours I spend in their home pouring over material on the Westside project. Mr. Grant was the project's chief design planner. Through his eyes, I was able to get a clearer idea of the overall plan and the loyalty the staff felt to Mr. Bell. To Lyle Scott for his input on Westside and to Fred Boutin, horticulturist on Westside from whom I was able to glean an appreciation for the many hours of work needed to enhance the beauty of the site. An additional thanks to George Kirby, landscape supervisor on Westside for his recollections. I am very grateful to Chris Holman who did restoration work and painting at Westside. She took me on a long walk one day along the old Turnback Creek Railroad which ran from Tuolumne to Yosemite and deposited customers at the beautiful Turnback Inn.

As the course of my work continued on Bell, I contacted a host of people referred to me by numerous friends and acquaintances. Among those were George Speaker of Tuolumne and Lenore Rutherford of the *Union Democrat* who wrote several articles on the Westside project. I benefited from Sharon Marovich's memories, as well as Stephanie Seuss of the Tuolumne County Planning Department and James Wood, of the Parks and Recreation Department who accompanied me to the site. Frank Cimino, Sam and Betty Gordon, Mary Etta Segerstrom and Joan Gorsuch gave me their points of view. And finally to railroad buffs everywhere for their love and appreciation of railroading.

For Otheto, there was Margaret Calderero who shared many of her recollections about Otheto and allowed me to view her very extensive collection of Otheto's paintings. My sincere appreciation to Sharon Grout and Columbia State Park for compiling such excellent resources on Otheto. I owe a debt of thanks to Susan Dunsmire and the Monterey Museum Association who gave me a good deal of insight into Evelyn McCormick, Otheto's birth mother. To my sister, Marion Cameron, for remembering her stories about Otheto when she visited her pet store. Otheto loved poodles and in exchange, my sister received two of Otheto's paintings, becoming in effect an art patron. My gratitude to Louise Young Ruiz, who shared her experiences of growing up in Columbia with Otheto's boys. My thanks to Carlo De Ferrari for information on the Burns family in Groveland, as well as to Mary Laveroni for her input. My thanks to Steve Parker at the Monterey public library and to the many people who appreciated Otheto and loved her work.

For Melvin Belli, I extend warm appreciation to Irving Symons, who has an incredible memory and spent many hours going over his recollections of Melvin as a young boy. To my sister, Marion Cameron, who shared her memories of the trial, Cameron vs. California State Division of Forestry. My enormous gratitude to Robert Cameron for his recollections of his brother, Butch. To the staff at Sonora High School who recalled their personal stories of Butch and to Judy Isaman, whose sister graduated the same year as Butch Cameron. And finally to the dozens of people along the way that gave me bits and pieces of Belli's colorful personality, too colorful oftentimes to print.

Clarence Ayers was a work of love and dedication. On one of my early visits to Sonora, I was drawn to the beautiful Red House next to the Red Church at the foot of North Washington Street. Research on Mr. Ayers proved difficult. I was confronted with the daunting task of looking in two separate research areas: Mining and Architecture. Here, the Genealogical Society, and specifically Nell Holloway, helped tremendously. From there, the search continued for months, leading to a first prize in the Writer's Award bestowed by the Tuolumne County Historical Society in 1994. Shortly thereafter, I discovered James Ludham, Mr. Ayers grandson. He provided me with lots of personal memorabilia.

Annie Kline Rikert proved to be a total surprise. Lyle Scott first mentioned her name to me. He put me on the right path and from there, research was somewhat routine. My first calls included Shirley Burman, railroad enthusiast, who put me in touch with Kyle Wyatt, whose thesis: Railroads in Tuolumne County, 1897-1917, provided excellent information on railroads in the Mother Lode. From there, I followed the trail to the Mississippi Department of Archives and History. Here, Gordon Cotton gave me invaluable information about Annie's early childhood and her Civil War exploits. When her plans to build a railroad went awry in Jamestown, the trail went cold. But the Tuolumne County History Center and Annex came to my rescue. I pursued their old newspaper files and found an item about Annie in Redding California. The Mt. Shasta Historical Society and Joe Haner took over from there and I was able to piece together her whereabouts after she left Tuolumne.

For John Studebaker, the Placerville Historical Society and Museum opened their files to me. My gratitude also to George Speaker of Tuolumne and to Fred Fox, who have written extensively on the Studebaker family.

The first time I heard the Goldwater name was as a very small child visiting relatives in Phoenix, Arizona. My aunt worked at the Goldwater store as did many residents in communities around Flagstaff. What a surprise to learn years later that the Goldwater family got their start right here in Sonora. Carlo De Ferrari shared his information on Goldwater's visits to Sonora. My sincere appreciation to the Arizona Historical Society Foundation and Mr. James Allen for sharing their extensive archival information with me. And Last, my appreciation to the Phoenix Public Library and the Phoenix Historical Society.

For Murphy, the Tuolumne County Genealogical Society had extensive files on the Luddy and Murphy families. Kay Murphy (wife of William Murphy's son) shared personal letters with me as well as generously donating many excellent photos. To Mary Robles, daughter of Mary Ellen Murphy, brother of William Murphy, I am grateful for the many invaluable letters she sent me. I am equally grateful to Ann Rooney, on the Luddy side of the family and finally to Bill Murphy, grandson of William Murphy who currently heads the Murphy Bed Company.

Albert Francisco, founder of the *Union Democrat*, turned out to be a gold mine. I happened to browse through Malcolm Rohrbough's recently published book: *Days of Gold*, 1998, when Albert's name jumped off the page. Without that source, I would not have known that twenty-six unpublished letters of Francisco's resided at the Huntington Library in San Marino, California. There, I discovered Peter Blodgett, curator of Western Historical Manuscripts at the Huntington, who sent me copies of Francisco's letters. I am grateful to St. Patrick's Church in Sonora for keeping archival records, and finally to Eleanor Davis, great-great granddaughter of Calvin Francisco, whose years of painstaking research on her family was so generously shared with me.

The Sonora Inn is a large and imposing landmark in Sonora. In the past, the Inn, now Days Inn, provided customers with menus that included a short history of the Inn and the man who built it, Captain William Nevills. Alas, that information is no longer readily available. Too bad. Mr. Nevills warrants our admiration for providing such a lasting memorial to the community of Sonora. I extend my gratitude to the Sacramento Public Library for their help in sending me the dozens of newspaper references from which I pieced together Nevills colorful years in the Mother Lode. To the Bureau of Mines in San Francisco and Gaylord Staveley, who married Nevills' great-granddaughter, my thanks.

A vital industry in the Mother Lode is film-making. How fortunate to be able to discuss this early era with one of the men responsible for shaping it, Irving Symons. It is hard to believe he is in his nineties. His memory is incredible and Irving is always accessible to historians like myself who need first-hand information on Sonora's past. I certainly appreciate the time he spent with me retrieving memories of early Sonora's contribution to film. I am also grateful to Larry Jensen of the Visitors' Bureau, who first told me about the 1947 De Soto and filled me in on the many films made here. He in turn led me to Jim Opie, Sr. and the story of the famous car. To my neighbor, Leonard Ruoff, my appreciation for his memories of Sonora during the early Hollywood years. And my thanks to the Tuolumne County Visitors' Bureau, who organize so many activities each year which welcome filmdom to the Mother Lode.

For information on John Curtin, I located Allan Masri's excellent paper on John Curtin located at the Tuolumne County Historical Society. My thanks to the Sacramento Public library and Bancroft Library as well.

Dave Brubeck. One only has to listen to his classic, *Take Five*, to be overwhelmed with appreciation for the music he wrote and continues to perform. A visit to his alma mater, The University of The Pacific, helped my research enormously. Dr. Donald Walker is in charge of the Brubeck archives on campus and oversees the newly established Brubeck Foundation. A visit to Mr. Brubeck's home town, Ione, put me in touch with many of his friends who shed information on his early years there.

My thanks to my editors: Sari Terry, Beth Hall, Carlo De Ferrari, Sharon Marovich, Alan Haack, and Carol Giordano, Graphics For Business. To Ruth Howard, and Foothill Business Cards for hundreds of hours of thoughtful solutions to xeroxing needs.

And last, I wish to thank all my business advertisers. This book would not be possble without their support.

Sonora of the 1890's
Washington Street Painting
by Archie T. Newsom
Courtesy Tuolumne County Historical Society

Introduction

Why does one take the enormous amount of time necessary to set pen to paper to write a book? Passion has something to do with it, a kind of historical obsession with sharing the spoils of discovery. For me, it was a simple request to put together a biographical file at the local museum.

I had not been in Sonora very long before my historic antenna led me to the Tuolumne County Historical Museum on Bradford Street. Not long after, I was working there on Fridays in the former 1866 jail turned museum. Fridays became very special for me. I enjoyed talking to historians, authors, visitors from all over the world and the locals who dropped by to share their own personal histories and stories with me.

One day, Dr. Pat Rhodes, one of the directors of the museum, came in with a huge pile of newspaper clippings. She explained that these were to be put into a new biographical file for researchers. Henceforth, my Fridays, for some time to come, were spent categorizing the names of men and women who found their way to the Mother Lode beginning at the dawn of the Gold Rush to the present. Some came west to find their bonanza in the earth; others came to begin businesses that would create and mold a new land that now stretched from the East Coast to the Pacific.

What surprised me most about these forgers of dreams, was how many were "spawned" right here. Perhaps that shouldn't have come as any great surprise. In 1848-49, when the world rushed into California, a great many outstanding men found their way to the Southern and Northern mines. If you glance at the guest's book at the old Murphys Hotel for example, you run across a microcosm of the great and the powerful. There was Mark Twain of course, Victor Hugo, Presidents Ulysses S. Grant, Teddy Roosevelt and many more. What I found in addition to these, however, were people who came here with nothing more than the clothes on their backs and subsequently made significant contributions to the world at large. There was John Studebaker, Michel and Sarah Goldwater, (Barry Goldwater's grandparents) Dr. Albert Michelson, Melvin Belli, Dave Brubeck and William Murphy. These men were known in their respective fields throughout the world, but few people were aware of their early years in the Mother Lode.

Then, there were the men and women who made enormous contributions locally, but were not well known outside the area. There was Clarence Ayers, architect and miner; Albert Francisco, founder of the *Union Democrat* newspaper; Captain William Nevills, owner of the Rawhide Mine and builder of the Sonora Inn; Otheto Weston, artist and preservationist; and Annie Kline Rikert, builder of a railroad.

Closer to the present era was Glen Bell, founder of Taco Bell. The chain which he began is very well known throughout the United States, but not so well known was his interest in historic theme parks and the one he founded in Tuolumne: Westside. There was John Curtin, a hometown boy who became a Senator and unsuccessful candidate for Governor. Perhaps most unique was the 1947 De Soto automobile, transportation for Hollywood celebrities.The car came to symbolize Sonora's early entry into an important industry which continues today. Almost anyone associated with films in Tuolumne County remembers the car and with it, an entourage of endearing stories.

Then of course, there were the colorful tales that inevitably found their way into the columns of the local papers. They portray as nothing else can, the personality of the age, the sensibility that characterized that era and the differences that make that time so memorable.

In looking back at the unabashed naïve 19th century, we

tend to romanticize the past. We have, perhaps, lost that supreme sense of adventure and surprise at encountering for the first time something totally new and different. Perhaps it is because we consign the past to oblivion, thus creating a withering of historical memory where man's very fate may lie.

It does the heart good to return occasionally to that less hurried past and see through the heart and soul of these men and women the kind of world they were creating for us. How well they fared can be judged by the reader.

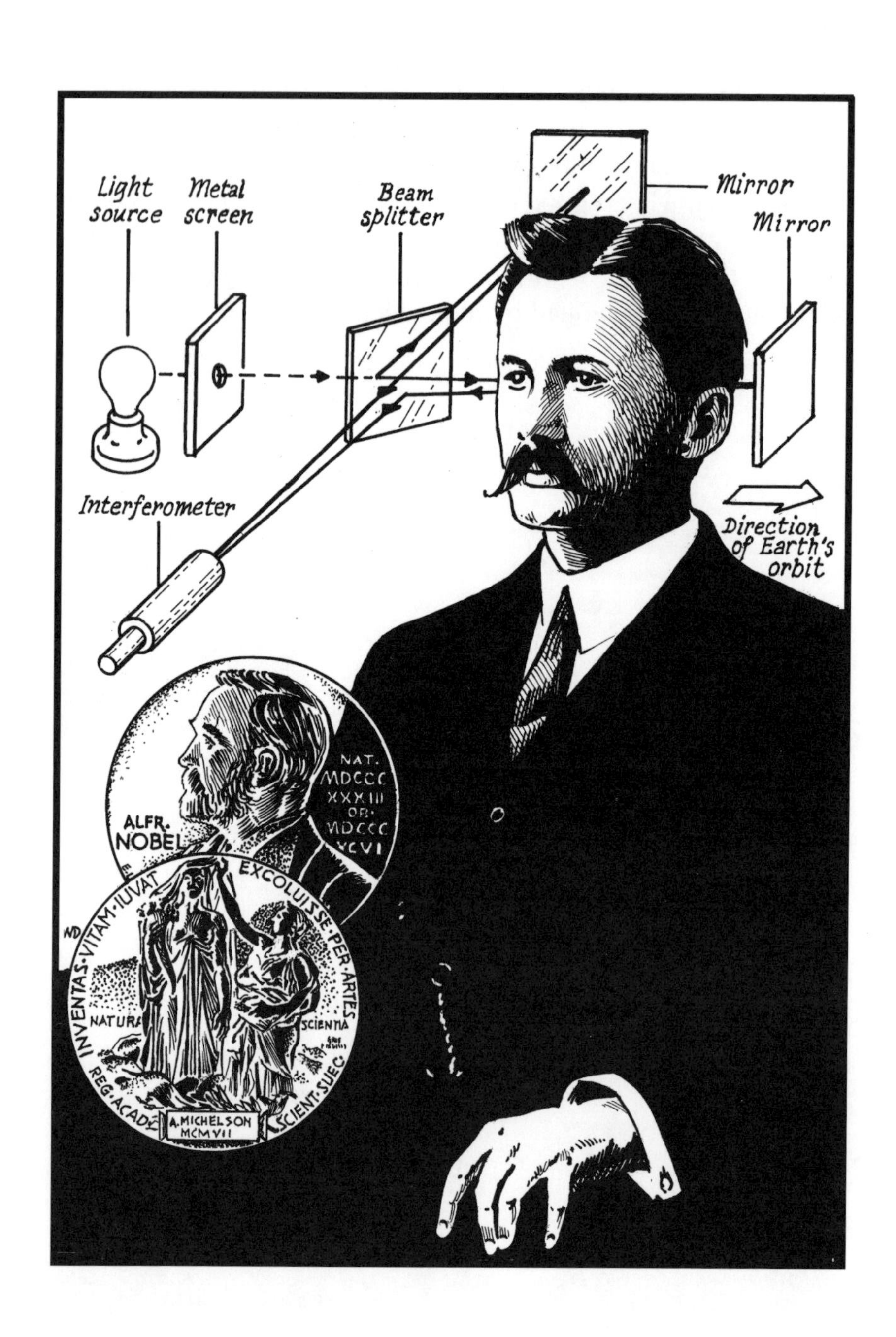

Light source
Metal screen
Beam splitter
Mirror
Mirror
Interferometer
Direction of Earth's orbit
NAT. MDCCC XXXIII OB. MDCCC XCVI
ALFR. NOBEL
INVENTAS·VITAM·IUVAT EXCOLUISSE·PER·ARTES
NATURA
SCIENTIA
REG·ACADE SCIENT·SUEC
A. MICHELSON MCMVII

Dr. Albert Michelson

Every astronaut knows his name. Any student of physics is familiar with his work. A crater on the moon is named after him.[1] A ship bears his name.[2] It has been said that if interplanetary communication were to occur it would be by means of his discovery of the length of light waves.[3] Albert Einstein said of him, "It was you who led the physicists into new paths and through your marvelous experimental work, paved the way for the development of the Theory of Relativity."[4] He was America's first winner of the Nobel Prize for physics in 1907, but few people in the Mother Lode realize that Dr. Albert Michelson was raised in Murphys, California.[5]

His parents, Rosalie Przylubska and Samuel Michelson were born in Poland. They met at a wedding party.[6] Her father was a noted physician. Samuel's father came from a Jewish family who worked in the dry goods business. Albert was born on December 19, 1852, in Strelno, what was then Prussia, near the Polish frontier.[7] The future scientist came into the world in a period of enormous upheaval. The political turmoil caused by the revolution of 1848, with curfews and ghettos for the Jews, led the growing family to make a profound decision to immigrate to America.[8]

After traveling across Europe, the Michelsons then went by steamer, probably from Hamburg, and landed in New York. The steerage lasted three long weeks.[9] Once in New York they went to the home of Rosalie's relatives, the Friedenburgs. There they first heard the news about the California Gold Rush. Samuel's sister and brother-in-law, Belle and Oscar Meyer, had been successful at "Murphy's Camp" in Calaveras County.[10] The stories of gold must have held out an enormous sense of hope for the new arrivals in a country where their children would be raised with opportunities unheard of in Europe.[11]

The Michelsons traveled from New York to Panama. Booking passage on a small ship to Porto Bello on the Isthmus, the family soon began to understand why the area had a reputation as the "grave of the Europeans." There were outbreaks of brain fever, cholera, malaria, and small pox. There were no police, no regulations of any kind, and no sanitation. Drinking water was extremely expensive. Prostitution, gambling and alcohol consumption were endemic. After an unpleasant sea journey of sixty days, the family finally arrived in the port of San Francisco. Although Albert was only three, he remembered it for the rest of his life.[12] The Michelsons were not gold seekers, and in any case, by the summer of 1856, the mania of gold fever had subsided. They remained in San Francisco a short time before embarking for the Sierras. Samuel secured supplies and boarded a stage for the slow and uncomfortable trek to Murphys Camp.

The little community where young Albert would spend his formative years was named after the Murphy Brothers, John and Daniel. They had come into the valley in the late summer of 1848. Here, they set up a trading post. When they left in December of that year, they had more gold than any other miners on the Pacific Coast, estimated at a staggering two million dollars! The placer claims at Murphys were reputed to be the richest of any in Calaveras County.[13]

One invariably wonders what conditions in young Albert's life contributed to the making of the future scientist. Murphys, like other Gold Rush communities, was still in the midst of change. Placer mining had waned, but hope held out its ineffable appeal to newcomers. Gold Rush communities were exceedingly busy, with an influx of new people from all over the world. There was Snowshoe Thompson, the mailman who carried letters across the Sierras in winter for twenty years.[14] He often visited Murphys. There was also a musician, who reputedly introduced Albert to the violin.[15] Across the street from the Michelson home lived a blacksmith and a few streets away, an apothecary, Dr. William Jones. Bee Matteson operated the first telegraph and her father, T.J. Matteson was a surveyor who laid out the route of the canal from the Stanislaus River. He also operated the stagecoach from Murphys to Angels.[16] The Sperry and Perry Hotel was next to the Michelson home and Samuel's business was located in a dry goods store immediately west of the present Murphy Hotel.[17]

According to family sources, Albert's mother, Rosalie was not well liked by the women in the area. She was called "proud."[18] Rosalie wanted her son to do well in school and she placed a high priority on learning. He did show an unusual proficiency in math, which was evidenced early.[19] She insisted he learn the violin, a skill he retained throughout his life. While the small community would not have been as rich culturally as communities in Europe, Rosalie saw to it that the children were not deprived of musical and artistic training.

When the Michelsons arrived in the small town, they brought a rare commodity with them—their children. The first residents of the camp were unattached miners. By 1852, there were wives and children, but no schools for them to attend. It is estimated that there were only twenty public schools in the entire state and none in Calaveras County.[20] However, several private schools were begun. There was "Pine Grove College," so nicknamed since it was "all the schooling you could get in Murphys and say you had been to college."[21] By 1855, there were several private schools. A Sister Louise operated a Catholic school on Scott Street. A Miss Powers ran a school in a private home. A Mr. Jaquity conducted a school in the first school house located west of the present Masonic Temple.[22]

According to Michelson's daughter, Dorothy Livingston, Albert's first grade teacher was Mary Anne Conway, a fourteen year-old Irish girl who came to Murphys via the Horn. She spoke Spanish as well as English.[23] The standard fare was taught: reading, writing and arithmetic. Young Albert collected colored ores from the men who had dug them out of the ground, but mining did not appeal to him. The colored minerals might have sparked an interest in art, however. Michelson would become an accomplished painter and throughout his life he continued to reach for his brushes.[24]

Today, a drive along Main Street in Murphys will take you to a house designated by E. Campus Vitus as the Michelson home. However, according to historian Judith Marvin, the original Michelson home was built in the early 1850's and was located where the Red Bud Bed and Breakfast Inn now stands.[25]

By the 1860's, young Albert would most certainly have been caught up in the news of the impending war. In 1862, 300 men passed through town and many miners left their claims to join the Union Army. Upon Lincoln's assassination, the family was so distraught that they bestowed the name Abraham, as a middle name, upon Albert.[26]

Mining around Murphys had begun to decline in the 1860's. Just about the time that silver was discovered in the Comstock Lode, the Michelsons made yet another important decision. They decided to move to Nevada to take advantage of the business there but Albert did not move with them. His education came first. He was thirteen, and another roaring mining camp with limited educational opportunities was not what the family planned for Albert's future. It was decided instead that he should remain with his cousins, the Meyers family, in San Francisco. There, he would attend Lincoln Grammar School.[27] In 1866, Albert then transferred to the well-regarded Boy's High School, today's Lowell High School.

Established in 1856, the school was exceptional, both in the classes it offered and in its philosophy. Begun as the Union Grammar School, students were admitted after passing a Board of Education examination. On August 25, 1856, the school opened in rented quarters on Powell Street. In 1860, another school was built in the same location near today's Fairmont

Hotel Tower. By this time, the name of the school had been changed to San Francisco High School. The graduates consisted of seven boys and four girls, the first beneficiaries of a public high school education in California. Within just ten years, it was apparent that the fledgling high school was producing outstanding graduates who went on to earn advanced degrees and pioneer outstanding careers. With the coming of the Civil War, the name of the school was changed to The Boy's High School. This was done because parents objected to exposing their young daughters to rude and disorderly boys. The study of Latin and Greek, higher mathematics, mineralogy and assaying was assigned to Boys High School and excluded from Girl's High School.[28] The San Francisco Bulletin noted the school as being "the crown of the public school system in our city."[29] This was the school were Albert would receive his basic education.

In addition to Latin and Greek, Albert learned chemistry, physics, French and German. He lived at the home of the school principal, Theodore Bradley. Bradley must have recognized the young student's unusual ability, because he placed Albert in charge of the school's scientific equipment and paid him three dollars a month to keep it in good repair.

In 1868, Albert graduated. By this time, it was obvious that Albert was deeply interested in science. But where to go from there? The opening of the University of California at Berkeley was still a year away. There were other colleges in California, but they were not noted for their science classes. Congress had just passed the Morrill Land Grant Act of 1862, which established many excellent colleges, but these were back east and were expensive. Colleges in the United States were on the brink of offering more scientific classes, but they tended to concentrate on philosophy and the arts. Classical learning was paramount. Science was still new. Yale had created the Sheffield Scientific School in 1854 by merging the schools of engineering and applied chemistry. Their report was issued in 1867-8 just as Albert was searching for a school. The Massachusetts Institute of Technology at Boston offered good science classes as did

Brown and Michigan University, but they were too far away.

In the meantime, Albert left California to be with his family in Nevada. The center of prospecting had shifted to Virginia City where, in 1859, silver had been found. The Michelsons had moved to Carson City which had a population of 30,000. Their home was located at 24 South "C" street, where Samuel Michelson kept a store on the first floor.[30]

One day, his parents were reading the local newspaper, the *Territorial Enterprise* of April 10, 1869. The article that caught their eye was a letter from the Honorable Thomas Fitch, Nevada's representative in Congress. The United States Naval Academy had just made available two new openings from the State of Nevada for boys between the ages of fourteen and eighteen.[31]

The Academy had been established twenty-four years earlier by scientist and oceanographer, Lt. Maury, U.S.N. Michelson's parents were attracted by the fact that the academy offered a first-rate education in the natural sciences, physics and chemistry and also provided traveling expenses. In addition, cadets received pay of $500 a year. Immediately, the family began planning.

On June 10,1869, Albert and nine other young men took the written examination for the Academy in the Virginia City Courthouse. However, in spite of tying for first place and with over 100 letters and telegrams on behalf of Albert, the coveted appointment went to fifteen year-old James Blakely. Sentiment may have been the reason. Blakely was the son of a poor Civil War veteran who had lost his right arm.[32]

For most applicants, being rejected by so prestigious a school would have meant the end of the matter, but not for Albert. Coming from a family where discouragement was often a centuries-old way of life, the final word on the part of the United States Government was not enough to make Albert change course. He wrote to his Congressman, Thomas Fitch. He wrote to the newly elected President, Ulysses S. Grant. He had decided to do the impossible—change the Government's decision.

Traveling first by carriage, then horseback, on foot and by

rail, a month before the Central Pacific and the Union Pacific were joined in Utah, Albert went to Washington D.C. to speak with none other than President Grant. With him were hundreds of letters of recommendation. With far less restrictions than today, Albert was able to wait for the President as he took his dog for an outing on the White House lawn. Albert approached the President and explained, "I would make you proud of me if I get the appointment."[33]

Like Albert, Grant had chosen a military academy, West Point, to pursue his schooling because there were few alternative avenues in education open to him. He had been stationed in California in 1853, so he shared many similar experiences from the Mother Lode. His three brothers-in-law, George, John and Lewis Dent had come into possession of Knights Ferry along the Stanislaus River. Ulysses had visited them and even erected a bridge across the river.[34] But Grant's hands were tied, as he tried to explain to Albert. He could only fill ten appointments legally and they had all been filled.

Then, a strange turn of events occurred. In a prophetic and unique twist of historic fate, Senator Fitch wrote the President an unusual letter.

Had I felt at liberty to be governed by considerations of political expediency, I should have selected him. His father is a prominent and influential member of Virginia City and a member of the Israelite persuasion, who, by his example and influence has largely contributed to the success of our cause and induced many of his co-religionists to do the same. These people are a powerful element in our politics. The boy is uncommonly bright and studious and is a pet among them and I do most steadfastly believe that his appointment at your hand would do more to fasten these people to the Republican cause than anything else that could be done.[35]

Grant may have known military tactics, but he was about to learn the nuances of political strategy as well. He turned Albert over to a naval aide who sent the boy to Annapolis to see Captain Napoleon, Commandant of Midshipmen.[36] Albert waited three days in Maryland. Discouraged, he thought of going back to Washington to make yet another plea to President Grant. Then a messenger arrived with a letter. Another opening at the Academy had been created, and Albert would receive an unheard of eleventh appointment!

Apparently, Grant had been persuaded by Vice Admiral David Porter, superintendent of the Academy, to bend the rules in this case. Many years later, Michelson loved to point out that his career as a scientist stemmed from "an illegal act."[37]

On June 28,1869, at the request of the Secretary of the Navy, sixteen year-old Albert Michelson presented himself to the medical board. A few days later, he filed an affidavit stating his loyalty and willingness to serve in the United States Navy for eight years.[38]

Albert graduated with his class on May 31, 1873. Out of a class that numbered ninety-two, only twenty-nine completed the training to midshipmen.[39]

His record during the four years was as follows: As a freshman, he stood seventh in a class of eighty-seven and took: fencing, mathematics, grammar, geography, history, French and drawing. In his sophomore year, he stood sixth out of forty-five. In his third year he stood sixth out of thirty-four students and took: astronomy, electricity, dynamics, French and drawing. In his senior year he graduated ninth out of twenty-nine students. He earned a first in optics and acoustics and was twenty-fifth in seamanship. He had completed thirteen months of sea duty.[40] The superintendent of the academy told him, "If you would give less attention to those scientific things and more to your naval gunnery, there might come a time when you would know enough to be of some use to your country."[41]

An incident occurred at the Academy which displayed clearly where Michelson's early genius lay. He was asked, during a classroom experiment, to go to the blackboard and outline the steps he had taken to resolve a difficult problem in optics, a field in which he showed a clear talent and which would ultimately lead to his promising scientific work. The problem was not difficult, but as he began to illustrate his own unique and original method for solving it, the instructor noted that he did not follow the outline in the text. Albert's solution was right, but his method for solving it was not according to procedure. The instructor was aghast. Cheating, he told Albert, would not be tolerated. Michelson was ordered to appear before a board of officers and professors. When the day came, Michelson tried to explain how he had arrived at his answer. One of the professors decided to assign him a new problem, and, again, Michelson solved the problem differently than the textbook indicated. Apparently, he convinced the board, because they rendered a verdict of not guilty and all charges were dismissed.[42]

Michelson had earned a much needed vacation. Before returning to the Academy to fulfill the requirement of going to sea for two years, he took a furlough to visit his family in Nevada. Everyone was very proud of the young cadet. Insisting that he put on his spectacular blue dress uniform, Miriam, his sister, wanted to show off her brother. They decided to walk to town for a pail of ice cream. The story goes, that as he stepped from the door, a group of ruffians appeared, offended at the bright blue uniform and shiny sword. Teasing turned into taunts, and Michelson, with as much dignity as he could muster and with proper military decorum, handed his long sword to his sister. He then proceeded to fight the hoodlums off with the ice cream pail. The town "toughs" left, but Michelson's beautiful dress uniform was ruined.[43]

He served his prescribed two years on board several ships and was perhaps, entertaining doubts about his future in the navy. The navy, however, had no doubts about Michelson's ability in physics, and they asked him to become a professor at the Academy in physics and chemistry.[44] Michelson was just twenty-three years old. He was asked to come into the

Commander's office for a briefing on the physics course, and it was suggested that he begin with a demonstration of the experiment on the velocity of light made with a rotating mirror, an experiment originated by French physicist Leon Foucault. Michelson felt he did not know enough about that particular subject so he went to the library and "boned up."

What Michelson learned was that the Greeks had been the first to ask, what is light? Aristotle believed that an object was seen because it emitted light. Ptolemy stated that rays of light emanated from the eye and extended to the object. An Arabian scientist, Alhazen, was the first physicist to give a description of the human eye and support Aristotle's view.[45]

In all of these theories, light was assumed to be instantaneous. In the history of the theory of light, however, there were two ideas about its nature which were advanced. One proposed that light was pictured as a wave motion, and the other, as a flight of fast moving particles. It was not until 1638, that anyone imagined that light might have a finite speed. That was the year Galileo attempted to measure the speed of light. By placing two lanterns on hilltops less than a mile apart, he stated that the naked eye was capable of seeing it.[46] Exact measurements would have to wait until scientific accuracy became more sophisticated.

In 1670, Claus Romer, a Dutch astronomer, discovered that light traveled at a definite speed. He was the first to estimate the speed at 138,000 miles per second.[47] James Bradley verified Romer's theory. He estimated that light reached the earth from the sun in eight minutes thirteen seconds. All of these attempts to measure the speed of light were based on astronomical observations.[48]

Aside from Galileo, only three men before Michelson had tried to find the speed of light by using terrestrial measurement: Armand Hippolyte I. Fizeau in 1849, Leon Foucault and Marie Alfred Cornu in 1874. Of the three, Leon Foucault found the most accurate value for the absolute velocity of light: 185,299 miles per second.[49]

With this inspiration, in 1877, Michelson believed that a modification of Foucault's finding was possible. He replaced the concave mirror with a plane mirror and, by altering the lens position and lengthening the path of light to 500 feet, the return of the beam would be deflected at a wider angle. In one swift stroke, Michelson had made a beautiful simplification.

Michelson had found his life's work. But he knew that he must continue experimenting. He was able to assemble most of the equipment he needed from pieces available at the Naval Academy. The apparatus for this experiment was set up along the sea wall of the Academy at Annapolis.[50] By 1878, he was ready to make a preliminary test. The change Michelson initiated made possible the use of a much greater distance between mirrors without too great a loss of light intensity. As a result, Michelson achieved an accuracy 200 times that obtained by Foucault. He was about to make scientific history.

By late spring, Michelson's new measurements had arrived at the figure of 186,508 miles per second for the speed of light.[51] By knowing the speed of the rotating mirror, the distance traveled by the light beam and the amount of deflection of the returning beam, he could use simple mathematics to calculate the speed of light.

What was unique is that for under $10, Michelson accomplished what another scientist, Simon Newcomb, had with thousands of dollars in money appropriated by the United States Congress.[52] When Newcomb heard about Michelson's experiment, he tried to help obtain government support for him. Unfortunately, Congress voted instead to fund even more money for Newcomb's work. Michelson would have to look elsewhere for funds.

In May 1878, Michelson published his first abstract of the experiment in *The American Journal of Science and the Arts*. Shortly thereafter, he was invited to present a paper to the American Academy for the Advancement of Science.

Just about this time, another door opened for Michelson. He met and married Margaret Hemingway, the daughter of a wealthy retiree who had trained in a legal career.[53] She was just eighteen, he was twenty-five. They exchanged vows on April 10, 1877. Michelson's father-in-law financed his new son-in-law with an advance of $1,000 for instruments to test the theories he was advancing. Michelson ran his tests on the Severn River in Annapolis. From these experiments, he was able to establish the speed of light at 186,380 miles per second. Two years later he corrected it to 185,355 miles per second.[54]

Like most scientific questions, the nature of the questions Michelson was attempting to solve invariably opened up other areas of exploration. We can look back now and see that the young scientist was standing on a precipice of scientific breakthroughs. But he could not easily proceed without tackling another monumental question—ether.

Ether was a hypothetical substance which, it was believed, filled space and served to transmit those forces which one material exerted on another. During Michelson's early work, the ether hypothesis was generally accepted. This had to be accounted for, since light, it was believed, went through some hypothetical substance which was responsible for slowing its speed. What was space composed of? This was a question that had baffled the best scientific minds of the last three centuries. How much friction did it exert on moving bodies and did it account for a lessening of the speed of light? Some physicists such as Augustin Jean Fresnel believed that the speed of light would indeed be affected by the motion of ether.[55] It was critical to solve the problem of ether because an accurate measurement of light could not be obtained without it.

Michelson stood at a cross road. He did not want to pursue a professorship of math at the Academy because he did not believe that he was an astronomer or a mathematician. He did believe that if he could devise an instrument that could count and measure light waves with an accuracy no one had yet obtained, he could measure not only the speed of the earth as it traveled through the ether, but also the speed of the whole solar system.

There was also a practical side to this—navigation. It was

necessary to know the exact distance of the sun from the earth. Scientists already knew the time required for light to reach the earth from the sun, but they could not calculate the distance until they knew its velocity.[56]

Michelson's work began drawing attention. In 1879, the *New York Times* made a prediction. "The scientific world of America is destined to be adorned with a new and brilliant name. Ensign Albert Michelson, a graduate of Annapolis and not yet twenty-seven years old is distinguishing himself by studies of optics in measuring the speed of light."[57]

The pressure was on, but Michelson felt he needed additional work in physics. Unfortunately there were no colleges or universities in the United States where students could do graduate work in the field in which Michelson was working. Johns Hopkins was just beginning to offer such courses, but its scientists had been trained elsewhere.

He decided to leave for Europe and take some basic courses at the University of Berlin to study theoretical physics with Hermann Von Helmholtz, the leading physicist of Germany.[58] With his family, Michelson sailed for Europe in 1880. In the meantime, his friend Samuel Newcomb contacted Alexander Graham Bell. Bell had also experienced funding problems before his patents came through. Bell took an immediate interest in Michelson's ideas and made arrangements to get him a Valta Foundation grant. When the funds arrived, Michelson was working at the University of Berlin designing his new instrument. It was called an Interferometer.[59]

Like all of Michelson's ideas, the concept was simple. He sought to project a beam of light in the direction in which the earth travels in its orbit and another beam at right angles to this. The first beam would be retarded by the flow of ether passing through the earth. The second beam, crossing the current at right angles (although the distance is the same), should arrive ahead of the first by a length of time determined by the velocity of the earth. The experiment could be compared to two swimmers, one swimming upstream and back, the other, crossing the river and returning. The second swimmer will always win, if there is a current in the water. These experiments were carried out at the Potsdam Observatory in 1881, the first of Michelson's ether-drift experiments.[60]

Michelson's instruments were so sensitive that traffic from the street threw the calculations off, so he worked at night. After six months of careful measurement, the facts were indisputable. The experiment offered a zero effect. There was no drag on the transmission of light in either direction. Either the earth was dragging the ether along or else ether did not exist at all. What Michelson could not have known was that he was setting the stage for the greatest scientific discovery of the 20th century, Einstein's Theory of Relativity. In one sense, his experiment failed. The results, however, pointed to the path that would lead to the second scientific revolution of the age—quantum mechanics.

In 1881, Michelson received an appointment at the Case School of Applied Science in Cleveland, Ohio. One of the incentives was a sum of $7,500 to be used for instruments for a new lab at the school. Michelson resigned from the United States Navy in 1882, having served twelve years and two months. He remained loyal to the service for the remainder of his life. Five of his patents would be used for optical range finders and one to protect the ear during gunfire. In World War I, he was in charge of the committee on scientific research at the University of Chicago and in 1918, he enrolled for four years in the United States Naval Reserve Force. He served as a lieutenant commander on active duty from June 21, 1918 to March 8, 1919.[61]

In 1884, the British Association for the Advancement of Science met in Canada. It was here that Michelson met Edward Morley, a chemist with the Western Reserve University. Their friendship marked a turning point in Michelson's career. The result of this collaboration was the now famous Michelson-Morley Experiments carried out in 1887.[62] By measuring the velocity of the earth through a theoretical ether, it could be established that all velocities would be fixed. The failure to detect any influence of the earth's motion on the velocity of light was critical. What these experiments proved was that the velocity of light was constant and the same in all directions for all observers and independent of the motion of the source of light or the motion of the receiver. In other words, the basic tenet of relativity. It was the only possible way to account for the negative results of the Michelson-Morley experiment.[63] Einstein did away with the idea that there was absolute motion. Motion, he said was relative and determined against other objects. There was then, no reason for the existence of ether.[64]

Beginning in 1886, Michelson received the first in a long line of honorary degrees.[65] By this time, his parents had moved back to San Francisco. Albert visited them and also made a trip to Murphys. He enjoyed a long delayed vacation. Almost a half-century had passed since the young boy had walked the streets of the little town. He explored an abandoned mine shaft and drove to the Big Trees for a picnic.[66]

In 1889, Michelson accepted a position at Clark University in Massachusetts, and in 1892, he was appointed professor and the first head of the Department of Physics at the newly organized University of Chicago.[67] Here, at last, Michelson found an institution that approached his own ideals and goals of education. Marshall Field, a wealthy department store magnate, had donated ten acres of land on what had been the former site of the 1893 Columbia Exposition. Among the 120 men and women on the first faculty, nine were former college presidents.[68]

In 1899, Michelson was asked to deliver a series of twelve lectures on light at the Lowell Institute of Boston. These lectures formed the basis for his first book on light waves and their uses. Following this, he won the prestigious Copley Medal from the Royal Society of London. Honorary degrees from all over the world followed. Nearly all scientific societies claimed him for membership.

Then came the momentous year, 1907. This was an important milestone for Michelson. He was summoned to Sweden. Here, he received the highest honor a scientist can achieve for a lifetime of work, the Nobel Prize. He was the first American to be so honored in the field of physics.[69]

Michelson was the ultimate Renaissance man. A composer of music, a player of the violin and an extremely accomplished artist, he was on one occasion asked to exhibit his water colors. A lady approached him and said she felt it was a huge mistake to have given up art for science. With as much containment as he could muster, Michelson explained that he had never abandoned art. He believed that in science alone was art able to find its greatest expression.[70]

Michelson continued to work on measuring the velocity of light as well as on a variety of other experiments which challenged him through the years. He determined the rigidity and elasticity of the earth. He measured the angular diameters of the satellites of Jupiter in the 1890's, and was the first to measure the star, Alpha Orionis' diameter in 1920. His interferometer made it possible for him to determine the width of heavenly objects by comparing the light rays from both sides and to determine how far apart their points of origin were.[71]

In 1923, in the southern California mountains, he surveyed a twenty-two mile pathway between two mountain peaks to an accuracy of less than an inch. Using an eight-sided revolving mirror, he set the value of the speed of light at 299,798 kilometers per second, correcting his own original measurement. By this time, however, ill health forced Michelson to leave the final measurement to others. In 1930, he was still working on the speed of light. It would be his last hurrah. At seventy-eight, he had come to Orange County, California, to follow the movement of light through a mile long vacuum tube. In so doing, he hoped to measure how fast light waves moved. His final measurement of the speed of light was 186,282 miles per second obtained in his last two sets of experiments.[72]

On May 9, 1931, Michelson suffered a fatal stroke. He had come to America and learned to work hard and make people proud of him. He gave back to the nation he loved so well, a scientific legacy. A generation after Michelson's death, with far more sophisticated instruments than he had, the accepted value of the speed of light was set at 186,282 miles per second.

Robert Millikan, winner of the Nobel prize in physics in 1923, characterized Michelson as a "pure experimentalist, designer of instruments, refiner of techniques, a man who drove the refinement of measurement to its limit and by so doing showed a skeptical world what far-reaching consequences can follow from that sort of process and what new vistas of knowledge can be opened up by it. The results of his work are reflected today in the extraordinary recent discoveries in the fields of electronics, of radioactivity, of vitamins, of hormones, of nuclear structure and others. All these fields owe a large debt to Michelson, the pioneer in the art of measurement of extraordinarily minute quantities and their effects."[73]

Footnotes

[1]Michelson Crater. The Lunar Orbiter Spacecraft V medium resolution camera took this crescent view of the backside of the moon on August 7, 1967 from an altitude of 5,000 kilometers. The Crater Michelson, named in honor of Dr. Albert Michelson, the U.S. first Nobel laureate in physics, 1907 is located on the back side of the moon and was formed more than four billion years ago. A copy of the plaque is located at the Albert Michelson Elementary School, Murphys, California.

[2]USNS Michelson. Other honors: Michelson Laboratory at Naval Weapons Center, Michelson Hall, Naval Academy, Annapolis, Maryland.

[3]Dorothy Livingston, The Master of Light: A Biography of Albert Michelson, (1973).

[4]"Professor Einstein at the California Institute of Technology," *Science*, Vol. 73, No. 1893 (April 10, 1931). pp. 375-381.

[5]We do have a school named after Dr. Michelson on Pennsylvania Gulch Road in Murphys. There are pictures, a video and files on Michelson located in the school library.

[6]Livingston, The Master of Light.

[7]ibid.

[8]Bernard Jaffee, Albert Michelson and The Speed of Light. (1960).

[9]Livingston, The Master of Light.

[10]ibid.

[11]Like the Goldwater family who left for California in 1852, both families experienced very much the same set of conditions in Europe.

[12]Livingston, The Master of Light.

[13]Kenneth Castro, Murphys California, (1972). Also Earl Schmidt, Murphys Camp. During an interview with Mr. Schmidt, he said Albert's father was a mine foreman. September 3, 1997.

[14]Jaffee, Albert Michelson.

[15]Livingston, The Master of Light.

[16]Jaffee, Albert Michelson.

[17]Judith Marvin, Letter, October 29, 1998.

[18]Livingston, The Master of Light.

[19]Jaffee, Albert Michelson and The Speed of Light. (1960).

[20]Richard Coke Wood, Murphys, Queen of the Sierras, (1952), p. 59.

[21]Castro, Murphys California.

[22]Richard Wood, Murphys, Queen of the Sierras. My thanks to Judith Marvin for the references here quoted. Letter October 29, 1998. An Album of the Pioneer Schools of Calaveras County, Compiled and Published by the Calaveras County Historical Society, 1986.

[23]Livingston, The Master of Light. The teacher was fourteen and had been educated at the Covent of Monterey. Michelson must have been familiar with German, Polish, and possibly other Slavic languages.

[24]Michelson was a superb painter. His work was similar to that of John Marin, a California Impressionist. He exhibited in various galleries throughout his life. In 1931, a major retrospective show was held at the Pasadena Art Institute. *Pasadena Star News*, May 13, 1931.

[25]Judith Marvin, Letter, October 29, 1998.

[26]Livingston

[27]Lincoln Grammar School was founded on July 1865 and located at Market and 5th Street. It was burned in the 1870's and rebuilt, then destroyed in the 1906 earthquake. San Francisco Public Library. Mr. Roberts, librarian. October 29, 1998.

[28]Paul A. Lucy, Lowell High School (1989), from Alumni Association, Lowell High School. Conversation, September 1997. The High School was named after Russell Lowell (1819-1891).

[29]Other graduates of Lowell include Nobel Laureate, Dr. Joseph Erlanger '92, winner of the *1945 Nobel Prize in Medicine* and two California governors, Pat Brown '23 and Clement C. Young.

[30]Livingston

[31]ibid.

[32]Blakely proved to be a poor choice. He apparently could not keep up with his studies and he was unable to retrieve his standing. In 1871, he was dropped from the Academy. The other candidate chosen for appointment was unnamed. (Author)

[33]Jaffee.

[34]Louise Nau, "Tuolumne County's Pioneer Ferries," *Chispa*, Vol. 10, No. 3. (January-March 1971), p. 346.

[35]ibid. Also, once Grant had exceeded his quota, he went on to appoint two more midshipmen at large, a total of thirteen in 1869.

[36]Jaffee.

[37]Letter from the Department of the Navy, James Cheevers, Naval Academy at Annapolis, October 9,1997.

[38]Livingston, The Master of Light.

[39]Cheevers. Letter.

[40]ibid.

[41]Livingston, The Master of Light.

[42]ibid.

[43]John Waldorf Taylor, Kid on the Comstock, (1968).

[44]D. McAlister, Albert Michelson: The Man Who Taught the World to Measure, (1970).

[45]Jaffee, Albert Michelson. The Greeks knew that light traveled in a straight line and understood refraction. Ptolemy compiled tables of measured angels of incidence and refraction. Aristotle thought that the speed of light was infinite. Islamic scientist, Avicenna, thought that the speed of light was finite.

[46]Isaac Asimov, Asimov's Biographical Encyclopedia of Science and Technology, (1982). Galilei Galileo (1564-1642) placed two lanterns on opposite hills in an attempt to measure the speed of light.

[47]Who's Who in Science From Antiquity to the Present, (1968). Romer, Olaus. (1644-1710), Danish astronomer. While at Paris, he discovered that the velocity of light could be determined by observing eclipses of satellites of Jupiter.

[48]S. P. Rigaud, Miscellaneous Works and Conceptions of James Bradley, (1832). James Bradley (1693-1762), an English astronomer whose observations mark the beginning of the modern era in physical astronomy.

[49]Leon Foucault, (1819-1868). He determined light's velocity in air and found that its speed in water and other media diminished in proportion to the index of refraction.

[50]*Scientific America*, May, 1930, p. 377.

[51]Albert Michelson, The Velocity of Light, (1902).

[52]McCrafy-Millington, Dictionary of American Biography, Vol. XII, pp. 593-596 (1933). Simon Newcomb, (1835-1909). Considered the greatest American astronomer of the 19th century. He had little formal education, but by seven years of age had published a book on arithmetic. In 1861, he received a commission in the Corps. of Professors of Mathematics, the United States Navy and was assigned to the Naval Observatory at Washington.

[53]Livingston, The Master of Light. Michelson was often invited over to their home for dinner. She described him as a handsome young officer with brilliant eyes.

[54]ibid. By using equipment he designed himself and altering the distance between mirrors, he found he did not suffer too great a loss of light intensity resulting in an accuracy of 200 times greater than that obtained by Leon Foucault.

[55]Asimov's Biographical Encyclopedia, pp. 405-06. Another talented observer whose overriding interest was light was Armand Fizeau. (1819-1896). In 1849, he set up a rapidly turning, toothed disc on a hilltop and a mirror on another, five miles away. From the speed of revolution at which the light was first reflected, the time required for light to travel ten miles could be calculated.

[56]Dava Sobel, Longitude, (1995). Sobel's small, but award winning book, explains the quest for a clock which would accurately measure time aboard ships. That search in turn led to an investigation into the questions of time and the velocity of light.

[57]*The New York Times*, 1879.

[58]Asimov's Biographical Encyclopedia. p. 411. Physician, mathematician, philosopher and lecturer on popular science. A pioneer in optics. Professor of Physics at the University of Berlin.

[59]A.C. Candler, Interferometer, (1951). Also, S. Tolansky, Introduction to Interferometry, 1955. No single instrument has more profoundly influenced modern physics than Michelson's Interferometer. With this, Michelson laid the foundation of the Theory of Relativity, established the existence of hyperfine structures in line spectra; standardized the meter in terms of light waves and measured the tidal effect of the moon on the earth.

[60]Jaffe, Albert Michelson.

[61]McAlister, p.6

[62]Candler, The Interferometer. In 1881, the experiment was carried out by Michelson. In 1887, it was jointly carried out with Morley. The Interferometer was placed on a heavy block of stone mounted on a disk of wood, floating in a tank of mercury. This allowed the apparatus to float smoothly. To enhance the light path, beams were reflected several times backward and forward. Four mirrors were used. What Michelson expected was that the two beams of light at right angles to each other ought to fall out of phase and show interference fringes. By measuring the width of the fringes, it would be possible to show the earth's exact velocity. Then the earth's absolute motion could be

determined. However, the effects were negative. The only possible conclusion was that there was no ether. The climax came in 1905 when Einstein proved that the velocity of light in a vacuum is fundamental and an unvarying constant.

[63]*Scientific America*, May, 1930. Vol. 142. p. 377. About the same time, Lorentz in Holland and Fitzgerald in Ireland proposed a theory to make Michelson-Morley experiment compatible with earlier theories. The Lorentz-Fitzgerald hypothesis formed the basis as well for Einstein's Theory of Relativity.

[64]McCrafy-Millington, Dictionary of American Biography. Michelson received over eleven honorary degrees.

[65]McAlister, p. 22

[66]References in various sources refer to Michelson's visits in both 1886 and 1930.

[67]Michelson was disappointed at Clark by the lack of support for his work, apparently caused by irreconcilable differences of opinion. At the University of Chicago, President Harper recognized the importance of Michelson's work and allowed him to take a leave of absence in order to continue his experiments on the standard meter. He also gave him freedom in selecting facility and lab equipment. Michelson was a member of the Renaissance Society at the University of Chicago. Its aim: to stimulate the love of the beautiful and to enrich the life of the community through the cultivation of the arts. Michelson was very much like Leonardo De Vinci, in that he was both artist and scientist.

[68]Livingston, The Master of Light.

[69]The Nobel prizes were begun December 10, 1901, on the fifth anniversary of Albert Nobel's death. The award for Michelson read: for "Spectroscopic and Meteorological investigation using precision optical instruments."

[70]Livingston, The Master of Light.

[71]McAlister.

[72]John Nielsen, "The Master of Light," *Orange County Register*, November 2, 1988. The experiment was carried out near today's John Wayne Airport between Armstrong Avenue and Alton Avenue in Irvine. Today's measurement of the velocity of light is 186,281.7 miles per second.

[73]Robert A. Milliken, "Michelson Memorial Address." U.S. Naval Ordnance Test Station Commemorating Michelson-Laboratory Dedication. China Lake, California, May 1949.

If a Scientist says that
something is possible,
he is almost certainly right,
but if he says that
it is impossible, he is
very probably wrong.

— **ARTHUR C. CLARK**

TACO

Glen Bell

Americans have a neurosis about success. We gloat over our self-made millionaires and billionaires. We feature their rags to riches stories on the evening news and we seem endlessly fascinated by their personal life. If there is scandal, so much the better. We vicariously relish the details in the sensational books that make the best seller list.

If I had a formula for this type of success, it would consist of one quality above all others, a will to never give up. In the end, however, there are just too many variables. The recipe for the right brew that denotes success or failure in the business world does not exist. There are exceptions to the rule and Glen Bell is a case in point.

The first time I heard the name Bell associated with Sonora was in 1979. A local realtor was attempting to re-introduce me to a community I had not visited in quite some time.

"Have you heard about Westside?" he asked.

" No," I responded. "What is Westside?"

He drove me down Tuolumne Road, about four miles east of Sonora. To our right stretched a huge parking lot which was deserted. A large sign with massive wooden beams hung lifelessly overhead as we drove through the gate. The western buildings that still beckoned were deserted and abandoned.

"What happened?" I asked curiously.

"You've heard of Taco Bell?" he asked. "That man, Glen Bell, had big plans here, but they turned sour."

"What was Bell doing here?" I inquired. It seemed a long way from the fast food restaurants I sometimes frequented in Los Angeles.

"Bell got started here," he replied. I had no idea that so successful an enterprise had its roots in Sonora. The truth, as it turned out, was very different.

Glen Bell was born September 3, 1923, in Lynwood, a small community near Long Beach. His grandfather had been lured to California by the popular novel, *Ramona*.[1] The story was written by Helen Hunt Jackson, who had written an excellent earlier book, *Century of Dishonor*. The book did not sell well so Mrs. Jackson turned her writing skills to something that she hoped would catch the public's attention. Compiling stories she had heard about Spanish and Mexican California, she flavored them with ample amounts of myth, romance and legends. Ramona was so popular that it became an overnight success and a California legacy was born.

Thousands of Mid-westerners flocked to southern California to "find" Ramona's birthplace or simply recapture the so-called halcyon days of the Spanish Dons. Apparently, so too did Glen Bell's grandparents, Ed and Maud Johnson.

The Johnson's invested in real estate, forming an investment company in Long Beach. At one time Mr. Johnson owned a sizable chunk of the city's Signal Hill Suburb.[2]

Their daughter Ruth met and married a handsome young man, Glen Bell senior, in 1921. The newlyweds were given a lot in Lynwood as a wedding present. By the time young Glen came along however, there were financial problems. Then, at only forty-nine, Ed Johnson passed away. The Great Depression followed and the Bells moved to Oregon.

Growing up, young Glen had to wear shirts made of cement sacks. Kids in school teased him because the wording, Portland Cement, faded through. When the hard times deepened, Glen made a promise to himself. He would someday become a successful businessman like his grandfather.

His grandmother Maud came to their rescue. She had purchased land in Cedar Springs, a small community twenty miles north of San Bernardino.[3] There, the growing family would have a home. Granted, there was no refrigerator, no electric lights, and water had to be heated on a stove for washing, but the family would be nearby where she could keep an eye on them.

Young Bell harvested potatoes and sold them. He and his brothers and sisters sold flowers door-to-door. It was probably during this time that Glen learned the basics of selling—how to sell a product as inexpensively as possible and still make a profit.

As a teenager, Glen began riding the rails just outside of San Bernardino searching for jobs. In the cities he passed through, restaurant owners let him wash dishes or mop floors in exchange for food.[4]

Once, he rode the rails all the way to Alexander, Iowa, where his father's family owned a large farm and a spacious home. He learned the advantages of self-sufficiency. The experience also created a life-long love of railroading.

Back home again, he heard that a neighbor wanted to go to Washington State. She asked if Glen could accompany her. While he was there, he could visit his great Aunt Mary who lived in a comfortable two-story Victorian farmhouse with a huge unused kitchen. Glen was fascinated. It was June and blackberries were in season.

"How do you make a pie?" Glen asked his aunt. He was already figuring out ways to make small slices that would sell for a nickel. Glen realized there might be a way to make money even during The Depression. He and his aunt named their new venture "Mrs. Dye's Homemade Pies."

Every morning at 5 a.m, Glen was off and running. Soon the business prospered. He and Aunt Mary hired salesmen. By summer's end, Glen and his aunt split $3,000. To Glen it seemed a fortune. At sixteen years of age, Glen had learned a few fundamental rules about running a business.

With the coming of World War II, the family's financial conditions improved. Glen Bell senior got a job at a shipyard in Long Beach. In 1943, Glen joined the Marine Corps. Shipped to the South Pacific, he landed on Guadalcanal shortly after the island had been taken by the United States military. Glen's job consisted of serving food in the dining room to large numbers of men. That taught Glen a valuable lesson in food preparation.

When the war was over, Glen returned to San Bernardino where his best friend, Neal Baker, offered him work. In 1946, Neal and his brothers opened an adobe brickyard. Unfortunately, government regulations specified that brick had to be reinforced and the changes were costly. Neal went broke.

Glen and Neal often talked over their mutual job problems at a new place in town called McDonalds. At the age of twenty-four, Glen knew exactly what he wanted to do—own his own business. How to begin however, was another problem. He had also met and married a young girl who wanted a secure future and a husband who would go to work in the morning and return at five. The two goals, self-employment and regular hours were simply not compatible. Dorothy Bell did not look upon her husband's dreams with eagerness. To her, it seemed he had not yet learned to "settle down."

Glen tried to make peace. He went to work for the Southern California Gas Company reading meters. After his daily routine, however, the idea of owning his own business kept coming back. On his route he happened to see a vacant lot opposite a public swimming pool. What a great place to put a miniature golf course, he thought. With a salary of $150 a month, he spent a hard earned $400 to lease the lot for a year. It didn't take Glen long to realize he had been somewhat over eager. A golf course would cost a small fortune to build and finance and it was simply beyond his means.

He discussed his ideas with Neal at their favorite eatery, McDonalds. One day, both men noticed the owner's new Cadillacs parked outside. They reasoned that their business must be pretty good to warrant such early prosperity.

At this time, fast food was a totally new concept. There were drive-ins but nothing like the idea of walking up to a stand, ordering food and walking away with your order minutes later. It was still foreign to people. Glen reasoned that his ill-conceived lot was four miles away, not too close to compete with McDonalds, but far enough away to take advantage of the kids swimming in the nearby pool. The opportunity to begin his own business beckoned again.

With his experience of making bricks with his friend Neal, he constructed a small brick building measuring 12 x 16'. In 1948, Bell's Hamburgers opened a short time later. Then disaster struck. The polio epidemic closed all public swimming pools. Also, Glenn found it was still hard to convince people to get out of their cars and place their own orders. When customers drove up they would honk their horns. Glen had to motion for them to come up to the stand. Bell was determined nevertheless that this could work if he put in the time necessary. He spent twelve to fourteen hours a day at his stand.

Dorothy complained about the long hours. "Get a normal job," she kept telling him. "How can we raise a family? I want someone who will be there."

Bowing to pressure, Glen sold his hamburger stand and once again found himself looking for a job with regular hours and a steady paycheck. The idea of owning his own restaurant however, would not go away. By this time, other competitors had entered the fast-food market. He knew he would have to offer the public something different. "How about tacos?" he asked Dorothy one day. She thought the idea was mad. Mexican food was too spicy, and who would eat it?

Glen persevered, however, and began again, this time selling tacos. The business prospered and in 1952, he bought a home for Dorothy. Again, Glen's hours were impossible. The Bell's also had new responsibilities. Their first child, a son was born. When Glen did not show up in time for his birthday party one evening, Dorothy was furious. The marriage was over. Glen wanted to make sure his son would be well cared for so he signed over his entire business, his only source of income, to his former wife.

Glen moved to Barstow and opened Taco Tia. It provided a modicum of success. Yet, because of problems with a partner, Glen sold his share of the partnership and headed for Los Angeles.

Now remarried to a schoolteacher, Marty, Bell opened El Taco with four partners. After only two years, he sold his interest. Glen wanted to be independent.

With years of experience now behind him, he was sure he could create a profitable chain of fast-food Mexican restaurants. In order to avoid confusion with all the other Taco-Tia's and El Taco's, Bell called this new venture, Taco Bell. For his first enterprise, he chose Downey, California. The year was 1962.[5]

Over the next two years, Bell built eight more Taco Bells. In 1965, he sold his first franchise, and in 1969, Taco Bell had its first public stock offering. He had built the organization to 462 restaurants in thirty-four states and in 1974, retired.[6] Bell was fifty years old and he had achieved his goal. Like most men with financial security, he looked around for other challenges.

His quest had begun in 1970 when he saw an ad in the *Los Angeles Times* which drew his attention. An auction of Hollywood memorabilia was scheduled to be sold. Fifty-six years of dreams from Metro Goldwyn Mayer Studios were going to be auctioned.

When the bidding began, Bell found himself vying with actress Debbie Reynolds for a 1931 Ford roaster that Mickey Rooney drove in several Andy Hardy films. "But what," Debbie Reynolds wanted to know, "will you do with the items you purchased?" Bell replied. "I don't know. Maybe display them in a museum or theme park." The idea surprised even Bell. The wheels were churning and Bell's fertile imagination went on fast forward.

For the next few years the Bells traveled, looking for some kind of "ideal" location. Family and friends shook their heads. "Does an Eden like this exist?" they asked. Glen and Marty visited Disney World in Orlando, Florida and searched for a place where Bell could begin a family-oriented theme park. The idea haunted him. He purchased thirty acres along the Rainbow River. His plan, he told friends, was to build a 500 seat deluxe restaurant in addition to a Mexican gift shop. He and Marty had been delighted years earlier when they went to Mexico and floated down the canals of Xochimilco in colorful little boats with flowers everywhere. The image never left him.

Then he purchased 160 acres further north in Florida known as Fanning Springs. Two years later, Glen was in Oregon and northern California. But nothing quite fit the picture.

In 1975, an ad appeared in the *Wall Street Journal.* It got Bell's attention. He wrote the following letter:

The Wall Street Journal
1701 Page Mill Rd.
Palo Alto, Calif.

Gentlemen,

Please send me information on The Westside and Cherry Valley Railroad per recent edition of the Wall Street Journal.

Very Truly Yours,
R. Bradley
Secretary to Mr. Bell.[7]

Suddenly, all the cumulative ideas that Bell had envisioned since childhood came together. The concept of an American community which had never been touched by The Great Depression intrigued Bell. That was an era of small town America, where families could enjoy being together, when America was at her best. This was Bell's most fervent dream. Most of all it resembled his childhood home in Cedar Springs. This just might be the place Bell was looking for.

Originally the home of the Miwok Indians, Tuolumne was also home to the Gold Rush in the late 1840's. A sizable camp had grown up around the famous Eureka Mine. The area became known as Carters, named for C.H. Carter, a local merchant. Rich timber had been transported from these mountains as early as 1850. Six years later, there were twenty-four mills, mostly devoted to the local mines.[8] When Franklin and Elizabeth Summers came to the area in 1854, around Turnback Creek, it became known as Summersville. Then came the inevitable decline of mining. As it waned, farming, ranching and logging began. But change was just over the horizon.

William Crocker, son of Charles Crocker, one of Southern Pacific's Big Four railroad moguls and Charles Gardner, William Newell and Thomas Bullock were scouting routes for an extension of the Sierra Railroad. Completed to Jamestown in 1897, the Sierra Railroad was built largely to gain access to Bullock's 55,000 acre timber interest in the area around Carters and Summersville. In August, 1898, these men met in Jamestown to devise plans for a tourist business, hotels and a thriving community, serviced of course, by their railroad. Promoting plans to build a three-foot gauge logging railroad from the timber land above Carters to the mills, they named their enterprise, The Westside Flume and Lumber Company.[9] The Sierra Railroad was extended to Sonora in 1899 and finally Tuolumne City, eleven miles away in 1901.[10] In 1899, construction on a sawmill began for the railroad.

Westside went through inevitable growth changes. In 1901, 850 people were employed by the lumber company. In 1903, Westside passed to W.R. Thorsen, J.R. Prince and George W. Johnson. It became one of the first large lumber complexes to operate in the county and was for a time one of the largest in the entire state.[11] There were eight locomotives, 150 logging cars and one passenger coach.

In 1915, *Sunset Magazine* described Westside as one of the largest lumber companies operating in California, with a saw mill-planing mill, cutting factory, box factory, mill pond, machine shops, car and railroad shops.

In 1925, it was known as Pickering Lumber of Kansas City, Kansas. With The Depression, Pickering closed. In 1934, it passed again to Westside and back again to Pickering in 1958. Finally in 1961, its glory days were winding down and the last of the old cars wound their way through the mountains for a final run.

Since that time, sporadic tries at reviving Westside as a local tourist operation were discussed. In 1968, Westside and the Cherry Valley Railroad was organized. Cars were reconditioned and made ready as tourist cars. These ran until 1971-73, when the line was closed down.[12]

Enter Glen Bell. He and Marty flew to San Francisco. They drove into the Sierras. For Bell, the magic had begun. The 340 acre site included a thirty acre mill pond, antique trains and lots of nostalgia. The hillsides were covered with pine and oak trees. Deer, coyote, squirrels, raccoons and birds of every species made their homes there. It brought back memories of a world he knew as a boy. Westside was about to be reborn. On October 14, 1975, Bell submitted an offer to purchase Westside. Shortly thereafter the offer was accepted.[13]

The *Union Democrat*, Sonora's weekday newspaper, was enthusiastic. The staff for the new project was chosen. Jim Summers became Westside's project manager. Bill Grant was hired as planning director. There were meetings with the local planning department and the Board of Supervisors. There were hearings and hundreds of townspeople attended. The small community of Tuolumne was about to undergo a vast change.

Bell assured the residents that this would not be a theme park like Knotts Berry Farm or Disneyland. From the beginning, Bell never envisioned that kind of commercial concept.[14] This would be an historic theme park, an "operating museum" with the emphasis on history. That alone made Westside unusual. The 340 acre site was expected to generate a million visitors by 1990 and over 500 employees. This denoted a long term goal that would require planning, patience and a great deal of investment.

The master plan consisted of a narrow gauge railway system throughout the park which would take passengers to a series of nine depots and stops along the way. These depots would serve as entrances to a logging camp: The Green Gold of California, a lookout mountain, an amphitheater, a Chinese Village, a Mexican Village and an Indian Camp.[15,16]

The waterway was essential to the project. The original millpond would be expanded into a thirty acre body of water. Several islands would be constructed and landscaped. The lake would provide a waterway for excursion boats. There would be paddle wheelers, workboats, Chinese sanpans, Chinese junks and a waterway that was similar to Mexico City's Xochimilco Gardens.

A road system was planned which would carry antique cars connecting various destination points. The vehicle storage and dispatch facility would represent a 1930's used car lot and gasoline filling station complete with hand operated gasoline pumps.

There would be horse drawn buggies, an antique car and truck collection of thirteen, a country village known as Glenbrook which would provide a variety of shops, working exhibits, a general store, candy, bakery shop, cafés and fast food facilities.

The Board of Supervisors approved the plan overwhelmingly. "This is one of the largest projects we shall see on this board," said Supervisor, Billy Marr.[17] "This is the right combination for a great project for the community," said Al Jespersen of Tuolumne.[18]

The headlines of the *Union Democrat*, August 5, 1976, read: Planners Endorse Westside Zone. Perhaps the greatest endorsement for the plan came from the Tuolumne County Historical Society. Most historians have become accustomed to seeing the word "history" attached to untold schemes and adventures, principally from highly skilled developers who understand the value of promotion, but care very little for authenticity. This is ironic because preservationists and historians alike realize, that in California, visits to historic sites and landmarks far outnumber the visits to all the theme parks in the state combined. Bell was giving Tuolumne County something it could be proud of, an idea whose time had come.

While the desire to preserve the county's native and historic landmarks had become increasingly important to the general public and local tourist economies, its implementation was still painfully slow. Bell's project was environmentally progressive and incorporated many state-of-the-art features. For example, the typical paved parking lot eye-sores seen in every large recreational facility would not be permitted. The 2,100-acre, 2,500 car parking lot at Westside would not be completely blacktopped. Instead, it would be interspersed with attractive rows of grass which would result in a softer impact. Signs directing people to "Please Park On The Grass" were a refreshing change. Large trees were planned which would create natural overhead shade.[19] Westside would also be self-sufficient, creating its own water supply. Only in the main office would local water be used.[20] More importantly, this would be a living history museum, a rare singularity in the state for the 1970's. There were theme parks, amusement parks and museums, but Westside combined what had never been done before—an historic park in its own natural setting. It would not depend on amusement rides or a carnival atmosphere to entertain its visitors but would satisfy the public's desire to experience the past firsthand.[21]

The gift shop, located in the nursery building adjacent to the Glenbrook Depot, featured a variety of hand-crafted items and turn-of-the-century reproductions. There was a wide selection of beautiful antiques representative of the 1900-1930's era, which were displayed in beautifully designed cabinetry.

Actor Michael Landon and the cast and crew from the television program, *Little House on the Prairie* visited Westside while shooting nearby scenes for their up-coming episodes. Landon was impressed with how well everything was crafted. It was, according to Sam Gordon, project public relations manager, very upscale. "With Bell, quality was uppermost."[22]

In order to insure the authenticity of the vehicle restorations, Glen wanted to involve local people. One of these was Joe

Speaker, owner of one of Tuolumne's gas stations. Glen purchased his entire service station in order to let Joe supervise the renovated garage's operations. Joe said he felt like he had died and gone to heaven.[23]

Bell's love of railroading was seen everywhere. The railway locomotive barn was filled to capacity starting with old No. 2 from Tuolumne Park. The restoration of a narrow gauge engine to operating condition became part of the museum's rolling stock. In addition, two logging engines would be restored, No. 12 and No. 15. Old No. 7, which had been on display at the entrance to Sonora, would be moved to Westside.[24]

The historic spin-off was contagious. Old timers began

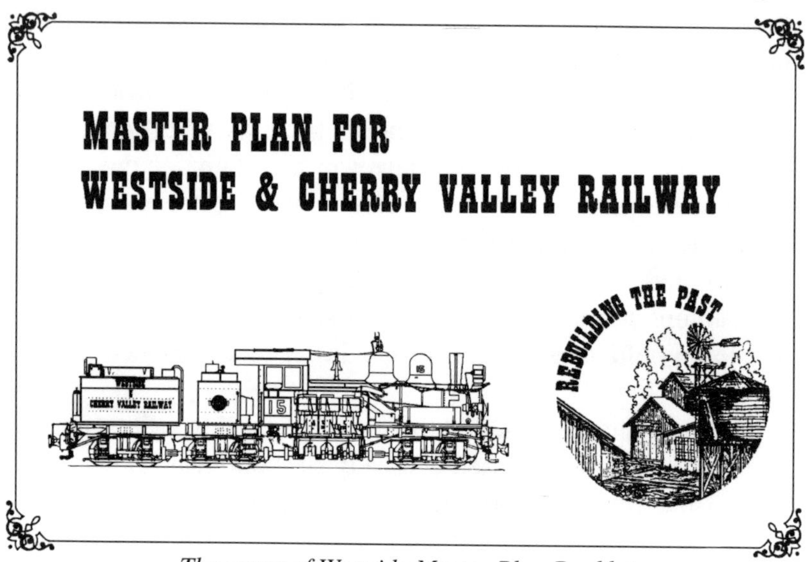

MASTER PLAN FOR
WESTSIDE & CHERRY VALLEY RAILWAY
REBUILDING THE PAST
15

The cover of Westside Master Plan Booklet

retelling stories of the way it was when they worked at Pickering or Westside. History was coming to life before one's very eyes.

Bell was also enormously generous. Half of Tuolumne's residents, he noted, were on welfare. He wanted to turn that around. He believed in sound business principles in the workplace. Trying to see others benefit from what he had begun was one of them.

Glen and Marty attended auctions throughout the United States. They purchased tour buses, antique trucks, delivery wagons, fire engines and limousines. The cost was mounting. They were spending over $100,000 a month to see Westside come to fruition.[25]

By the fall of 1978, the theme park was 5% completed.[26] There were unavoidable set-backs. Scheduled to open in May, nature pulled out all the stops in the spring months prior to the grand opening. Rain deluged the new park. Finally, the grand day arrived. Westside officially opened on September 30th of that year. It was an unabashed success. Those that knew and appreciated railroading were thrilled. "Glen Bell has done it right," a railroad enthusiast said to his friend. Over 1700 people thronged the new addition to the county. As a gesture of friendship, Bell turned over the entire proceeds from admission tickets to the Tuolumne County Historical Society and the Tuolumne City Memorial Museum. It was a much appreciated gesture.[27]

The cost of admission was small, $2. Bell felt that since the park was not yet fully operational, the entrance fee should be kept small. After the Disneyland hype, Bell was reticent about advertising. He was afraid that too much advertising might disappoint people.[28] "People came from every state in the Union and from European countries, and local support was overwhelming."[29]

Glen and Marty put down roots. They purchased a home in Sonora and began commuting from Rancho Santa Fe Springs in San Diego County to Tuolumne. Glen collected books about the history of the area, the beginnings of an excellent reference library which he encouraged the staff to use. He purchased the Mountain Lily Mine on Italian Bar Road. In effect it was the picture perfect fairy tale mine.[30] He also purchased a restaurant, Station 108, with a railroad theme. [31]

Employees who worked at Westside, found it ideal. "The camaraderie was wonderful," Mary Etta Segerstrom recalled. "There were no time clocks, we signed in and often as not, we were there early. Bell wanted perfection in everything. There was no cutting corners. And we all wanted that too."[32]

Yet, just one year later, Westside came to an end. Why? Several reasons were cited for the sudden withdrawal of Bell.[33] One was the fuel shortage of the 1970's. Bell was sometimes pictured as a man oblivious to the hardships of average people who were faced with the expensive fuel costs. Getting to work required planning. If people drove up from Sacramento or San Francisco, how and where would they get gas for the drive home?

Then there was Marty. The flights back and forth from San Diego to San Francisco were taking a toll. The flights were relatively short, but the planning beforehand and the long drive to Sonora took the better part of the day. Then, just five days before Westside opened in 1978, PSA flight 182 crashed, killing 144 people. It had been the flight just before Marty's.[34]

Also, Glen had, by this time, spent over five million dollars on Westside.[35] By the time the project was scheduled to be completed in the 1990's, the cost could easily soar to $20 million. Was Westside worth this and would it jeopardize Bell's other financial assets?

There had also been delays. Problems arose with off-site expenses. Improvements called for by the County Road Department due to the potential number of tourists anticipated had to be addressed.[36] Bell personally responded to the county's request.

"I feel very fortunate that I am able to withstand the financial pressures brought about by the capital expenditures required in a project of this type before the first ticket can be sold. We are opposed to moving the railroad to another location even though sites are available. We feel its historical significance is best served in Tuolumne County. Hardly a day goes by that we do not have a visit from locals who have worked on this railroad and we truly want to preserve this memory. However, in the event we are forced to abandon the project, I do make this commitment to the local people. I shall leave the property in a condition that will be an asset to the community."[37]

In December, 1979, a meeting was called in Westside's main building. It was, Bill Grant recalled, a beautiful room, but "that day was one of the saddest in my life."[38] Jim Summers walked to the platform, and, in front of a surprised group of employees, broke the news. Mr. Bell had decided to sell Westside. Mr. Richard Colburn, Westside's new owner would take over at the first of the year. Glen Bell was conspicuously absent from the meeting.[39]

On January 2, 1980, the general public was told of the sale. For awhile, it looked as if the entire Westside project might be donated to the Tuolumne County Historical Society. However the park was only partially finished, so how could the small historic group possibly take on the job of completing it? In the end, Bell withdrew his proposed gift.

Colburn's Los Angeles based Henley Management Company operated Westside until 1982. The property was then sold to Quality Resorts of America.[40] The locomotives, antique cars and equipment were sold. In 1991, Q.R.A. sold Westside to Ken Cox and Bud Loveless who planned a golf course, shopping center and residential lots.

Today, Westside is snarled in a legal quagmire. On the drawing board is a proposal for almost 240 homes, a nine hole golf course, an assisted Senior living facility and a small commercial center, but the plans are far from being finalized.[41]

Recently, I was driven around the site by James Wood of the Department of Parks and Recreation. I wanted to see first hand what remained of the vision that Bell had tried to create. We met in Tuolumne and Mr. Wood and I walked to the offices of the old Westside Lumber Company. They had been built originally in 1899 by the prominent architectural firm of Bliss and Faville, graduates of the University of California at Berkeley's School of Architecture. Their plan incorporated a design that reflected Westside's growing importance in the community where timber was "king."[42]

Mr. Wood explained that when Bell first arrived he found

the building in almost total ruins. The two story structure had been devastated by fires in 1902 and 1918. Only the first floor remained. Nevertheless the building had been rebuilt each time. After the Westside and Pickering departures, however, vandalism and neglect had taken its toll. By the time Bell first viewed the offices, they were in complete shambles. Glass lay strewn about, the windows were broken and the roof had caved in. Bell hired a team of carpenters and worked seven days a week to restore the building. When completed, it was gleaming. There was also an eighty foot passenger car which had been brought to the project. Bill Grant recalled that this was where he and Bell discussed their ideas for Westside.

When I peered inside the structure, my heart sank. Windows were broken, the roof had caved in, gaping holes were visible in the floor and glass was everywhere. It was hard to believe that only twenty years had passed since Bell's painstaking effort had been so lavishly expended to bring Westside back to life.

Meanwhile, Bell refused to let his dreams die. In southern California, on a 115 acre site in San Diego County, he turned an old ranch into Bell Gardens. It is a working farm which sells a variety of produce.[43] There are trains, of course, an old Model A Ford, a tractor, barn and antique trucks similar to the ones he grew up with in Oregon. It is an idealized concept of what a farm was like in that era before The Great Depression and, more importantly, of the childhood Bell always wanted to re-create.

Footnotes

[1]Helen Hunt Jackson, Ramona, 1939.

[2]Debra Baldwin, Taco Titan: The Glen Bell Story, (1999), p. 2.

[3]ibid, p. 13.

[4]ibid, p. 29.

[5]Downey Historical Society. Letter, August 12, 1998.

[6]Baldwin, p.115.

[7]Glen Bell, Letter, November 5, 1974.

[8]Mallory Hope Ferrell, Westside: Narrow Gauge in the Sierras, (1979).

[9]ibid.

[10]The names Tuolumne and Tuolumne County are often confused. Sometimes residents refer to Tuolumne City to denote the town as separate from the county.

[11]"Early Tuolumne Life Focused on Westside Flume and Lumber." *Union Democrat*, August 2, 1978.

[12]ibid.

[13]Tuolumne County Recorder's Office. Corporation Grant deed. December 17, 1979. Vol. 596, p. 466.

[14]According to conversations between Mr. Fred Boutin, (horticulturist for Westside) and Bell, Glen said, "What you're building here isn't going to be financially rewarding—it will depend on a constant infusion of money." July 17, 1998.

[15,16]Frank Cimino, employee at Westside, used this terminology to define the importance of logging in California. Conversation, April 20, 1999. Master Plan for Westside & Cherry Valley Railway brochure. Courtesy, the Grants.

[17]Randy Seelye, "Master Plan Endorsed for Great Project," *Union Democrat*. August 5, 1976.

[18]ibid.

[19]*Union Democrat*, October 10, 1977.

[20]Westside dug twelve wells and installed five pumps at a cost of $50,000.

[21]The attempt to build a replica of Venice, Italy, in southern California by Abbott Kinney in 1901, highlights what has so often been the unfortunate chain of events that seem to typify this kind of effort. Kinney dug

a number of elaborate canals and imported authentic gondolas from Venice. His Venice by the Sea was meant to revile the real Venice of Italy in the Renaissance era. Alas, visitors increasingly preferred the side shows to the performances of Sarah Bernhardt and eventually, a carnival-like atmosphere took over Kinney's dream city. (author).

[22]Sam Gordon, public relations employee at Westside. Interview, April 21, 1999.

[23]Baldwin. Joe Speaker's garage began in 1908.

[24]*Union Democrat*, December. 11,1977.

[25]Bill Grant interview, July 2, 1998.

[26]*Union Democrat*, December 22, 1978.

[27]"Westside Turns over $4,800," *Union Democrat*, October 1978. Also, *The Historian*, monthly newsletter of the Tuolumne County Historical Society, October, 1978.

[28] Bill Grant interview, June 30, 1998 and July 2, 1998.

[29]Sam Gordon interview. "They were coming five years after Westside closed down," April 21, 1999.

[30]Boutin interview, July 17, 1998.

[31]ibid.

[32]Mary Etta Segerstrom, interview, April 21, 1999.

[33]In the dozens of interviews I conducted, I received a variety of reasons for Bell's withdrawal from the project. I thought Debra Baldwin's comments were probably as close to the heart of it than anything else. "Bell's decision to sell Westside illustrated how his talents lie more in envisioning things than in running them. He's more dreamer than businessman. Glen finds satisfaction in conceptualizing how property might be developed for others' enjoyment—something that has been consistent in his character throughout his life and certainly is true today. Once Westside was up and running, like Taco Bell, Glen turned his creativity, which also is his source of greatest pleasure, to developing new properties and projects." Letter, April 21, 1999.

[34]"San Diego Air Crash Kills 136," *Union Democrat*, September 25, 1978.

[35]Amounts vary considerably regarding what Bell actually spent on Westside. From $10 to $15 million were the sums quoted to me. (Author).

[36]*Union Democrat*, October 10, 1976.

[37]ibid.

[38]Grant interview, July 2, 1998.

[39]ibid.

[40]Mr. Speaker overheard a remark that Richard Colburn's father made to his son. "The only value here is the unencumbered 300 acres." Interview with George Speaker, July, 1998.

[41]Lenore Rutherford, *Union Democrat*, April, 1999.

[42]*Documentation and Evaluation of Historic Structures*. Judith Marvin, Planning Dept. p.414. In July, 2001, the *Union Democrat* stated that the Cherry Valley Development Liability Corporation filed for bankruptcy in San Francisco. Lenore Rutherford. "Bankruptcy Puts Off Sale of Westside," *Union Democrat*, July 10, 2001. p.1

[43]Baldwin, p. 223.

Otheto

Otheto Weston

One of my first tasks when I arrived in Sonora, was to clean out our parent's home which both my sister and I described as "uninhabitable." It was filled to capacity with furniture, boxes, and what I loosely described as past dreams, lost hope. My parents were pack rats. Mother was an indoor pack rat, my father's realm of expertise was the outside. Absolutely nothing was thrown out, including used brillo pads. Andy Warhol would have been ecstatic.[1] I counted sixty cans of the rusting foul-smelling wire balls in the garage, not to mention 600 pounds of bottles, assorted engines, motors, machines, tools, trailers and hundreds of boxes of broken spare and used parts. It had all been put away on the off quoted word my father used to justify the mess—temporarily. Temporarily had stretched to forty years and nothing that I recall was ever retrieved from that graveyard of possibilities. I was not in a mood to sort out or lay aside. Everything had to go.

"Do you want that?" I asked my sister, who had joined me in an all out effort to return my parent's residence to house beautiful. I nodded in the direction of a small oil painting hanging slightly askew on the wall. "That's an Otheto," my sister replied. "What's an Otheto?," I asked, pushing the last of the boxes into the hall. The painting consisted of a small cottage and an old miner amid a forest of trees. It was meant to exemplify the life and times of what was once the sublime and simple ways of a bygone era in the Mother Lode.

"She's a painter from this area," my sister explained, noting my lack of enthusiasm. "Her mother wouldn't let her have crayons as a child, so she really had to struggle to paint." I knew where my sister was coming from. As a child I had made a terrible fuss in first or second grade over some crayons my beleaguered teacher had somehow failed to let me have. I placed Otheto's painting in my closet and proceeded to forget about the Mother Lode artist. Several years passed. The house was restored and life became somewhat normal again.

As I began to compile information for this book, my thoughts returned to the small picture of Otheto's now hanging in my bedroom.[2] Perhaps it was my interest in finding out how Otheto overcame her parents unfavorable attitude to her art that sparked my interest.

Otheto's journey began on September 30, 1895, in Pacific Grove, California, among the beautiful wind-swept vistas of the California coast. It was an ideal setting for the future artist. She was christened Elizabeth Stoddard. Her father was Charles Warren Stoddard, poet, travel writer and author. Among his many books were: *South Sea Idylls, The Lepers of Molokai, Hawaiian Life*, *In the Footprints of the Padres* and many more. He came from a privileged family in New York, his father being a paper manufacturer. Young Stoddard began traveling early, arriving in San Francisco at the age of twelve. He attended schools in the east and in California. At fourteen, he rounded Cape Horn on the legendary ship *"Flying Cloud."* Several trips to the South Seas followed. There was the obligatory European tour. In London, he met Mark Twain, becoming his private secretary. Later, he took the post of professor of English at Notre Dame, and lecturer of English literature at the Catholic University of America in Washington D.C., holding the chair from 1889 to 1902. During the last years of his life, Stoddard worked in California for *Sunset* magazine, writing about the California Missions. His final years were spent in a small cottage in Casa Verde. He was laid to rest on El Estero, a tile as his eternal pillow from the mission he loved the most, Carmel.[3]

Otheto's mother was Evelyn McCormick, one of the most

prominent and gifted artists in California. Born in Placerville, California, her family moved to San Francisco. She attended art school at the California School of Design and after a tour through Europe, enrolled in the prestigious Academie Julien in Paris.[4] At the opening of the Del Monte Gallery in Monterey in 1907, she was only one of a handful of women to be represented in its inaugural exhibition. She was also one of the first American women artists to be invited to exhibit at the Paris Salon. Her work was exhibited in Berlin, New York, Washington, and Philadelphia and in 1915, at the Exposition in San Francisco. Critics at the time compared her to Claude Monet.[5] Later Evelyn moved to the Monterey Peninsula and established a studio on the second floor of the Customs House. Commissioned by the City of Monterey to paint local buildings, her works are still displayed at the Carmel Art Association and Monterey's City Hall.[6]

Evelyn was a natural-born Bohemian. She was petite and chic and had the reputation of being the belle of the ball. As a child her instincts for play interfered violently with all attempts on the part of her parents to give her a formal education. When finally allowed to study at the San Francisco Art Association, "it was," she confessed, "like heaven."[7] She sought out freedom and expression in her life at the expense of everything else. "It's all electricity with us. We are mad with life."[8]

Otheto's father, was, in the words of one biographer, a "self-indulging old sybarite who neglected his great literary talent."[9] Robert Louis Stevenson described him in his novel, *The Wrecker*, as a man who so loved the South Seas that it re-kindled his own interest and resulted in making Samoa his home.

Bohemian life before the San Francisco earthquake was devoted to the association of like-minded artists, musicians, writers and other free souls who shunned traditional roles that society had imposed upon its inhabitants.[10]

When these two Bohemians met, sparks flew. Stoddard was much older than Evelyn, who was already well-known as a vivacious young artist in the Monterey area. Their meeting was uniquely recorded. "It is funny, for three weeks we have seen each other daily. She is bright and Bohemian and free."[11]

Unfortunately this Bohemian lust for life did not leave much room for the responsibilities of parenthood. Evelyn and Charles chose to remain faithful to the precepts of a lifestyle which left no room for Otheto.[12] "My mother did not like babies," Otheto said later.[13]

For the first eighteen years of her life, Charles Stoddard and Evelyn McCormick's daughter did not know of her biological parents. Like a fairy tale set in an enchanted forest, Otheto believed she would find her real home if she just searched for it. But the illegitimate princess did not begin her quest for her real parents until free of the restraints of what must have been a somewhat confining upbringing.

Why Otheto finally initiated the search for the two most important people in her life is unclear. What she eventually came to learn however, in an era when illegitimacy bore a terrible stigma, was that birth records of children born in a private home, did not have to be legally recorded.[14] She wrote the following letter, hoping to unravel the mystery.

State Dept. of Public Health
Bureau of Vital Statistics

Dear Sir,

I am trying to establish the true date of my birth and true name, if possible.

I am female...Was born to Evelyn McCormick at Pacific Grove September 30, 1895.

I was "christened" Evelyn Stoddard...at age two months, I was given to Minnie Couey, unmarried, to raise or place in [an] adoption home. I was raised by Minnie Couey...My father was said to have been Charles Warren Stoddard.

My efforts to get information from Salinas was unfruitful as I [also] told the Court.

My house had burned with all records, shortly after my birth.

I will be grateful for any help you can give me.

Sincerely Yours,

Evelyn Otheto Stoddard[15]

Otheto's adoptive mother, Minnie Couey, had been a former friend of Evelyn McCormick.[16] She married a Mr. Hinton and the young Otheto began life in the Monterey area.[17] According to a 1978 interview, she started painting in 1901, when she was only five or six. "I would sit on the steps overlooking the ocean and paint postcards. I would do sketches of the beach, then walk down to the beach and peddle them for ten cents apiece."[18] Since her foster parents did not approve of painting as a career, she decided rather willfully to earn her own money. A crayon cost a penny, hence the young entrepreneur could afford to finance her own enterprise! An example of this came to light when Otheto broke away from home one day and sneaked down to the beach to paint. When her foster father, a policeman, found her, she was roundly punished.

The family moved in 1907 to Oklahoma and in 1910, to Colorado. In 1912, Otheto made front-page headlines in the local Colorado papers, when she got "lost." Otheto became separated from her three companions while picnicking and hunting for wild flowers, losing her way in the Nipple Mountains.[19] Everyone was terribly worried. The area was honeycombed with abandoned mines and there was fear that Otheto had fallen into one of them.

However, the following day, the newspapers revealed that Otheto had stayed in an old barn overnight, then walked to town the following morning. Another article stated that the family intended to leave Leadville, Colorado and go to Berkeley where Otheto planned to enter art school. Apparently she had won her parents over, since by the age of seventeen, Otheto's work had gained enough attention to be mentioned in several newspapers.[20]

By 1914, Otheto had become a very attractive young girl and was modeling bathing suits in San Francisco. She also won the lead role of "Eve" in a pageant in the California 1915 Exposition held in San Francisco.[21] It is interesting that her biological mother exhibited her work there, as well as, winning a bronze medal. Also in 1915, at the age of twenty, Otheto married Harry George Weston. She continued modeling, this time for the Maxwell Car Company. In 1917, her first son, Robert Weston was born, followed by a second son in 1921. In 1922, she discovered Columbia for the first time, probably because of visits to her foster parents who had moved to Groveland.

At some point Minnie Couey married Lou Burns. "They ran a small grocery store on the north side of Main Street, several doors from the Hotel Charlotte."[22] County historian, Carlo De Ferrari recalled hearing that he (Mr. Burns) once delivered freight, possibly during the Hetch Hetchy Dam construction in the 1920's.[23] The Burns family had a store and "Otheto returned to Groveland and either purchased or rented what we always called "the adobe." She had a little studio there for a year or so."[24]

In 1929, Otheto was in Hollywood. She earned a speaking role in a movie "Wagon Wheels" with the famous actor, Jim Thorpe.[25] In 1930, she returned to Columbia, having found the community which would inspire her for the rest of her life. But Otheto was not a woman who could settle down for long. Returning to Los Angeles she found a job with the Broadway Department Store. She had seen their ads in the paper and knew she could do them. When the art director asked to see her portfolio, she replied "I had none." "What experience have you had," he asked. "None" she replied." Well," he said, "Anyone with that much crust ought to have a try." So Otheto got hired. She was good, and eventually moved from the basement to an upstairs office.[26]

After three years in artwork and copy writing for several Los Angeles stores, Otheto decided she couldn't take the confinement. "That little piece of sky [above her office], taunted me," she recalled, "and I had great hunger for open spaces." In 1930, she and her two boys headed for the hills.[27] She returned to the Sierras, camping at Pinecrest, doing sketches of people and teaching art classes.[28]

In the fall of 1933, at the height of The Depression, Otheto was back in Columbia. The town, with its historic ambiance, was beginning to work its magic on Otheto and the work that emerged during this time was forming a lifelong theme of her art. As she painted old buildings, their history began to take on a life of its own. She visited museums and photographed buildings everywhere in the Mother Lode. This work would give birth to a classic, *The Mother Lode Album*, her greatest contribution to the preservation of California history. Published by the Stanford University Press in 1948, the book represented pictures she had photographed over the previous fifteen years and would leave an excellent record of the area's architectural heritage.[29]

In 1934, she was working at Sutter's Fort, Sacramento, perhaps to glean more history from California's past. She sold one of her paintings, "Sleepy Hollow" to first lady, Eleanor Roosevelt.[30] That was followed by work for the Works Progress Administration. This was a unique government project that in part paid young and gifted artists a monthly stipend. While the idea of subsidizing artists was attacked and maligned by people who believed it was not the governments place to subsidize art, the concept was responsible for launching many now famous artists' careers, including Otheto's.[31]

In 1940, she was in Coloma, where James Marshall first spied a small nugget along the American River in 1848. There, she rented a small studio and published *Historical Buildings of the Mother Lode*.[32]

In 1939-49 Otheto wrote a series of articles for the *Union Democrat* called *"Tailin's From the Diggins."* These charming tales, part folklore, part history, have become invaluable additions to the area's colorful past.[33]

Then came World War II. Her two sons served on Naval cruisers and Otheto went to work at McClelland Air Force Base as a photographer. In 1943, she decided to sketch the entire Mother Lode from Murphys in the south, to Downieville in the north. She bought an old station wagon which served as an artist studio and living quarters. At least thirty renderings of Wells Fargo buildings were the result of this effort.[34]

In 1950, Otheto returned to Los Angeles and the suburb of Buena Park. What was then only a fledgling idea in the mind of Mr. Knott was beginning to take shape. The area was comprised of a vast stretch of farms. Mrs. Knott made jams and jellies and sold them at a small neighborhood fruit stand. Like thousands of other farms in southern California then as now, farmers often sold their produce along well traveled by-ways, usually nothing more than dirt roads. The Knotts' products, however, were special. Mrs. Knott added home fried chicken to her other homemade items and it too became widely popular. So popular, that slowly, a few western buildings were added next to the nearby restaurant. Today, of course, Knotts Berry Farm bears little resemblance to that early beginning.[35]

Otheto worked for Mr. Knott, designing and painting murals for the western buildings. Paul Klieben, an artist from Columbia and Sonora, was hired to work on the concept of the Knotts' western town. When he became sick, Otheto was placed in charge of the entire project.[36] One mural alone was ten by forty feet. The masterpiece of her work were the stories of the founding of California and the Gold Rush depicted in eight large paintings. In 1954, she worked free-lance for an amusement park in Arizona and in 1955, she was at work in Calico, a historic ghost town outside of Los Angeles.[37]

But Otheto could not be tied down for long to any project. In 1956, she was back again in Columbia where she purchased land on Parrotts Ferry Road. After that, Otheto's heart and soul remained in the Mother Lode.

It was here that her true life's passion emerged. Otheto, along with several other preservationists, had initiated a campaign to save Columbia. The memories of those first experiences in the Gold Rush community haunted her. The town was pristine, untouched by the growth that had overtaken other gold mining towns. They had lost most of their connection to their historic past, but not Columbia. The past simply hung about the place like an unrelenting seduction.

Governor Earl Warren signed a $50,000 appropriation bill for restoration and development of Columbia. Unfortunately The Depression intervened and plans had to wait until after World War II. At that time, the Columbia Historic Park Association became an advisory group to the State Historic Park Commission. Columbia officially became a State Park in 1945.[38] Otheto was designated as the Historical Director for the up-coming Centennial Celebration Committee (1848-1948).[39]

The little girl who longed to be accepted had fulfilled a dream. She was, perhaps ironically, very much like her biological mother, a free spirit. It was said that when Evelyn McCormick died in 1948, on her lap was a letter from Otheto. While she never recognized her daughter openly, she must have been aware of her only child's enormous contribution to the history of the Mother Lode.[40]

Otheto remained proud of her real parents. In 1955, she went to the Carmel Mission where her father was buried and joined the Catholic Church. That decision was based, in some measure, on her desire to be buried next to him. She purchased a burial plot to safeguard that decision.[41]

In a letter which Pellie (Martinez) Palmer, wife of famed artist Xavier Martinez and friend of Evelyn McCormick, wrote in 1953, she described Otheto's strong resemblance, both physically and psychologically to her father, Charles Stoddard. "We are greatly impressed with the very strong resemblance to her father. I, Pellie, knew her father personally, and I can assure you she not only looks like him but has so many qualities that were his. Her gentleness, her love of humanity, her talents and her intelligence that made her fine books and her work possible. The very lovable qualities she had were the ones that made life difficult for her, just as he had difficulty. But Otheto was a woman who did not get the protection that was given him and did not have the aggressiveness and temperament that seemed to go with the success of well-known women artists and writers I have known."[42]

These gentle qualities were evidenced in small things. Once, Otheto found a sparrow in the road and drove miles out of her way to bring it to a friend who she knew would nurse it back to health.

While at Knotts Berry Farm in 1954, she wrote a letter to a friend:

> *Today, I'm going to rent a tape recorder to catch a mocking bird who sings all night above my trailer.*
>
> *I do want to tell you about him. He's the most remarkable bird I've ever known. If I can get his continuous songs I'll try to interest the museum of Natural History in having records made. Where do you suppose one little bird picked up so much in a birds life."*[43]

Footnotes

[1]Next to Jasper John's infamous "Beer Cans," probably Andy Warhol's "Brillo Pads" ranks as a work of art which offends more people than any other contemporary art piece. (Until recently that is).

[2]Charles Surrendorf, 1906-1979. Painter, printmaker. He had a studio in Columbia for years, but often disagreed with the concepts of the State of California in their plans for a State Park in Columbia. He felt their restoration plans actually compromised the ambiance of what Columbia should represent: a real Gold Rush community, not a watered-down version of the past.

[3]Laura Bride Powers, Old Monterey, p.262. He lived in a small cottage on Van Buren Street.

[4]*Six Early Women Artists, a Diversity of Style*, Carmel Art Association, August 8 through September 3, 1991.

[5]Monterey Museum docent file. Monterey Peninsula Museum of Art, 1982.

[6]ibid. For years, Evelyn lived at the Royal Hotel in Monterey.

[7]Irene Alexander, "Last Link With Bohemian Past Broken," Monterey, California, May 7, 1948.

[8]ibid.

[9]Bonnie Gartshore, notes on Stoddard.

[10]"Stoddard Is Mourned by Bohemian Club Members," *San Francisco Chronicle*, April 15, 1909. It was Stoddard who was one of the best-known of the early members of the Bohemian Club. He himself produced the patron saint of the club, John of Nepomuk, confessor of a thirteenth century Queen of Bohemia, whose husband suspected her of infidelity, but could not force the secrets of the confessional from the lips of the priest. The saint who wouldn't tell, became the club's patron saint. The statue of the saint was one of the most valued possessions of the club, being a remembrance of Charles Stoddard.

[11]Mayo Hayes O'Donnell, "Stoddard's Death," *Peninsula Diary*.

[12]In an interview with Elvira Mahoney, she recalled that Otheto said that she remembered Stoddard coming to visit her and bringing a new dress when she was a little girl. Album compiled by Elvira Mahoney, Columbia State Park, 1984. There is also a story that Otheto found out about her birth parents when she was about eighteen. Otheto lived two lives after that, one in the Sierras, the other, in the Monterey Peninsula. She was also said to have visited her birth mother and said, "I am your daughter." Two versions of this story remain. One, that the door was

slammed shut, the other that Evelyn McCormick opened the door and apologized. From papers at Columbia State Park. Otheto biographical file.

[13]Mahoney interview.

[14]"A Tribute to Evelyn McCormick," *The Sunday Herald*, May 2, 1993. See also "California Artists and Their Work" *Overland Monthly*, January 1, 1908, pp. 25-33.

[15]Letter from files on Otheto at Columbia State Park.

[16]Otheto may have been placed in an orphanage until, at two months of age, Minnie took her. Minnie Couey has been described as a friend and housekeeper to Evelyn McCormick. Another source called her a nurse. From Otheto files, Columbia State Park.

[17]Otheto describes going down to the beach, so I assume that was most likely in Monterey. (Author).

[18]Mahoney interview.

[19]Several Colorado newspapers carried articles. Columbia State Park files.

[20]"Mrs. Hinton Leaves for Leadville." 1913. Article states that local residents are familiar with some of Mrs Hinton's work which was in the shape of window cards, advertising Knights and Ladies. "The cards were not only artistic but were also attractive."

[21]Chronological file on Otheto. Columbia State Park.

[22]Carlo De Ferrari, Letter, September 1, 1998.

[23]ibid.

[24]ibid.

[25]Biographical file, Columbia State Park.

[26]Mahoney interview.

[27]John Upon, "Otheto Weston, Mother Lode Photographer Here," January 7, 1949.

[28]Margaret Coffill, Files on Otheto, Columbia State Park. July 10, 1995. Carlo De Ferrari states that she and her husband and two sons returned to Groveland for a time and then to Columbia. "I know she left Groveland in the fall of 1933. Later in the 1950's, she opened an art shop in the "adobe" which my father had sold to Carl Harris." Letter, Carlo De Ferrari. November 24, 1998.

[29]Otheto Weston, Mother Lode Album, (1945). The Story and Sketches

of Columbia. 1948.

[30]Steve Hauk, "A Tribute to Evelyn McCormick," *Sunday Herald*, May 2, 1993.

[31]It is interesting that Evelyn McCormick was also employed by the Works Progress Administration in 1930. Letter, City of Monterey, February 1998.

[32]Otheto rented a number of studios throughout her life in Groveland, Columbia, Coloma and elsewhere.

[33]These stories are delightful and well written. This is more surprising when you realize that Otheto had no formal schooling. "I tried to go to the 2nd and 3rd grade, but I would bawl so hard they would send me home." Mahoney.

[34]The Wells Fargo buildings are perhaps the single most identifiable symbols of the '49er era.

[35]As a teenager in Ontario during this time, I remember Knotts Berry Farm was a very popular place to go on a date. (Author).

[36]*Union Democrat*, September 28, 1995. Otheto privately told friends that she believed Paul had been poisoned.

[37]Hero E. Rensch, Historic Spots in California, (1996), Lying at the base of the Calico Mountains in the Mojave Desert, Calico became a ghost town. In the 1880's silver mines brought 3,500 people to the area and Calico was known as one of the wildest camps of the Southwest. p. 326.

[38]"Columbia Sees Hope Realized," *Stockton Record*, July 16, 1947.

[39]*Union Democrat*, June 30, 1939. There were many people involved in the plans to make Columbia a State Park. Among them were Dr. James and Geraldine McDonnell.

[40]Evelyn apparently never openly acknowledged Otheto. In her will she stated that she left a sister, E.H. Parrish of San Francisco and two nephews. She was known to have given generously to many young artists. From Steve Park, librarian. "Clippings" file at Monterey Public Library.

[41]Margaret Calderaro interview, February 5, 1998.

[42]Letter of Pelli (Martinez) Palmer, January 26, 1953. Files, Columbia State Park.

[43]Mahoney interview, February 18, 1953. Otheto painted lots of pictures of Groveland and always a little old man. Her father? Mary Laveroni. Otheto died June 2, 1990.

Butch
Melvin Belli
WD

Melvin Belli

In the Sierras in northern California, there are acres and acres of natural forest, timber interests, national parks and wildlife. There is great natural beauty. In summer however, forest fires jeopardize that beauty. In the summer of 1959, Sonora experienced a devastating heat wave. The air vibrated with thick layers that shimmered in waves as it hovered along sidewalks and streets. Throughout the Sierras, the firefighters went on red alert.

In July, the *Union Democrat* ran the following story: "Hot spell enters 5th straight day. Fire Danger."[1] Throughout June, the hot spell sent temperatures soaring to an unprecedented 106 degrees. One's skin bristled and tin roofs seemed to glow with an eerie sheen. By July 20th, almost 1000 acres had burned.

On July 25th, twenty year-old Butch Cameron, a recent graduate of Sonora High School, drove to Columbia Airport. Butch loved flying. He began soaring in gliders, sailing along the windswept coast of San Diego. Back in Sonora, he decided to get his private pilot's license and soloed in a record breaking four hours. He was a natural pilot and won award after award for spot landings in Tuolumne County. His instructor, Leonard Strand, ran a flying school at the small airport nestled in the Central Sierras. Butch typically "hung out" there. His older brother, Bob Cameron, planned and talked about buying a single-engine J-3 Cub. Almost fifteen years separated the two brothers, but rarely did one of them go anywhere without the other. This morning Butch was aching to get back to the airport.

My phone rang early the following morning awakening me from a rather peaceful slumber as I awaited another scorching day in Hollywood. It was my mother. "Butch has been killed," she said. "Oh, no," I remembered saying, sitting down, stunned. Memories flooded back to my teenage years in southern California. The five of us—Bob, Butch, and Don Cameron, my sister and I used to visit the local park picnicking together. Butch was only seven or eight at the time. More poignant was my recent visit in 1958 to Melones Lake in Tuolumne County. I had not seen Butch in over ten years and I was surprised to meet a handsome nineteen year-old youth on the verge of manhood.

"What happened?" I asked. "He was in a plane crash. We don't know for sure. He hitched a ride with Mr. Strand. They were throwing out supplies to fire fighters in Groveland and something went wrong."

That was over forty years ago, but the memories of that day in July, so many summers ago, still linger. Only now, as I return to piece the fragments together, have I been able to understand the events more clearly.

In the *Union Democrat*, days after the crash, the headlines read: "Rites Set For Two Plane Victims Monday. Billowing parachute blamed in air disaster. The two are Everett Hayward forty-five, and Edward Allen (Butch) Cameron, twenty. Recovering is Leonard Strand, forty-four, pilot of the Cessna 180. The crash occurred at Big Oak Flat Fire Station."[2] Soon thereafter, Leonard Strand decided to bring suit against the United States Forest Service and the Camerons joined with him. They hired attorney Melvin Belli to bring clarity to the unique circumstances and justice to the victims.

I had heard the Belli name by then. In Hollywood, Belli's name was listed alongside other attorneys who had gained a reputation for themselves by defending famous movie stars. Errol Flynn, Lana Turner, Mickey Cohen and a host of other notables were Belli's clients, often living in real life parallels close to their film roles.

I did not know that Belli was a native Sonoran, born in the heart of the Mother Lode on July 29, 1907.[3] He was an only child. His grandfather was Swiss. His father, Caesar, spoke six languages, among them Chinese, and had attended Bern College in Switzerland. He had dabbled in a number of projects, everything from vineyards to irrigation canals, banking and investments. The family had a reputation for being "flamboyant." His maternal grandfather had been a doctor, his grandmother, Leonine Mouron was the first woman pharmacist in the State of California.[4]

Belli attended Sonora Elementary School until the 6th grade. Among his classmates were Irving Symons, whose father was a partner in Hales and Symons Lumber and Hardware.[5] The family then moved to Stockton. As a teenager, Melvin worked with his father on their ranch, producing grapes, raisins, and pears.

In 1925, he was scheduled to graduate from Stockton High School. He had been chosen Valedictorian of his class. Belli loved oratory. The speech which he had prepared was entitled "Respect for Law and Order." It would prove to be somewhat prophetic. The brash young graduate began celebrating his graduation early and somehow some windows in town got broken. The principal informed Mrs. Belli that there would be no diploma, no Valedictory. Young Belli's first experience with the law was about to begin.

The elder Belli went to the judge whose job it was to hand out writs, bench warrants, subpoenas, bail bonds and other paraphernalia. Caesar Belli grabbed a wad of legal papers, bound them together with a very official-looking seal and topped it off with a red ribbon. He then marched over to the school and (accounts vary), slammed the papers down on the principal's head. Be that as it may, the outcome was a victory. Young Melvin got his diploma, whether reluctantly or under duress is not clear. The incident made a deep impression on the young student. At that point he thought about becoming a lawyer, but not just any lawyer—he would be the very best lawyer in the land.[6] Along with his desire to practice law came another natural affinity, attracting attention to himself.

Belli attended the University of California at Berkeley, and while there, met his old childhood friend, Irving Symons. It seems that Irving had a car, a rare thing to have in those days. During a recent interview, he admitted that his father had been somewhat indulgent because he had been such a good student and had earned excellent grades. Hence, his scholastic merits had been rewarded.

One evening, Mr. Symons recalled, he and Belli and another friend went out on a date with three young ladies. In those days, in order to get back to Berkeley, one had to take the ferry from San Francisco. As it so happened, the six young students missed the last ferry. Alas, Berkeley required its young women to be safely back in their dorms by two a.m. The six cohorts in crime parked across the street from the sorority house (in the early morning hours), trying to figure out how to get their dates back into their dorms without getting caught. This was serious. They could face suspension or possibly expulsion, not to mention what their parents might do. They began to discuss their dilemma and the conversation wound around to the topic of the current headlines. Apparently there had been a very bad dude known in the local papers as "the strangler." In the midst of recalling all the gory details, Belli suddenly burst out of the car without a word. He ran to the dorm, climbed up a vine-covered trellis to the second story and rapped loudly on the window. The lights went on. As the matron approached, Belli yelled. "It's the strangler." The girls sneaked back into the safety of their dorm. Belli escaped and the three men fled the scene. At ninety-two years of age, Irving chuckled when he recalled that night so long ago.[7]

Belli maintained a "colorful" career in his student days at Berkeley. On a dare, he swallowed moths. It was even said he made bootleg alcohol for $10. He ran nude, long before it was called "streaking." He was a practical joker and spent most of his college days on probation. The dean accused him of unbecoming behavior.

One day, casually reading a magazine, Belli was struck by the advertiser's warranties. He sent away for anything offered free, and received so much mail that the local post office had to hire an additional postal worker.[8]

Melvin Belli graduated in 1929, at the dawn of the Great Depression. Jobs were scarce, so he hired on board *The S.S. Kentuckian*, bound for New York. He had always longed to travel. As a student, a classmate's father had offered him a job in far-off Tibet, importing silver. Unfortunately, just as his appetite for world adventure was whetted, an international crisis in silver brought an end to that dream.[9]

Life stretched before him like a great adventure. For a salary of $25 a month, he learned seamanship and saw the sights of New York. He earned his Able Seaman Certificate, then found another job as an ordinary seaman and sailed for Europe. After that, the Orient beckoned and aboard *The S.S. McKinley*, he sailed east as a seaman with the Dollar Steamship Lines. Here, he noted extreme differences in wealth.[10] Having been gone a year, and probably spending many a day and night musing about his future, he made the decision to visit the U.S.S.R. The grand experiment in Communism was under way. One could assume perhaps that Belli was interested in knowing how well the problems of ordinary people were being addressed in a nation that expounded radical changes between the haves and the have nots. In America, at least in theory, these changes could be addressed legally.

In the fall of 1930, Belli entered Berkeley's Boalt Hall with the idea of fulfilling his boyhood dream—becoming an attorney. He studied hard and graduated 13th in his law school class. He was twenty-five years old and the year was 1933, not a particularly good time for finding jobs.

Belli was offered $75 a week from the National Relief Association, a governmental program initiated by President Franklin Roosevelt. The government was concerned with the appeal and growth of communism in the United States and wanted to observe this phenomenon more closely. Belli rode boxcars across California and met a lot of hobos. Arrested in San Diego for vagrancy, he learned early in his career what it was like if you were poor and in trouble. You pleaded guilty, otherwise you landed in jail.[11]

He began to identify with the underdog. When he returned to Berkeley, he wrote up his report for the National Recovery Administration. The report was used to steer groups of youthful vagrants into positive endeavors. The following year, the State of California instigated the California Conservation Corps. Belli passed the bar and married his first wife, Betty Ballentine. Then he got what he hoped was his first big break.[12]

Yearning for publicity to enhance his career and having a decided theatrical flare, he decided that a prison break at San Quentin offered him the opportunity he was looking for. Among the inmates was a British subject. With great creative gusto, he daringly called none other than Prime Minister Anthony Eden of Great Britain and pleaded on behalf of his client. But the outcome was devastating. His client, along with several other convicts were found guilty and hung. The horrified Belli came away from the event sadder, but wiser. It seemed as if it was easier in our system of justice to hang someone for stealing food than it was to bring the law down on a wealthy person floating phony stock schemes. The Bill of Rights and the United States Constitution were seemingly just scraps of paper written a long time ago. Justice was a theory still not available to everyone, and in America during The Depression, still a dream. That particular kind of jurisprudence made a great impression on the young lawyer.

Over the next several years, Belli forged a reputation for going after the "Big Guys," principally corporations and insurance companies. The fixers in Washington, it seemed to him, never went to court but were nevertheless culpable.

In San Francisco, Belli opened offices at 722-728 Montgomery Street where Lola Montez once danced and where Bret Harte wrote his *Luck of the Roaring Camp*. He restored the building, thereafter known as the Belli Building. Here, he brought a bar from his hometown in Sonora that had traveled around the Horn in the 1850's for the old Alsbee's Saloon. Here also was an armadillo statue of a Madonna with ostrich feathers imported from South America. Also from Sonora, there was an old apothecary jar from the local drug store, run by Belli's uncle, Otto Mouron, until well after World War II. As a child he had haunted the drugstore where his grandmother worked, learning about the contents of jars and wondering about the surgical instruments. There was a cuckoo clock from Germany, a demon mask from Nepal's Katmandu, and buffalo heads from Nigeria. On the wall was a certificate from E. Campus Vitus, a historic organization, signed by the colorful Emperor Norton I of San Francisco. And there was his famous skeleton, Elmer, which would figure importantly in many of the trials Belli handled.[13]

Belli believed in the principle of absolute liability in which manufacturers were automatically liable for injury caused by their products. It set the stage for later consumer protection litigation. Belli was bringing insurance companies into the very mainstream of the law. Before Belli, corporations could bend the law toward their own property rights and they had ample funds to do so.[14]

The up and coming attorney was gaining a reputation. "He could," someone said, "charm a cobra out of its basket." But Belli's real claim to fame, and something that is often overshadowed by his bravado was the fact that he was changing the business philosophy of the legal profession in America. Before Belli, it was difficult for an injured plaintiff to get a fair shake.[15]

In order to influence juries, Belli introduced demonstrative evidence. He felt the jury often did not really understand what it was they were hearing from attorneys who relied on legalistic jargon. Belli initiated what has become standard practice today, bringing in the actual physical evidence to show to the jurors. The jury, after all, is supposed to make valid judgments. But Belli knew that in order to make those judgments, they needed better examples of the evidence. "I learned," Belli said, "that jurors learn through all their senses, and if you can show them too, let them feel and even taste the evidence, then you can reach the jury."[16] His aim was to make due process open to everyone.

The American Bar Association often frowned on Belli's methods and his courtroom dress of scarlet suits and snakeskin boots. But more important to him was the fact that he was in the *National Law Journal* list of America's 100 most important lawyers.[17]

In 1960, in Sonora, the wrongful death suit against the U.S. Forest Service vs. the Camerons was getting underway.[18] According to the files of the case, "The defendants owned, operated and maintained a model Cessna 180. Equipment, and a parachute located in said plane was installed, thereby permitting the strap from the chute that should have been attached to the equipment (that was to be dropped from said aircraft), to be attached instead to the aircraft. These circumstances resulted in a dangerous condition, which existed at the time of the drop, and that was a result of the negligence and carelessness of the defendants. While the equipment chute was dropped from said aircraft, the chute failed to fall free from the plane, which was then flying at a low altitude, causing the canopy of the chute to become entangled in the empennage of the aircraft and directly causing the plane to crash, thereby resulting in the immediate death of Edward Cameron. Furthermore, Fred and Ruth Cameron have been deprived of the care and comfort, companionship, society, support and maintenance of said Butch Cameron."[19]

On March 3, 1965, a jury of ten women and two men began deliberating in the civil suit resulting from the 1959 plane crash near Groveland. Attorney Richard Gerry, one of Belli's partners, summarized evidence presented by the plaintiff to support the charge that negligence of the State Division of Forestry employees caused the crash of the plane.[20]

When Butch arrived at the airport that fateful morning, Strand told him that a fuel pump had to be dropped from the air as soon as possible, since a fire truck was stranded in a critical fire area without it. Three men had to be in the plane. One to fly, the other to hold the door open, and a third to throw out the parachute containing the pump. Ordinarily, the door of the plane would have been removed in order to facilitate a drop. But time was of the essence and when Butch arrived at the airport, he said he could be the "third" man. During the trial, there was candid admission from a forestry employee that "he did something wrong." He delivered to Mr. Strand a package and parachute that was allegedly improperly attached.[21] The jury entered in favor of the plaintiff in March, 1965.

On a softly rolling hill in Mountain Shadow Cemetery in Sonora, lies the Cameron family plot where Butch lies beside his parents. The headstone reads simply: Edward A. Cameron "Butch" 1938-1959. On another hill at the opposite end of town in Odd Fellows Cemetery lies Melvin Belli's grave. The tombstone reads:

The most important lawyer of the
20th century for Victims Rights.
A living legend
An American folk hero.
Buccaneer of the bar, master of cross-examination.
Father of Demonstrative Evidence.
The King of Torts.[22]
Born July 29, 1907. Died July 9, 1996.[23]

Footnotes

[1]*Union Democrat*, June 23, 1959.

[2]ibid. July 27, 1959.

[3]McMahon, Mae Bromley, "Memories of Old Sonora," *Chispa*, Vol. 22 No. 4. April-June, 1983. p.758.

[4]Robert Wallace, Life and Limb, The Fabulous Career of Melvin Belli. (1956).

[5]Irving Symons, interview, April 6, 1998.

[6]Melvin Belli, My Life on Trial, (1960).

[7]Symons Interview.

[8]Belli.

[9-12]ibid.

[13]ibid. In order to learn more about malpractice, Belli donned hospital gear and attended autopsies. Elmer often accompanied him.

[14]ibid.

[15-16]Harriet Chiang,"Melvin Belli, The King of Torts is Dead," *Los Angeles Times*, July 10, 1996.

[17]*The Economist,* Obituary, July 20, 1996.

[18]Richard Gerry, of Belli's firm, represented the Camerons. Belli attended the trial occasionally.

[19]Judgement Book, Vol. O, No. 246. "Camerons vs U.S. Forest Service." Tuolumne County Courthouse.

[20]Marion Cameron, Interview, April 1997. "There were two hooks on the parachute. One fastened on one end, the second one, on the other end. They reversed it." Interview, resident of Jamestown May 2, 1997. "Also when asked to pack the chute during the trial the same person packed it again, incorrectly."

[21]*Union Democrat,* March 3, 1965. My thanks to Robert Cameron who filled me in on more details of events as they occurred. Interview, October 5, 1999.

[22]That particular phrase was coined in a *Life* magazine article, 1954.

[23]"The King of Torts Dies," *U.S.A. Today*, July 10, 1996. Belli wrote and co-authored 72 books.

Someone once said:
"He (Belli) could charm
a cobra out of its basket."

— UKNOWN

Clarence Ayers

Clarence Warwick Ayers

Sometimes the smallest incident can stamp an indelible impression on one's memory. For me, such an incident occurred in 1967, when my husband and I flew into an unexpected snowstorm in the Sierras. We left Van Nuys Airport an hour before in good weather, but by the time we approached Sonora, our visibility was suddenly obliterated. Out of the whiteness of that unforgettable day loomed the Red Church, and to its immediate left, the old Red House. With our bearings intact, we landed at Columbia and drove back into Sonora, momentarily pausing by the two historic structures.[1] It was from that point in time that I formed an emotional attachment to the Red House. I vowed to learn more about the home, but as it turned out, almost twenty-five years would pass before I was able to keep that promise.

In 1990 I returned to Sonora. The promise I had made so long ago came to mind. When I began my research, however, I found that information on the Red House, or the Street-Morgan Mansion as it was more correctly called, yielded more information on the home's owners than on the man who built it. His name was Clarence Warwick Ayers.

Clarence was born in Mauston, Wisconsin in 1857.[2] He was descended from a rather renowned family on his mother's side. His father, Charles Wesley Ayers, was a school teacher. There were four children in the household: Clarence, Edward Layton, born at Lake City, Minnesota about 1862; a third son, Littleton Fenimore, born in Chicago in 1867; and a sister, Viola Lois, born in Chicago in 1869.[3]

By the time young Clarence had reached his teens, the '49ers trek to the California gold fields had begun to fade from memory. Like the proverbial stone thrown into the lake, the waves of excitement caused by the initial discovery of El Dorado eventually ebbed. Many of the original '49ers left California and returned to their original homes. Prentice Mulford noted, they became "an object of curiosity if they brought money with them, or rather, as long as the money they brought with them lasted."[4] Then came the Civil War. That tended to bring a dramatic conclusion to the memories of the California Gold Rush.

By the 1860's, the Ayers family was living in Chicago. One of that city's famous architectural pioneers, Frank Lloyd Wright, had arrived to work under America's architectural doyen, Louis Sullivan. By the late 1880's, these two men brought pivotal changes to American commercial and residential architecture. While it is doubtful that Wright had any influence on Ayers' work, the fervor of architectural activity centered in the Chicago area could not have escaped Ayers' attention.[5]

By Clarence's twenty-fifth birthday, he had moved to Ashland, Oregon.[6] There, he married Elizabeth "Lizzie" Hargadine. The Hargadines were noted pioneer Oregonians.[7] Their wedding was the social event of the year and most of the prominent citizens of the community attended. The Ayers' left on a honeymoon trip to San Francisco and southern California.[8]

What brought Clarence to Ashland may have been the old placer mines near Phoenix, Oregon, the property of Ashland's most prominent citizen, E.I. Anderson.[9] In 1890, Mr. Anderson employed Ayers to build a home for his family. Termed the "finest country residence in Oregon," the two-story home cost an astronomical $5,000.[10] While engaged in this project, Ayers left for Albany, Oregon, where he furnished plans and specifications for the new Linn County Bank Building. According to the *Democratic Times*, of Oregon, February 13, 1890, "He (Ayers) is a first-class architect as well as mechanic."[11]

In 1893, "the greatest fair in United States history" opened in Chicago. Known as "The Great White City," it was supposed to represent the ideal city of the future.[12] Thereafter, Ayers' letterheads read: "Clarence W. Ayers, Engineer, Mining, Mechanical and Architectural. The man who does things, Commissioner to the World's Fair, Chicago, 1893."[13]

In whatever capacity Ayers participated in the Chicago World's Fair, it would have a profound effect on his work. Today, we view the architecture of the fair much as Louis Sullivan did at the time, "an event which would set (American) architecture back fifty years."[14] It produced a chilling effect on an entire entourage of aspiring young architects, like Wright and Irving Gill, who were attempting to produce an indigenous American architecture, free of precedents based on European historicism. For most American architects, however, men like Ayers were more inspired to provide the more traditional choices their clients preferred, principally Queen Anne Victorianism, a flamboyant and popular style of the time.[15]

While Ayers' career was moving along rapidly, his domestic life was not. A petition for divorce was filed. By 1895, when Ayers was already in California, he was granted a final decree of divorce. He would never return to Oregon.[16]

Soon thereafter, both the *Union Democrat* and the *Tuolumne Independent* in Sonora recorded his activities.

From the day of his completion of the first building erected from a design by him and under his supervision, he has easily held the honor of being the best who ever came to the county. A man of fine artistic taste and conscientious in everything he undertakes even to the slightest detail, Mr. Ayers, by blending these two cardinal virtues in connection with his rare talent of creating beautiful effects has gained the confidence and admiration of the entire community.[17]

In 1895, Clarence Ayers began the first in a series of spectacular homes that would mark his career as Sonora's finest architect. Commissioned by William Frederick Bradford, son of wealthy lumberman S.S. Bradford, Ayers was asked to build a home on a hill above Sonora, overlooking the earlier residence of his father.[18] Known as the Bradford-Rosasco home, it has maintained its stateliness for a century of residents who have called it home. It is a rare and lasting tribute to its designer and builder.

In 1896, an enormous change occurred in Ayers' life—romance! An attractive widow, Charlotte Ellen Lynn, operator of a fashionable millinery shop in the Sonora Neubaumer Building, caught Ayers' attention.[19] The *Union Democrat* carried the following announcement.

WILL RETURN MARRIED

C.W. Ayers, our prominent architect hired himself away to the big town on the bay this week and when he returns congratulations will be in order. Friend Ayers was very shy about it all, but it was no go, the ubiquitous Democrat reporter caught on, as usual, and a little inquiry revealed the reason for his departure.[20]

Ayers' work blossomed. It was during this time that he designed the homes that would elevate Sonora's reputation from that of a former Gold Rush community into a town worthy of its title, Queen of the Mother Lode.

Ayers began work on the Street-Morgan home, popularly known today as the Red House. Begun in the summer of 1896, the first story was already up by August of that year.[21] Ayers was extremely busy in 1896, 1897 and 1898, but it would be the Red House that would establish his reputation in Sonora.

The Street-Morgan home can be described as Queen Anne-Eastlake at its best. However, to describe it only in these narrow architectural terms is to miss the underlying purpose and meaning of the Victorian style which permeated the age. The rules and precedents of what had constituted good taste in architecture were laid aside. Greek and Roman ideals of perfect symmetry, cool rationalism, and balance vanished. Here was a style that was romantic, ostentatious, emotional and picturesque. It was an architecture of choice for a new class of men and women who were not afraid to express themselves as individually as possible. The style was as diverse as its owners—as challenging in its display of design as its adherents could make it.[22]

Shortly after completion of the Street-Morgan home, Ayers took on yet another important commission, the John B. Curtin home on Columbia Way.[23] In many ways the Curtin home is by far Ayers' most outstanding work. While the Street-Morgan home occupies a pivotal location next to the Red Church, dramatizing its apex at the north end of town, it represents an earlier flowering of the popular Queen Anne style. The Curtin home, on the other hand, depicts a maturing of that style which is more monumental and stately.[24]

Somewhere during the incredibly busy year of 1897, Ayers completed the new County Hospital. The *Union Democrat* reflected the interest in the new, much needed hospital.

> *Our new hospital is now complete and ready for occupancy. Mr. Ayers has shown his ability and skill in both this and many other buildings designed and built in this city under his supervision and the modern and handsome class of improvements made within the past year mark his advent among us.*[25]

Ayers next project was unique and somewhat of a diversion. It gave him an opportunity to display his artistic side. He created a float and an arch which was designed for the Native Daughters of the Golden West Parade. The float represented the mining industry. The gold output of the area was proudly depicted by four pyramids, showing the yield up to the year 1897. He also created an elaborate arch across Washington Street which was a reproduction of a Norman gateway of the Federal period in England. It was beautifully decorated with carnival flags and the Stars and Stripes and presented an exceedingly handsome and massive appearance.[26]

Toward the end of 1897, Ayers took on what would be, for all intents and purposes, his last major project in Sonora.

Architect Ayers says that if the supervisors are willing, he will furnish the county with as handsome a courthouse as any in the state.[27]

For a man who was touted as a "hometown boy," it must have come as somewhat of a shock when, three months later, the firm of Mooser and Company of San Francisco was chosen to be the architects for the new building. Why Ayers' plans were bypassed is unknown. According to Carlo De Ferrari, Tuolumne County Historian, his plans were described as true "French Renaissance or Old Colonial style and considered to be the acme of artistic architecture."[28] After this, Ayers' architectural work ceased in Sonora. He had two other small commissions for work in 1897, but there is no evidence that they were completed by him.[29]

In March 1898, he and Charlotte visited San Francisco, probably for their first wedding anniversary.[30] From this point on, Clarence Ayers' life and work was devoted principally to mining.[31] At some point between 1894 and 1895, Ayers had purchased a portion, if not all, of what was known as the famous Omega Mine. Located in the vicinity of Table Mountain between the famous Rawhide and Alabama Mines, the Omega had a long history dating back to 1857.[32] In March of 1897, the same month that Clarence and Charlotte got married, Ayers sold his interest in the Omega to a Scotch syndicate, as reported in the *Union Democrat*.[33]

A $40,000 MINING DEAL

The Omega Gravel Mine owned by C.W. Ayers and S. Bradford has been sold by them to a Scotch syndicate for $40,000. Mr. Ayers may assume the superintendency but probably will decline to serve, owing to much pressure from other businesses.[34]

The Omega Mine continued to be in the news, in spite of the

mine being worked by others.[35] Then in December of 1900, an article appeared in the *Progressive Association of America* which stated that the Grand View Mining Company Articles of Incorporation were filed in the county clerk's office, by Mr. Ayers. The object of the corporation was to buy, sell and operate mines, generate and sell electric power and to buy and sell merchandise and to conduct hotels and boarding houses. It was an adventurous project with a stock capitalization of $250,000.[36]

Ayers took yet another turn in his already busy schedule. He began to deal extensively in oil stocks from his home in Bakersfield.[37] From articles that appeared in both the *Union Democrat* and the *Tuolumne Independent* newspapers, Ayers made trips back and forth from Bakersfield to San Francisco and Sonora. Known originally as the community of Mariposa, a name derived from a group of miners who came from the Mother Lode after the turn of the century, the town of Taft experienced a flurry of activity centered around the oil industry.[38]

Compared to the frenzy in oil, Ayers may have become somewhat discouraged with his mining claims in Sonora. By 1903, he had abandoned the working of a gravel claim at Montezuma to handle oil lands in Taft. Then, again, while on a trip back to Sonora, he stated that he was seeking capital investment to restart his gold mining activity. From 1903 until 1915, the local newspapers kept up a lively record of Ayers' activities in mining and the work at the Omega.

Ayers, however, was going to surprise everyone once again. His talents seemed endless. The following article was printed in the *Union Democrat.*

> *Mr. and Mrs. Ayers, formerly of this city but now residing in San Francisco, visited Sonora this week. Mr. Ayers, who is owner in the Omega Mine recently invented an oven which is revolutionizing the bread-making industry.*[39]

In 1916, a front page article appeared in the *Union Democrat* with the following news about the Omega Mine:

BIG STRIKE OF HIGH GRADE ORE IN THE OMEGA MINE

The Omega Mine, whose development had been chronicled in the Union Democrat for the past three months is in bonanza ore, tons of it so far. The existence of this ore body was no secret to Mr. Ayers, who is now directing operations for Lance and Hussy who hold the mine under a bond to purchase. The mine, which is owned by Messrs. Ayers and Harter was bonded to Lange and Hussy, whom we understand are the representatives of a large and wealthy mining syndicate operating mines throughout the West.[40]

In 1918, Ayers again returned to the Taft area and his adventures in oil. In 1929, he and Charlotte returned to Sonora for a reunion. "Mr. and Mrs. C.W. Ayers, well-known here, have been shaking hands with many friends in Sonora this weekend."[41] They had just returned from a spectacular cross-country trip from Los Angeles to Detroit in the love of Clarence's life—a Knox automobile. Clarence had made a bet of $1,000 with his fellow Knights Templar that he and his trusty Knox would show up in Detroit faster than his friends traveling by the more conventional train. And he did it![42] Then came an event that closed a chapter of Clarence's life.

MRS. AYERS DIES SUDDENLY

Mrs. Ayers, wife of mining man dies suddenly in the southland of Santa Barbara. Mrs. Ayers was well-known in Sonora, having come here and settled where she conducted a millinery establishment opposite the City Hotel. In 1897, she married Mr. Ayers, the mining man and ever since the couple lived happily.[43]

In 1935, Clarence wrote to his sister, Viola. "The time is fast approaching when old Father Time is snooping around with his scythe to mow down us old fellows who have lived out our allotted three score years and ten."[44] He went on to express some hope that the United States Congress would pass the Townsend Plan or some other provision that would help older people.[45]

Clarence moved to Los Angeles a short time later. In 1937, *The Banner* disclosed that "Mr. Ayers is selling a machine invented by him which makes cubes out of large cakes of ice, one of which will be installed in the local ice plant."[46] In that same year, Clarence visited Sonora again. He was eighty years old. Arriving in his twenty-seven year old Knox automobile, with 270,000 miles on the speedometer, he claimed that he sometimes had to call the police "in order to make his getaway from the crowds."[47]

During World War II, Clarence is pictured in the *Los Angeles Times*, well into his eighties, donating rubber tires off his beloved Knox automobile for the war effort.[48]

In 1945, Clarence passed away and was buried in Forest Lawn Cemetery next to his beloved Charlotte.[49] Thus passed one of Sonora's brightest luminaries. Ayers left behind a lasting legacy in Sonora including the Street-Morgan home, the Curtin home and the Bradford-Rosasco home. All three structures still remain in the Sierra community. His mining map of 1897, is displayed prominently in the planning department of the Albert Francisco Building, and the Omega Mine Road still leads to the site of the famous mine.

It has often been said that men and women can only do one thing well, but Ayers proved them wrong. He was an architect, a mining engineer and an inventor. Some of his finest work is located in Sonora, true architectural treasures of the Mother Lode.

Footnotes

[1]The Red Church, or the St. James Episcopal Church. Built in 1860. The Red House in 1886-87.

[2]Letter from Clarence to his sister Viola, February 16, 1935. "I do not have more than a vague idea that I was born somewhere near the town of Mauston in the State of Wisconsin, about 1857 or 58."

[3]David Clinton Higby, "Edward Higby and His Descendants". From his Ph.D. dissertation, 1927. Ayer's mother was Amelia Laura Higby. Her family dates back to New York, 1795 and to a distinguished line in England.

[4]Malcolm J. Rohrbough, Days of Gold, The California Gold Rush and the American Nation, (1997).

[5]Frank Lloyd Wright was born less than fifty miles from Ayers, in Richland Center, Wisconsin. Sullivan's beliefs attracted young architects from all over the U.S., spawning what became known as the "Chicago School."

[6]Debbie Harrison, Oregon. Letter, September 16, 1994. Apparently the entire Ayers family had moved to California around this time. Clarence's mother, Amelia Ayers died in Fresno in 1891. His brother, Edward, farmed in Fresno and later worked for Clarence in Tuolumne County. His sister Viola, was married to Henry Musick in Fresno in 1888 and died in Pasadena. Edward Higby and His Descendants.

[7]*Rogue River Genealogical Society*, September, 1994. The Hargadines took a grant of 640 acres in Ashland and owned and operated the first general store there. A cemetery is named after them. See their publication, *Sons and Daughters of Oregon Pioneers*. Letter, October 8, 1994.

[8]James Ludham. Letter April 13, 1994. Two daughters were born of this union: Mabel in 1884 and Bernice.Mabel Musick moved to Los Angeles, and Bernice Ludlam, to Sebastopol. James Ludlam of Los Angeles is a grandson of Clarence.

[9]*Rogue Valley Historical Society*. The best known placer mine in the district was known as the " '49er Diggins" about two miles from Ashland. E. I. Anderson leased many of his mining properties to San Francisco capitalists.

[10]*Ashland Tidings*. Ashland, Oregon, Vol. 5, January 1890-December 1891. The Anderson Home bears a striking resemblance to the Street-Morgan Home.

[11]The bank was located at: 327 West 1st Street, Albany, Oregon. The

reason for Ayers being in Linn County may have been due to mineralization discovered in 1863 in Linn County. Letter from Dick Milligan. January 11, 1995. According to Carol Harbison, library manager at the Southern Oregon Historical Society, Ayers moved to Oregon just for the Linn Bank Building. Letter of December 14, 1994.

[12]Harris, Rydell, Robert DeWitt, Grand Illusions: Chicago's World Fair, (1994). The title, "Great White City" was due in part to the fact it marked the first large public display of electric lights, debuted at the Philadelphia Centennial of 1876. Built with all the optimism that America possessed in the late 19th century, it would, by the 1920's, be seen as an architectural embarrassment. Stylistically, it brushed any hint of modernism aside. Its Neo-classic imitations denied the real genius of American enterprise, character and originality.

[13]The Chicago Historical Society could not find any reference to Ayers as a commissioner. Oregon did not have its own state exhibit buildings as did California, but it did have several other exhibits. Unfortunately, no references I found mention Ayers. James Ludham writes: "I saw a reference to Clarence Ayers, Commissioner of Mines and Mining, State of Oregon, and a reference to a diploma with medal, Chicago World's Fair, 1893." Letter, July 11, 1994.

[14]Louis Sullivan, 1893. "The damage wrought by the World's Fair will last for half a century from its date, if not longer."

[15]Wright, and those architects who attempted to create an indigenous American style of architecture were not popular. Ayers would have been, like most architects of his time, in the very center of the popular and highly ornate Gothic Revival, (Victorian) a style that a rising middle class adopted as their own.

[16]James Ludlam. Letter, April 13, 1994. According to James Ludlam, Ayer's grandson, the family was deserted by Ayers. "There was not a great deal of love lost between them and their grandfather. I can recall his appearing on rare occasions and he was quite a flamboyant character."

[17]*Union Democrat*, June, 1897.

[18]Sharon Marovich. "The Old House". Fifth in a series, "The Bradford-Rosasco Home," Unpublished paper, March 1992.

[19]Mrs. Lynn was a widow with a small child, Miles Bert Lynn. Her millinery ads ran July 1897 through December in the *Union Democrat.*

[20]*Union Democrat*, March 1897. March 13th was the date of Clarence's mother's birth. Apparently Ayers tried to keep the romance news quiet, but something was afoot when Edward, Clarence's brother arrived in January for a visit. The fact was mentioned that Ayers left for

San Francisco on Tuesday, March 13, 1897 (possibly for his marriage?).

[21]*Union Democrat*, 1896. The paper ran continuous articles on the progress of the home.

[22]Tuolumne County Genealogical Society. Voter's Register, 1896. Ayers may have been busy but he took time out to register to vote in 1896. He gave his birth date as 1858, his height as 5'11", with a light complexion, blue eyes, brown hair.

[23]Queen Victoria's long reign, 1837-1901, lent her name to the era known as Victorianism in England. In America, the architectural style known as Gothic Revival, often became known more popularly as the Victorian style. It flourished after the American Civil War and found its way to the West Coast after its appearance at the Philadelphia Centennial of 1876. It was also the result of the Industrialized Revolution. The new scroll and jig saws enabled homeowners to produce a dazzling array of gables, dormers, towers, turrets, pinnacles and other elaborate ornamentation.

[24]J.B. Curtin was born near Gold Springs in 1867. See Chapter on John Curtin.

[25]*Union Democrat*, September 25, 1897.

[26]*Tuolumne Independent,* January 9, 1897. What happened to the elaborate structure is unknown.

[27]ibid.

[28]Sharon Marovich, historian. Conversation, January, 1994. She suggested that Ayers may have designed a courthouse utilizing wood rather than stone—something that the supervisors were opposed to in fire-hazardous Sonora. Also see, Carlo De Ferrari, "The Tuolumne County Courthouses," *Chispa*, Vol. 39, No. 2, October December 1999. p.1379. An excellent sketch of Ayers' proposed courthouse was made by C. L. Sears, Sonora photographer.

[29]*Tuolumne Independent,* April 17, 1897, April 19, 1897. The McCormick Brothers Meat Market, the Jamestown Jail, and the Topping Home.

[30]*Union Democrat*, March, 1898. Ayers also owned interest in the Green Gold Mining Company, the Grand View Mining Company, and the General Hooker Quartz Mine. Minutes of the Sonora City Council. Oct. 17, 1894. The Green Gold Mine yielded $200,000 in 1897.

[31]Islam Temple. Letter, September 10, 1994. Clarence was a Noble of Islam Temple. He was initiated in 1901 and paid his dues through 1945. He was a 32nd Degree Scottish Rite Mason and a member of the San Francisco Consistory, Ancient and Accepted Scottish Rite of Freemasonry. Letter, October 3, 1994. He was also a member of the

Republican Party. *Tiding*, Ashland, Oregon, Vol. 4. January 13, 1888-89.

[32]*Union Democrat*, March 13, 1897.

[33]I am indebted to Mr. Johnstone of the Sonora Mining Company who sent me information on the mine.

[34]*Union Democrat* March 13, 1897.

[35]Under the Indexes of Deeds and Liens at the County Recorder's office, there is a stream of records relating to mine activity under Ayers' name.

[36]*Progressive Association of America*, December, 1900, p.40.

[37]*Union Democrat* June 21, 1904.

[38]The name "Taft" was not given to the town until 1910. Oilmen like E.L. Doheny and others made incredible oil strikes there. "It was family lore that Clarence built an Opera house in Taft, California." Letter, James Ludham, April 22, 1994. All attempts to locate this building or references to it have been fruitless. (Author).

[39]*Union Democrat*, October 23, 1915.

[40]*Union Democrat*, October 21, 1916.

[41]*Union Democrat*, June 29, 1929.

[42]*Mother Lode Magnet*, March 20, 1929.

[43]*Union Democrat*, March 1, 1930. It is ironic that March was the month the Ayers were married. Perhaps they were celebrating their 33rd wedding anniversary. (Author).

[44]Clarence Ayers. Letter to Viola Gulke, February 16, 1935.

[45]ibid. During the hard pressed years of the depression, many plans were advocated for helping people down on their luck. Most were basically unemployment compensation. The Townsend Clubs claimed almost a million members. Politically astute, President Roosevelt enacted the Social Security Act in August, 1935, stealing the thunder right out from under Townsend's proposals.

[46]*The Banner*, November 12, 1897.

[47]ibid.

[48]Courtesy, James Ludham.

[49]On Charlotte's tombstone was the inscription: "Beloved wife of Charles W. Ayers. Brightest light of my life went with her." On Clarence's tombstone, it reads: " Beloved Husband." Forest Lawn Cemetery. Vale of Memory, Burbank, California.

Sonora
Tuolumne
Jamestown
The "Women's Railroad"
Oakdale
Annie Kline RIKERT
WD

Annie Kline Rikert

Some women have always marched to a different drummer, even in the Victorian Era. And while most women in the 19th century preferred or were politely urged by societal pressure to trod the well-worn path of "expected" female behavior, a few daring souls chose other directions for their lives. One of those was Annie Kline Rikert, builder of The Stockton-Tuolumne Railroad, more popularly known as The Women's Railroad.

Given the era she grew up in, perhaps it is no wonder. The United States Civil War produced a great many Scarlet O'Haras. They were willful, independent, rebellious and resourceful women who felt compelled, due to circumstances beyond their control, to take a stand.

Annie Kline's origins reach deeply into the South. Her grandmother, Sarah, was a Kentuckian. Her grandfather, David Kline, moved to an area along the Big Black River, in Mississippi Territory before 1815. Exactly when they purchased their Warren County land is unknown, but the Klines were well established by 1815.[1]

In 1827, Sarah Kline was named executor of her husband David's estate.[2] The young widow not only had the responsibility of managing a 640 acre plantation, but also the care and education of her six children. One of those children, was Nineon E. Kline, Annie's father.

In 1836 Sarah died, and in 1837, Nineon Kline, her son, purchased the estate.[3] The following year, 1838, Nineon married

Patience M. Lynche. By this time Nineon was a wealthy planter in the Ashbury community. He and Patience had seven children. Annie was the oldest. Emma, Virginia, Minerva, John, Thomas and Nineon Jr. were Annie's younger brothers and sisters.[4]

War clouds were descending on a nation divided and with the firing on Fort Sumter, South Carolina in 1861, a way of life was about to end. Nineon Kline was forty-five years old, too old for Confederate service. But it did not take long for the reality of war to loom precipitously close to the Kline homestead.[5]

In 1862, Admiral David Farragut's Union fleet captured New Orleans and Baton Rouge and made their way upriver to Vicksburg. Jefferson Davis, President of the Confederacy, ordered that all the cotton stored in barns be burned to keep it from falling into enemy hands. No doubt the Kline plantation was included.[6] The fighting was fierce and the family could hear the roar of cannon from gunboats at Vicksburg.

In the ensuing struggle to take Vicksburg, Confederate troops camped in the Kline's pasture. Fearing a battle would take place soon, Nineon sought to protect his family by sending them into town to stay with friends, the Lum family. Ironically when Vicksburg fell on April 4, 1862, General Ulysses S. Grant chose the beautiful old Lum homestead as his quarters. Annie and her siblings were relegated to rooms upstairs. Thomas Kline, Annie's brother, remembers that his sister was an ardent rebel. She refused an introduction to General Grant.[7]

Apparently Annie took the war very seriously indeed. Her brother maintained that she was a spy for the Confederate Army and was arrested by the provost marshal and jailed in Vicksburg.[8] She was accused of smuggling supplies to the Confederacy. "Many a time I swam my horse across the Big Black River carrying information. I knew Jefferson Davis, of course, and asked him if he couldn't give me something else to do." "Well," he said, "I know of but one thing that we can give you and that is the task to burn the railroad bridge between Chattanooga and Nashville. If you can do that it will cut off the Yankees' supplies."[9]

Indeed, the entire Kline family was under suspicion by the Union forces and orders had been sent out by Union General James B. McPherson that these "outlaws should be entrapped and caught."[10] McPherson was emphatic. "I am also well satisfied that the Kline family and especially Miss Kline are guilty of acting in bad faith toward our Government and imparting information to the enemy. You will, therefore, take immediate steps to put the whole family across the Big Black River, not to return to this side without written permission from the proper military authorities under penalty of being dealt with as spies."[11]

Annie never wavered. At one point, with the city under Federal occupation, she hid a detailed plan of the federal fortification in her dress. Unfortunately, she was captured and the papers discovered. Imprisoned, she was tried by court martial, convicted as a spy and sentenced to be shot.[12] General Dana, offered to pardon her if she would disclose the names of the persons who had given her the papers. Annie defiantly told him, "You have it in your power to murder me, but not to make me murder the friends that trusted me. Execute the sentence."[13] However, Brevet Major C. P. Gooding intervened and succeeded in having her pardoned and freed.

Annie's narrow escape from death, however, did not alter her determination. She continued to help the Confederacy. After Abraham Lincoln's assassination, she was accused of being a possible accomplice in the plot. A warning order was conveyed to her. Annie fled. "My father was uneasy about me and sent me to Texas with my married sister. There I married."[14] Annie married Will Townsend and subsequently moved to San Francisco.[15]

In the City by the Bay, she began a highly successful business making artificial flowers.[16] Unfortunately, in 1877, a riot occurred in a business near by and when a fire broke out, everything she owned and worked for burned. She and her husband and their daughter, Maud, barely escaped. A short time later, her husband died.

Due perhaps to her widowhood, Annie Kline hired an attorney and tried to win back her claim against the city of San Francisco for $1,700. The case was dismissed. Depressed and, some feared, suicidal, Annie Kline vanished.

In the April 22, 1879 issue of the *San Francisco Chronicle* these headlines appeared. "Mrs. Annie Kline Townsend and her Daughter Maud Disappear." The *Chronicle* announced their mysterious disappearance and that no trace of either mother or daughter had been found. The paper asserted that there was reason for her friends to fear that she may have sought suicide as a relief from pressing temporal difficulties. The paper went on to describe Annie's talents and her successful business at the corner of Geary and Leavenworth Streets. There was, the paper continued, the unfortunate fire and her unsuccessful lawsuit and, finally, Annie's disappearance. The paper asked anyone who knew of her whereabouts to write Messrs. Lightfoot and Carter at 230 Montgomery Street, San Francisco. The writer added. "It is known that the lady could not leave the city as she was utterly penniless."[17]

Where had Annie gone? The details are conspicuously missing. However, when she did reappear, her circumstances had been altered considerably. She described these events as follows:

"How did I happen to go into mining? From necessity. Seventeen years ago, I was left a widow in San Francisco, without means and with my little girl to care for. I was not fitted for any ordinary work. I couldn't entertain the thought of going east again and being dependent on my father. I preferred an outdoor life and being in California, mining was the only thing I could see to turn to. I had never associated with mining people and knew nothing more about mining than I had of geology and mineralogy as a girl. I went to San Bernardino, got a tent, a little sheet-iron stove, a camp bed and provisions enough as I supposed [*sic*] to last a year. Then I hired a teamster to take me, my little five year-old girl and my outfit out on the Mojave Desert within three miles of the Silver King Mine. One day at sunset, as I was getting ready to start back to our tent, I was discouraged and almost ready to give up, I heard my little daughter screaming. Mama, Mama. I went to her as she called out. I have found some rock exactly like the specimen Mr. Pearson had at San Bernardino, Maud said enthusiastically. Mr. Pearson was a man who had come up from Mexico and had shown me specimens of silver ore. Sure enough, she was right. I knocked off some of the outcroppings and took about twenty-five lbs. back to my tent. It assayed at $9,000 to the ton. I had six pillowcases. Every day I went over and got as much of the ore as I could and when I had the pillowcases filled, I had them taken to Oro Grande to be milled. That is how I found and worked my first mine. Six months later, I had $40,000 in the bank, and owned several valuable mines."[18]

Annie went on to explain that there was a drop in silver mining and, hence, it was not worthwhile. She read up on reports of the state mineralogist and found out the yield of gold from the different counties for the past forty-five years. Traveling to Columbia in Tuolumne County, she asked if there were any houses for rent. "The town was dead, and I leased a pretty seven-room cottage with fruit and flowers around it for two years at $2.50 a month. I hunted up government land and in time, I located the Mascot, Midas, Alhambra, (the pride of Tuolumne) the Utopia, Lucky Star, Sarah Frances, Pina Blanco the Big Gun and the Oro Madre Mines."[19]

During the time she left her mining operations in southern California and Mexico, Annie had married a Mr. Rikert of Jamestown. A wealthy relative of the famed Vanderbilt family, Mr. Rikert was apparently not interested in the millions from that distinguished family, but preferred the anonymity of a quiet, less publicized existence.[20]

The relationship was unique, even looking back at it from the changed mores of our own era. While Annie was forging the rough and tumble life as a railroad executive, her husband seemed content to operate a livery stable in Jamestown.

In 1897, Annie Kline Rikert, the ardent former Confederate spy, was about to launch herself into history. Articles of Incorporation for The Stockton Tuolumne Railroad were filed.

The company had a capital stock of $1 million dollars divided into 10,000 shares, each valued at $100. The company proposed to construct a railroad from Stockton which ran in an easterly direction through the counties of San Joaquin, Stanislaus, Calaveras and Tuolumne to Summerville (Carters). The directors of the company were: Annie Kline Rikert, Maggie Downing Brainard of San Jose, Robert S. Clark of Alameda, Hannah Lewella Lane and Jabish Clement of San Francisco.[21]

It would take an iron will to accomplish her goals. Where the resources for this monumental undertaking came from in an era that had few, if any, female executive role models is not altogether clear. Granted, the Civil War played a role in shaping a steely personality that had learned to stand up to insurmountable odds. And if Grant and the entire Union Army was not enough to alter Annie's course, I doubt that she would have been intimidated by the thought of running a railroad. Still, it takes more than determination to plan and organize a project that required inordinate amounts of capital. Annie must have picked up a substantial amount of information not only about railroads, but about the requirements of mine owners as well. It was apparently enough to convince influential and powerful people that her endeavors were feasible. She was able to garner support from a wide variety of people, one of whom was Congressman James A. Louttit.[22]

There were a few other things in Annie's favor. The country was weathering scandal upon scandal against the Transcontinental Railroad. There was the Mussle Slough tragedy of 1880, the passage of the Sherman Anti-Trust laws of 1890 and, the incendiary book by Frank Norris, *The Octopus*. However, the fact that most of her support came from wealthy and powerful women may have proven less beneficial than it initially might have seemed.[23]

Through the latter half of 1897, publicity on what was becoming known as The Women's Railroad was enthusiastic. The railroad was scheduled to pass through Copperopolis, across the Stanislaus River below Bostwick's Bar, to Rossland,

Sonora and, finally, to Summersville. Judge Brainard of Sonora was to be in charge of the engineering. He had been a railroad engineer, having built The West Shore Road in New York State.[24]

Close behind this news, came the announcement that the road would cost $700,000 and that the management was principally composed of women. Mrs. Rikert did not seem to flinch when it came to criticizing the men. Taking aim at what she labeled a "next week" attitude toward work, she called them too slow to get the job done. Fast upon the heels of this rebuff, she took aim at her competitor, the Sierra Railroad whom she said had paid almost nothing for their right of way. "The Sierra Railroad was not well constructed," she declared, "and freight costs were too high."[25]

At the beginning of 1898, optimism ran high in Sonora for the new road. Judge Brainard held meetings in Sonora to which the public was invited. Attorney F. W. Street also made a convincing argument in favor of the road.[26] This was followed by a long editorial in the *Union Democrat.*

> *"The Stockton Tuolumne Railroad will positively be built. We have this straight from a source that is practically the main spring of the venture. Ever since the road was even mentioned, a skirmish line has been thrown out from the camp of the objectors, whose only purpose appears to be to ridicule as preposterous the idea that anything with women at the head can ever reach a successful climax. The same old nonsensical talk has been going on for centuries. When the Sierra Railroad accepted Jamestown as a terminus, the people of Sonora at once saw the need of a competing line that would transverse this district. Another thing we can vouch for is that this will be a people's road."*[27]

Mrs. Rikert spoke glowingly of the perspective plans and possibilities of what a new Railroad would mean to the affected communities. Thousands of tons of ore remained in dumps, she said, because it could not be shipped. Annie maintained that the costs the Sierra Railroad charged were outrageous. She went on to predict that on her line, costs of transporting ore would be reduced from twenty dollars a ton to nine dollars.[28]

Others pointed out that in the Gopher Range of hills (Gopher Diggings, Calaveras County) lay large deposits of gold, which the road would open up to exploration. Tuolumne County was reputed to be the greatest gold producing region in the state, but it needed access to rails. There were copper mines in Copperopolis, timberlands in the Sierra and limestone deposits used in the sugar beet industry.[29] All of these would be accessible with the new road.

In March, construction of The Women's Railroad or The People's Road as it was often called, was underway. Judge Brainard told Sonorans that when the road was finished, businessmen could go to Stockton in one day and return the same day for $2.50.[30]

On April 2, the *Union Democrat* ran a large article entitled:

> *A ROYAL WELCOME AWAITS*
>
> *A portion of Erickson and Company's crew, consisting of over thirty men are raising the road bed. This work was being done by a day's pay and no contract would be let until fourteen miles of road had been built and was ready for track laying.*[31]

On April 9, 1898, Mrs. Rikert promised to equip the road with first class passenger coaches with a seating capacity of fifty to sixty passengers. She would only use First Class box and flat cars, which would carry loads with a capacity of twenty-five to thirty tons.[32]

Also on April 9, it was announced by the *Union Democrat* that "it is no longer a question of raising the capital with which to carry on the work. Enough money had been pledged." Since Monday of last week the paper claimed that Erickson's crew has made rapid progress and everything was being done as fast as was commensurate with first class work and there would be no stopping until the road reached its destination.[33]

In May, construction of The Women's Road was progressing nicely. The first shipment of rails had arrived in Stockton from the Pennsylvania Steel mills.[34] Behind the scenes however, events were unfolding which would cause problems for Annie.

The Sierra Railroad had been incorporated in February 1897. Its planners were Thomas Bullock, railroad builder, Prince André Poniatowski, a promoter of European capital, William Crocker, son of the Big Four Southern Pacific founder, and Sidney Freshman.[35] Their plans initially outlined a route to be constructed from a point in Stanislaus County, on or near the town of Oakdale, in an easterly direction to the town of Angels Camp. Intermediate branches were to be built to Modesto, Knights Ferry, La Grange and Coulterville.[36] Their offices were located in San Francisco in the Crocker Building and the company was capitalized at five million dollars.[37] On November 10th, 1897, the Sierra Railroad reached Jamestown and a Grand Opening was held for a party of over 5,000 people.[38]

Partnering with the wealthiest citizen of Jamestown, the investors of the Sierra Railroad drew Captain Nevills into their plan to develop and promote Jamestown. He built the imposing and elegant three-story Jamestown Hotel with sixty guest rooms adjacent to the new depot, on the promise that Jamestown would be the terminus of the road. By April, his hotel had opened. Bullock assured Nevills that Jamestown would remain the terminus for the Sierra Railroad for at least five years and agreed to repay a $25,000 improvement loan should the railroad extend its line before that time.[39]

Earlier that year, Henry Crocker of the Big Four had purchased $515,000 bonds for the Sierra Railroad, one of the largest financial transactions ever made in California up to that time. The total issue of stock was $634,000. In effect, the bonds constituted 75% of the railroad.[40]

The real stake, however, in this war between two competing routes, was the valuable 55,000 acres of timberland to the east of Sonora, where the Sierra Railroad planned to construct the East Side Flume and Lumber Company. Owned by Mr. Crocker, neither he nor the promoters of the road could risk having another railroad reach these valuable timber holdings first and certainly not a group of high-handed women. In order to move their plan forward, The Sierra Railroad had to reach Sonora and Carters in Tuolumne as quickly as possible. In addition to timber interest, these men were also involved in enlarging the Standard Lumber Company of Sonora by developing logging and lumber operations. Another factor was a desire to get a line to the Columbia Marble Works, incorporated with Prince Poniatowski and Bullock of the Sierra Railroad. However, residents of Sonora and the *Union Democrat* favored The People's Road over that of the Sierra's "out-of-towners." The question was, who would reap the benefits of the service offered, the miners and The People's Road or the lumber interest of the Sierra Road?[41]

On July 23, the bubble burst when it was announced that The Women's Road was mortgaged. "Last Tuesday, a mortgage was filed for the record by Secretary A.S. Clark of the Stockton Tuolumne Railroad by which the property is mortgaged to Maud Townsend, daughter of Mrs. Rikert for a loan of $25,000."[42]

On August 4, 1898, the *Stockton Evening Mail* printed what appeared to be the first signs of trouble with the road. Mrs. Rikert's rails had been delivered and paid for in full, but for some reason, graders had been induced to quit by Charles Erickson, Annie's man in charge of road construction. She maintained that the trouble was coming from one source, The Sierra Railroad.[43]

On August 20, another surprising announcement stated that the Sierra Railroad people decided to desert Jamestown and extend their road through Sonora. For some time, they declared, the company had seriously contemplated deserting Jamestown as a terminus and pushing ahead to Sonora, and onto Summerville.[44] This news must have come as some surprise to

Captain Nevills who immediately filed suit against the Sierra Railroad for a breach of contract.[45]

The lines were drawn in the sand with the entry of Mrs. Rikert's road and its favorable acceptance by Sonorans. The Sierra Railroad's planned extensions to Sonora and Carters in the Sierras had to be put on fast forward.

As events began to heat up, Rikert refused to let the dream die. "We are going to build it," she boasted, "if we have to build it with a brigade of women."[46]

The voices raised in opposition to The Women's Road grew increasingly hostile and vocal. *The Mother Lode Magnet* of Jamestown referred to the railroad as Annie's Aerial Road, which began nowhere going over impossible routes and ending somewhere in the Nevada Mountains. "We have it on good authority by one of the best and oldest engineers in California that the road as proposed by these ladies is absolutely impossible to build owing to engineering difficulties in the crossing of mountains. There certainly is some hidden scheme in this proposed railroad. Is it the foisting of worthless stock upon a credulous public or the selling of town lots of a town yet on paper?"[47]

The town that the newspaper referred to was Rossland, or Rosslyn, located at the end of French Flat road, north of Rawhide. A post office was established there in May 1898. It was later discontinued and moved to Jamestown.[48]

In August 1898, the *Stockton Evening Mail* was not quite as ardently enthusiastic about The Women's Road as it had been initially. What lay at the heart of the problems, according to Mrs. Rikert, were some dirty tricks that the Sierra Railroad had cleverly instigated. "The Ericksons," Mrs. Rikert argued, "were induced to quit my road by the Sierra people who were offering them better pay. Do you suppose he (Erickson) cares whether the men got their pay or not? Of course he doesn't. It wasn't on their account at all that he induced them to quit, but to injure our company. The rails had been paid for and were waiting to be sent on. However, an attachment was levied on the rails for one purpose alone, to hold up work on the railroad."[49] If indeed the Ericksons had been hired away from Annie's road to work on the Sierra Railroad, that delay was enough to buy the time needed to proceed with their plans. Also, in order to sell shares of stock in her company, it was critical that the credit of the company remain unimpaired.[50]

Erickson's graders put an attachment on Mrs. Rikert's line for unpaid wages and immediately began work for the Sierra Railroad. When Mrs. Rikert cried foul, *The Mother Lode Magnet* said: "This is all twaddle. Mrs. Rikert's road fell in the consommé simply because laboring men must be paid."[51]

The Women's Railroad had secured the right-of-way out of Stockton as far north as Copperopolis and was actively continuing to sell stock by popular subscription at $100 a share. Its proposed route was still via Columbia to Sonora and Summersville where Bullock was not only determined to go, but to arrive first.[52]

The controversy mounted. While some people believed that Annie's line would bring better service than that offered by the Sierra Railroad, others called the line a purely promotional scheme. Bullock was quoted as having called Mrs. Rikert "a high tone thief and mesmerizer of large-figured checks." [53]

Then, Rikert's engineers ran into trouble on the bridge proposed to cross the Stanislaus River. Grading crews were also running into delays which put them neck and neck with the surveyors.[54] In addition, there were cash flow problems. By August 1898, crews were leaving The Women's Road and joining the Sierra Railroad.[55]

In September, the Sierra Railroad announced that they would extend their line to Sonora. And they would do so by using the very rails paid for by The Women's Road. There had been an attachment for some time on the rails, placed there by Sheriff Cunningham to secure any judgment which might be procured in four or five separate suits brought against The Women's Road by Erickson, McCormick and other creditors. It was known that the Sierra Railroad was anxious to make a deal

THE PROPOSED STOCKTON-LODI R.R.
GRADING ON THE "WOMEN'S RAILROAD"
RIGHT OF WAY ON OR NEAR
WHAT IS NOW ARGONAUT STREET,
IN WEST STOCKTON.
ABOUT 1895
RALPH O YARDLEY

This is a wood cut illustration of Mrs. Rikert planning the proposed route of the railroad.

for the rails to be used in their extension to Sonora.[56]

If all of these problems were not enough, Annie had to deal with men lured away by news of the Klondike gold strike in late 1897 and early 1898. Also, others were volunteering for the Spanish American War.[57]

Mrs. Rikert complained. "I want to show you the greatest exhibition of nerve I ever heard of. You remember the

Ericksons who sued me and attached the grading outfits and hampered me in every way they could—claiming that I owed them a great deal of money? Well, these same people want to work for me again. It strikes me as rather singular that men who think I am a fraud and unable to pay my debts want to work for me again."[58]

In January 1899, the *Stockton Evening Mail* ran the following: *"Damages demanded. McCormick Bros. sues for $80,000 by Women's Railroad."* The McCormick Brothers were sued by Mrs. Rikert for preventing the building of the road by maliciously prosecuting it for an unjust claim. When the case came to trial, judgment was rendered in favor of Mrs. Rikert. However, while attachments were dissolved, the railroad's credit and financial standing prevented them from selling $75,000 worth of bonds and added further expenses of $5,000 for attorney's fees.[59]

The *Union Democrat* explained that the McCormick Brothers conducted a butchering business in Stockton and had given Mrs. Rikert a bill for $5,710 for meals furnished to her for her crew. There was no cash on hand, so McCormick was given a note signed by Mrs. Rikert. The brothers brought suit to recover the amount and had attachments placed on the assets of the company, principally the rails that were worth $48,000. The court later claimed that this was invalid and ruled in Mrs. Rikert's favor. However, the butcher didn't think that a female owner of a railroad was good for the money so he took the case to a higher court.[60]

Almost a year later, the *Stockton Evening Mail* ran the following headline. *"Did It Block The Women's Road?"* Allegations claimed that the Sierra Company did just that. "Sometime ago, Mrs Rikert, President of the Stockton Tuolumne Railroad declared that the Sierra Railroad was back of the financial troubles into which she has been plunged."[61] Annie explained that when the Sierra Railroad intended to extend the line from Jamestown to Summersville, they had to stop The Women's Road because they also had Sonora as their objective point. Hence if The Women's Railroad was built, the Sierra bonds could not be sold.

In the end, the Sierra Railroad won its battle against Mrs. Rikert. On August 1898, *The Mother Lode Magnet* announced that the Sierra's extension eastward would be built.[62] On February 26, 1899, a jubilant crowd greeted the new road and complementary speeches by Mayor Burden, Attorney Crittenden Hampton, Prince Poniatowsky and Thomas Bullock were made.[63]

Tuolumne City (Carters) was reached on February 1, 1900. The site for the mill had been purchased on March 8, 1899, and the Westside Flume and Lumber Company was formally incorporated on May 31, 1899. Today, far beyond what the original builders expected, the Sierra Railroad is one of the longest lived railroads in the country. It still uses most of the original line, and continues to serve the lumber industry.[64]

The women put forth a courageous effort, given the attitudes and general suspicion of the time, that the so-called weaker sex could not undertake such a grandiose scheme. Annie Kline Rikert may have had the determination to get the job done, but she was stopped by the financial forces lined up against her. It would take the Women's Movement of the 1960's and years of legislation to alter people's perception about women's roles in society.[65]

It is ironic that Mrs. Rikert's nemesis, Charles Erickson's widow would play a part in railroading. Upon Mr. Erickson's death, Mrs. Erickson took over her husband's line, The Amador Central Railroad, becoming a railroad president in her own right. The line ran from Ione, where it connected with the Southern Pacific, to Martell, a distance of twelve miles. In addition to the freight business, the Amador Central did a profitable passenger business. It also operated two automobile stage lines out of Martell.[66]

Indeed, the honor of being the only woman railroad president was held by a Mrs. S. A. Kidder, of Grass Valley, California. She later resigned the presidency of the Nevada County Narrow

Gauge Railroad.[67]

And, in southern California, May Rindge founded and built her own railroad in Malibu, California. It ran along the same route as today's Pacific Coast Highway.[68]

What happened to Annie Kline Rikert? She left the area around 1900 and moved to a ranch in Shasta County. There, she received some publicity in the local paper for being arrested while guarding her garden path with a shotgun in order to prevent the neighbor's hogs from destroying her property. Never one to back down, she remained adamant and willful. The case was eventually dismissed.[69] From Shasta, she moved to Trinity County and a short time later, sought a divorce from Mr. Rikert in Sonoma County. In December 1906, Mrs. Rikert died in Sacramento.[70]

A rare and forceful woman of great courage, she would no doubt have been pleased at the careers women have found in today's world, though somewhat surprised at the length of time it has taken to achieve them.[71] Annie was simply a woman a century ahead of her time.

Footnotes

[1]Gordon A. Cotton, Asbury: A History, (1994), p. 91.

[2]ibid.

[3]ibid. Also, a neighbor, the Lums, posted a $40,000 bond as guardians of Annie and the children. The Lums would figure importantly in Annie's life during the Civil War. p. 92.

[4] The Kline family children were well educated. Nineon's brother, John, attended Jefferson College, and Sarah Ann, his sister, attended Elizabeth Female Academy. Nineon was referred to as a wealthy planter in the community. Asbury, p. 92.

[5]Wailes' Private Diary, 1962. Warren County. Wailes lived nearby on an adjacent plantation.

[6]Mississippi Department of Archives and History, 1862.

[7]ibid.

[8]ibid.

[9]Helen Dare, "Up Grade and Down Grade on The Women's Railroad," *San Francisco Examiner*, August 21, 1898.

[10]Cotton and Mason, With Malice Toward Some, "The Smoked Yanks," Quotes, p. 173.

[11]ibid.

[12]Asbury, p. 95

[13]ibid. p. 95

[14]*San Francisco Examiner,* August 21, 1898. Annie's sister Emma was also imprisoned along with Annie.

[15]Apparently, William was an invalid. Perhaps he had been wounded in the Civil War. (Author)

[16]"Apprehended Suicide," *San Francisco Chronicle*, April 22, 1879.

[17]ibid.

[18]*San Francisco Examiner*, August 21, 1898.

[19]ibid.

[20]"Woman Miner and Railroader Dead," *Union Democrat*, December 22, 1906.

[21]"That New Road Line," *Stockton Evening Mail*, December 24, 1897.

[22]"Honorable James Alexander Louttit," *History of San Joaquin County*, p. 559. Born in Louisiana in 1848, Louttit's family moved to Mokelumne Hill in Tuolumne County. He studied mining in Colorado and was admitted to the bar in California. *Stockton Record*, July 27, 1906. In support of Annie's road, Louttit purchased a section of road bed. *Union Democrat*, April 2, 1898.

[23]Phoebe Hearst, wife of William Randolph Hearst, founder of the *San Francisco Examiner*, was also an enthusiastic contributor to The Women's Railroad. "That Railroad to Sonora," *Stockton Evening Mail*, December 19, 1898.

[24]ibid. Note, the spelling of Rossland seems to vary in many of the sources. (Author).

[25]"The Lady Railroad Builder," *Stockton Evening Mail*, December 31, 1898.

[26]*Union Democrat*, January 15, 1898.

[27]*Union Democrat*, January 29, 1898.

[28]"The Lady Railroad Builder," *Stockton Evening Mail*, December 31, 1898.

[29]"Help the New Road Along," *Stockton Evening Mail*, April 19, 1898.

[30]*Union Democrat*, March 19, 1898.

[31]*Union Democrat*, April 1, 1898.

[32]"The New Railroad Project," *Stockton Evening Mail*, April 9, 1898.

[33]*Union Democrat,* April 9, 1898.

[34]"Progress of the New Road," *Stockton Evening Mail,* May 14, 1898.

[35]Dave Connery, "The Sierra Railroad. A Centennial Tribute, 1897-1997," *Chispa*, Vol. 36, No. 3. January-March 1997. p. 1258.

[36]ibid.

[37]"That Railroad to Sonora," *Stockton Evening Mail*, December 12, 1898.

[38]*Chispa*, "A Centennial Tribute," p. 1266.

[39]ibid.

[40]*Union Democrat,* February 12, 1898.

[41]"A Railway at Last," *Union Democrat*, February 12, 1898.

[42]*Union Democrat,* July 23, 1898.

[43]"May Pull Through it All," *Stockton Evening Mail*, August 4, 1898.

[44]*Union Democrat*, August 20, 1898.

[45]*San Francisco Call*, October 31, 1899. Nevills sued Prince Poniatowski, Thomas Bullock and the Jamestown Improvement Company for $25,148.50, the alleged amount to have been expended by Nevills for the defendants.

[46]"The Lady Railroad Builder," *Stockton Evening Mail*, December 31, 1897.

[47]*Mother Lode Magnet,* August 1898.

[48]Lyle Scott interview, July 24, 1997. Lyle said that a hotel was built on the site, and that various dignitaries were wined and dined there. The new city was also adjacent to a great mountain of Quartz in the Pinon Blanco group of mines. *Union Democrat*, December 1906.

[49]"May Pull Through it All." *Stockton Evening Mail.* August 4, 1898.

[50]*Union Democrat,* September 24, 1898.

[51]*Mother Lode Magnet*, August 1898.

[52]Dorothy Deane, Sierra Railway, (1960).

[53]ibid.

[54]*Union Democrat*, January 27, 1898.

[55]*Chispa*, p.1265.

[56]*Union Democrat*, September 24, 1898.

[57]"The Road Will Go Through," *Stockton Evening Mail*, November 1, 1898.

[58]ibid.

[59]"Damages Demanded," *Stockton Evening Mail*, January 14, 1899.

[60]*Union Democrat*, January 21, 1899.

[61]"Did It Block The Women's Road?" *Stockton Evening Mail*, December 9, 1899. Annie also had problems with J. Lorentzen, who she claimed took the corporation's books and sold supplies to people outside of her employ. *Mother Lode Magnet*, August 10, 1898. In September of 1899 Annie was fined and sentenced to jail for contempt because she could not produce the corporation books. *Mother Lode Magnet*, Sept. 9, 1899.

[62]*Mother Lode Magnet*, August 1898.

[63]*Chispa*, "A Centennial Tribute." p. 1266.

[64]ibid.

[65]Under President Eisenhower and at the urging of famed flyer, Jacqueline Cochran, a program was begun to find qualified women pilots to undergo the same training as the men for a women in space program. While the women proved their ability, often out-performing men on both physical and mental tests, their lack of jet fighter training was seen as a barrier and the program was scrapped.

[66]"The Only Woman Railroad President," *Sunset, The Pacific Monthly*, Vol. 31, No. 3., September 1913.

[67]ibid.

[68]Malibu Historical Society Clippings. May Rindge rode "shotgun" on her 44,000 acre estate in Malibu in order to bar people from trespassing. Her three mile narrow gauge railway was built in order to impede further infringement of what she perceived as an abridgment of her property rights.

[69]"Mrs. Rikert Again," *Union Democrat*, June 30, 1904. She also owned the Massot Placer Mining Claim in Mt. Shasta. John Haner, researcher, Shasta County Historical Society,. May, 1999.

[70]"Woman Miner and Railroader Dead," *Union Democrat*, December 11, 1906.

[71]In railroading, there are far more women in the field than in Rikert's era, but, "it is not a job women are swarming into." Patricia Ripoll, dispatcher on the Union Pacific. "One Good Railroader," March 1999. From *Women in Transportation*, an organization based in San Francisco.

Studebaker
WD

John Studebaker

On a warm Sunday afternoon in 1967, a young California Highway Patrol officer got an urgent call from his dispatcher. "There is a car out there," she radioed, "traveling very fast." In hot pursuit at ninety miles an hour, the officer tried to apprehend the culprit but just couldn't keep up. The Studebaker Avanti was traveling in excess of 120 miles per hour. The officer radioed back. "Tell them," he chided, "that if they can't catch him, he sure is fun to watch fly by."[1]

"Studes" enthusiasts can ramble on forever about the wonders of their favorite automobile. There are automotive museums sprinkled throughout California, Nevada and Washington D.C. that proudly display vintage Studebaker cars.[2] This would, no doubt, have come as a surprise to the founders of the company, the Studebaker brothers who came from a world away, both in distance and in philosophy.

In 1736, in Rotterdam, Holland, a ship, *The Harle*, left port heading to Philadelphia. Aboard was the Studebaker family: Peter, Clement, Henry, Anna Margetha and Anna Catherine. From Switzerland originally, the family had lived in Holland for a number of years.[3] There, they worked as wagon makers and blacksmiths, trades that had their origin in the Medieval era.[4]

By the time of the American Revolution, John Studebaker, son of Peter Studebaker was living near Gettysburg, Pennsylvania in a sturdy brick home. Close at hand was his wagon shop. Records reveal that he sired five boys, three of whom would give birth to an automotive dynasty. They were: Henry, Clem, John, Peter and Jacob. Their training and personal beliefs were forged early. "Owe no man anything, but to love one another."[5]

Mother Rebecca Mohler Studebaker set down the rules. Go to church and practice what you hear there. Her family, the Mohlers, had been honored by William Penn, founder of Pennsylvania with a grant of land.[6]

By 1834, the movement west was underway. John Studebaker, senior, decided to inquire about buying land in Ohio. Building his own four-horse Conestoga Wagon, he moved the family to Ohio. By then, the family had already lived one century in Pennsylvania.[7]

When John's boys grew up, they fell naturally into the profession of wagon making. They worked hard, from dawn to dusk with the admonition of their father always spurning them on. 'I'll tell you when it's time to go to sleep. Duty comes first."[8]

As the Studebaker sons approached manhood, the necessity of forging their own independent roles in life began. Henry and Clem moved to Indiana in 1852. John followed. They pooled their resources which consisted of sixty-eight dollars and established their own firm of H.C. Studebaker, Blacksmiths and Wagon Makers.[9]

Most of their work involved shoeing horses and repairing wagons and buggies. By the end of 1852, they had built three covered wagons.[10] Their motto: Founded in 1852 with willing hands, stout hearts, and no capital.[11] With that shaky start, they could not have envisioned that their business would last 114 years, or that Studebaker would produce road vehicles longer than any other car company in American history.[12]

John, the youngest and perhaps the boy with more wanderlust than his older brothers, thought about working in his brother's shop, but somehow the lure to head west was simply too strong. By this time, 52,000 emigrants were already making plans to depart for far off California. In 1853, he learned that a group of men from South Bend, Indiana were forming a company with the Golden State as their destination. Following the tradition of the family and with the help of his brothers, the very first wagon young nineteen year-old John made, a Prairie Schooner, was used in the trek west.[13]

His mother kissed him and bid him to take care. She gave him sixty-five dollars, which he carefully sewed into his belt and buckled securely around his body. The South Bend Company began their journey on March 23, 1853. Unfortunately, John fell in with a "bad" crowd of smoothies, shell sharks, who easily beat him out of his cash.[14]

It was an object lesson not wasted on the young pioneer. The emigrant train numbered about 1,000 men. They wanted to put an end to the gambling that John had fallen prey to. In rounding up the culprits, an eyewitness identified one of those who had killed a fellow passenger. The doomed man confessed. "My dying advice to all you boys is to never play cards for money."[15]

Five months later, John reached the small town of Hangtown (Placerville), California. All he had left in worldly assets was 50¢, not much for a grubstake. John had learned a valuable lesson. "In journeying across the country, I saw hundreds of wagons that had been wrecked and abandoned. Neither material nor workmanship were what they ought to be to stand the strain of such a trip. I never forgot this object lesson showing the importance of excellence in production."[16]

Alighting from the grueling journey, he heard someone yell. "Is there a wagon master in the lot?" This was Joe Hinds, who immediately offered young Studebaker a job in his shop. However, at that point, John had other plans. He had come west to find gold, not make wagons. [17]

In the crowd was an old timer, Dr. Worthem, who approached John with some rather sound advice. "Take that job and take it quick." He went on to explain to John that many a man who had tried digging for gold had failed. Also, there was plenty of time later to dig for the yellow ore. John thought about what the good doctor had said and since "I was broke," he noted, "I decided to go to work for the wagon master."[18]

Actually, John would not make wagons after all. What were really needed were wheelbarrows for the miners. His first order was twenty-five wheelbarrows to be sold at $10 apiece. The next morning he went to work.[19]

Apparently the wheelbarrows also served another interesting and somewhat unusual purpose as well. It seemed that the local Adams Express Company was in financial difficulty. Joe Hinds was concerned that some of the money deposited in Placerville would be used to cover the overdrafts in other offices. At two a.m. in the morning, Joe and John saw four men move the company's deposit accounts. Hinds and Studebaker had no intention of losing their savings. So, early in the morning, they contacted the sheriff and said they wanted to levy an attachment on the safe in Joe Douglas's store, since that's where they saw the company men move their money. They got one of John's wheelbarrows, counted out the money that was theirs, loaded it up and went home.[20]

John was learning some very practical lessons during his early years in Placerville.[21] After making one hundred wheelbarrows, he repaired stagecoaches and made picks and other equipment for the miners. He also wrote to his brother's back east with his ideas on how Prairie Schooners should be built for the eager miners heading west.[22]

Meanwhile, back in South Bend, his brothers were having cash flow problems. Clem and Peter began pleading with John to join them. John had been gone for five years. He had already amassed a small fortune, $8,000. The best the brothers could do was build one dozen wagons a year and they had to do all the work themselves. With John's added financial help, they could build 100 wagons a year.[23]

In April 1858, John packed his belongings, said a sad farewell to his employer, Joe Hinds, had a farewell drink at the Golden Nugget Saloon with friends and boarded a stagecoach for Sacramento. He took a last, long farewell look at the old town and left. John did not know that he would not return for

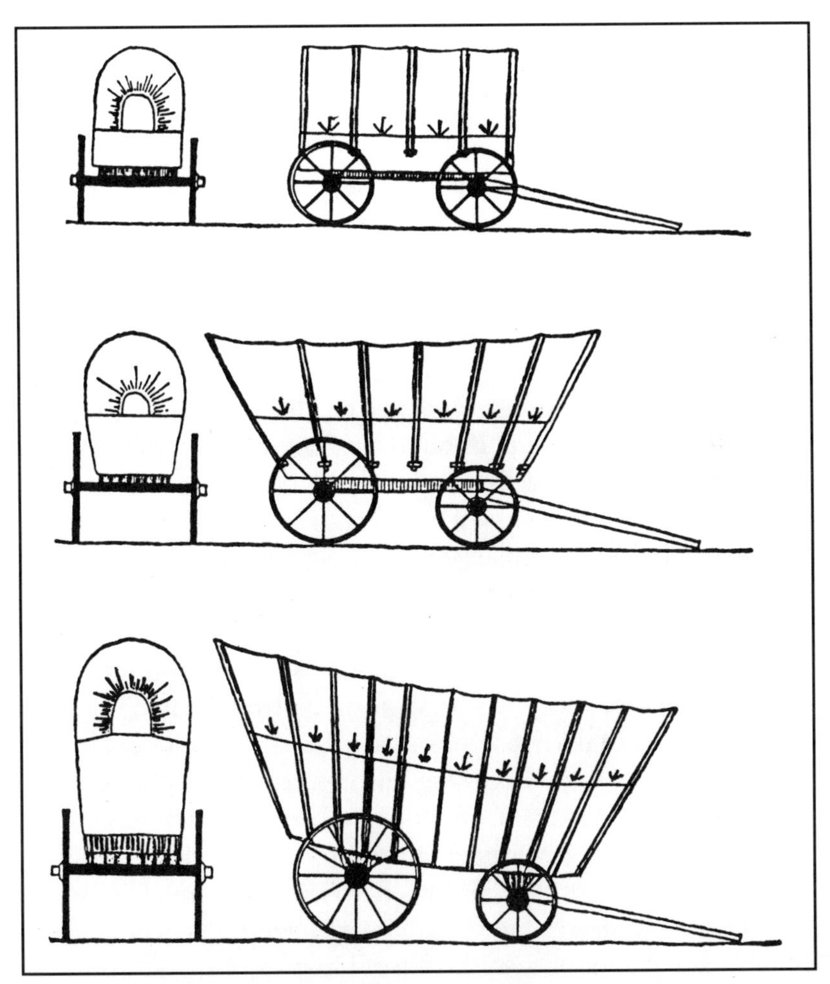

Assorted wagon styles designed by John Studebaker.

another fifty-four years.

Remembering the incident five years earlier regarding his money belt and now having a significantly substantial sum of money, he was far more prudent. He not only sewed his money securely to his person, he vowed not to remove his clothes. No one would be able to engage him in any card games this time!

On April 27th, 1858, he boarded the steamer, *Golden State*. Unfortunately, soon after leaving, the steamer lost its main shaft and had to return to San Francisco. It was there he received news of a new gold strike in British Columbia. Almost everyone but John left the ship to go north. He had had enough news about gold to last a lifetime, however, and on May 7th, he left California. The trip took twenty-one days.[24]

Arriving home he greeted his brothers, anxious to share with them new ideas about building wagons. He now realized that his was a business that had a future. Together, the brothers targeted Indiana pioneers who were heading west. Since the best place to drum up business was in St. Joseph, Missouri, they established an outfitting post there. This became the very first Studebaker branch.[25]

They built carriages for everyone, from the well-to-do to the average person. They built Victorias, Broughams, Landaus Barouches, the Tally Ho, Rockaways and Wagonettes.[26]

By the time of the Civil War, the company turned to erecting and equipping buildings for military service. Clem and John signed their first governmental contract. They had so much work, they could not fill all the orders. [27] They built freight wagons, ambulances, gun carriages and beer wagons. It would be a Studebaker Wagon that would carry President Lincoln from the White House to the Ford Theatre.

With the peace came even more work. Now there were orders from Oregon, New Mexico and California. Buildings at the plant were enlarged, and dealers placed in six cities. [28]

In 1868, Joe Hinds, John's former employer in Placerville came to South Bend, Indiana. He was looking for a job. John embraced him with open arms. "You'll be my assistant foreman,"

John assured him.

By 1881, 500,000 people in the United States were using Studebaker wagons.[29]

Through the Spanish Civil War and World War I, the company flourished. The brothers built wagon depots in Chicago and Minneapolis.[30]

The greatest change for the Studebakers, however, still lay ahead—the horseless carriage. John was against it. He looked upon the new contraption as dangerous, a new toy. "If cars are using steam," he said, "they'll blow up. If electric, they'll run down. If using gas, they'll catch on fire."[31] But others in the company persisted. "What if we get an order for a horseless carriage. What are we going to do?"[32] John told his brothers that he had just been in Detroit and met a thin, smart, soft-spoken fellow who expects to be the biggest man in the auto business. "What was his name?" everyone asked. "Henry Ford," John answered. "Never heard of him," snapped his brothers.

Cooler heads prevailed. Fred Fish, an advocate of combustion engines met and married Grace Studebaker. He wanted to convince John once and for all that the time had finally come to build one of these new cars. Already on the market were the Apperson, Maxwell, Oldsmobile, Franklin, Packard, Cadillac, Peerless and Ford motor cars.[33] John kept complaining. "To me," he said, "the gasoline auto is a clumsy, dangerous, noisy brute of a vehicle. People will be killed. They'll blow up, the damn thing stinks to high heaven, they break down, they'll be a public nuisance."[34] But he also added. "Nothing is going to stop it. I want us to build a solid, substantial powerful hell of a good truck as well!"[35]

The factory in South Bend grew to a capacity of 200,000 automobiles and employed over 25,000 people.[36] John continued to preside over the business for forty-five years. He had a reputation as a stickler for precision, strength and perfection.

In the history of transportation in the United States, Studebaker was the only company that had gone from horseless carriage to automobiles and survived for 100 years.

On April 16, 1912, a grandiose celebration took place in Placerville, California. The streets were decked out as if it were Christmas. Garlands swayed in the early morning sun. Freshly picked pine boughs from the pine trees in the nearby hills filled the air with their pungent aroma. What was the purpose of the celebration? John M. Studebaker was coming to town! The pioneer automotive genius had, fifty-nine years before, stepped down from an emigrant wagon train and took his first look at a country where he had come to make his fortune.[37] Today, it was time to make a triumphant return.

Passing through the streets that unforgettable day, eighty year-old John Studebaker read with delight the signs in the shop windows.

We are glad you came back.
Welcome John Studebaker
Home to Hangtown.
If the city had a key, You'd get it.
Welcome, Wheelbarrow John.
Gold is where you found it.[38]

The memories of that day, so many years before, flooded back. An elder John Studebaker retraced the steps he had once taken in coming west. He revisited the shop where he began his first job as a young, impressionable boy still in his teens. He shook hands with the men there to welcome him—men who had dressed "down" in honor of their distinguished visitor, in overalls and boots. Standing in front of anvils and benches, John looked around at the same old wagons, the same old tools that brought back so many memories. "Boys," he said, looking around at the dimly lit shop. "I never did better work in my life than I did in this shop."[39] He was handed the very same brown hammer he had once used for years as a memento. He was given specimens of gold quartz and placer dust and nuggets as souvenirs, but none meant as much to him as that old hammer.

Later that night, a huge gala celebration was held in the

Ohio House where the banquet hall was elaborately decorated. The menu was creatively enhanced for the evening's repast. There was Chili Gulch Rib Warmer, Sluice Box Tailings, Cedar Ravine radishes, Lady Canyon Chicken with Hangtown dressing, Shirt-tail peas, Dead Man's asparagus, Texas Hills fruit, Pay Day Smokes, and assorted nuggets.

The homages, the cheers, the tributes and toasts and the speeches of that evening flowed like wine. Studebaker himself stood after the many commemorative accolades and addressed the group. Sounding more like a minister than a mogul of industry he told the audience:

By coming back and giving you this farewell dinner, it is my desire to show my respect for you my friends, and to offer a last tribute to those who have gone before. We who are here have seen the years that usually span the term of human existence. God created this beautiful world for his children to live in and make more beautiful and better. The man who goes through his allotted time in this old world without trying to make it better amounts to little. When I look upon your kindly faces, that time has touched so gently, thoughts come to me of the early struggles of us all. We shared our burden together then more than is the custom now, and all of us were the better for it; but after all no one knows a man's life except himself. No one can look into the heart of his nearest companion and read the secrets. No one can judge. Therefore we must all be compassionate; we must be considerate to our associates, making due allowance for mistakes of head or heart...and this we must all ask of one another.[40]

By the time John died in 1917, the Studebaker Corporation had undergone enormous changes. His brother-in-law, Frederick Fish came into the business in 1901, adding an incredible genius for industrial organization. It would be needed in the years ahead. Later, Fish became treasurer of the company. With the last of the five original brothers gone, two men, Fish and another partner, Erickson, would carry Studebaker through the turbulent years ahead. The last horsed-drawn wagon was made in 1919. By 1913, Studebaker became the 3rd largest producer of trucks and cars in America. The company reached its peak period of production in the 1950's, producing 335,000 cars and trucks.[41]

The family, through thick and thin maintained one unbendable rule, they gave to educational and charitable causes, regardless of sect or condition. They came from the old school, learned in the back of their pioneer blacksmith shop. "Owe no man anything, but to love one another."[42]

Footnotes

[1]Former C.H.P. officer, "Letters," *Turning Wheels*, The Studebaker Driver's Club, Inc., Vol. 29, No. 2, October 1997.

[2]There are several automotive museums in California, Nevada and Washington D.C. All of these museums exhibit various Studebaker models. They include: The San Diego Auto Museum; Merle Norman Nethercutt Collection in the San Fernando Valley; the Imperial Palace Collection in Las Vegas, Nevada; Harrah's; The National Auto Museum in Las Vegas; The Towne Ford Museum in Sacramento; the Petersen Auto Museum in Los Angeles; and the Smithsonian Institute in Washington.

[3]El Dorado Historical Museum, Placerville, California. They have a very complete group of files, books and information on John Studebaker. Prominently displayed is one of Studebaker's original wheelbarrows.

[4]From Medieval times, trades became frozen and passed down from father to son in merchant craft guilds which lasted well into the 18th, 19th century.

[5]Edward Woolley,"Conquerors of the Roads," *Review of Reviews*, 1930 Vol. 82:26, p. 310.

[6]ibid.

[7]ibid.

[8]ibid.

[9]"Studebaker: A Cavalcade of Wagons, Autos and Dividends," *Newsweek,* February 20, 1937.

[10]ibid.

[11]Fred Fox and William Cannon, Studebaker, the Complete Story, (1981).

[12]ibid.

[13]ibid.

[14]Fred Fox, "John Mohler Studebaker's 1852 Overland Journey from Indiana to California," *Overland Journal,* Vol. 8, No. 4, 1990.

[15]ibid.

[16]ibid.

[17]ibid.

[18]Carlock, Faust & Miller, The Studebaker Family in America, 1736-1976. (1976).

[19]Wells Drury, To Old Hangtown or Bust, (1912).

[20]ibid. By this time, John had saved a few dollars.

[21]Hero Rensch, Historic Spots in California, (1966). At first known as Old Dry Diggins, then as Hangtown, the community was founded in 1848 by William Daylor. On May 13, 1854 the town was incorporated under the name Placerville.

[22]El Dorado History Museum, Placerville.

[23]Edwin Corle, John Studebaker: An American Dream (1948).

[24]Woolley. John's destination would have been Panama. Where he disembarked is not stated. (Author)

[25]Corle.

[26]The Brougham was named after the first Lord Brougham 1778-1868. It was a large closed carriage with seats for two or four. The Landau-A was a four-wheeled, covered vehicle with a top divided into two sections. The Barouche was a four-wheeled carriage with a driver's seat in front and two double seats inside. The Rockaway was a light, low four-wheeled carriage with standing top open at the sides. The Tally Ho was a pleasure coach so called from a fast coach formerly plying between London and Birmingham. The Wagonette, was a kind of wagon with two facing seats along the sides behind a transverse seat in front. The Victoria was a low four-wheeled pleasure carriage with a calash top. (From the Kolesa Czech)

[27]Corle.

[28]"The Studebaker Brothers," *Newsweek,* Vol. 39:77, February 25, 1952.

[29]"The Studebakers: A Span of History," *U.S. News,* Vol. 55:59, December 23, 1963.

[30]Corle.

[31]Fox, *Overland Journey,* p. 12. Oldsmobile went out of business in the year 2000. (1897-2000)

[32]Corle

[33]ibid.

[34]"Studebaker gas car makes its bow," *Hobbies,* Vol. 58:41, August 1953.

[35]ibid.

[36]*The El Dorado Nugget,* The El Dorado History Museum.

[37]Wells Drury, To Old Hangtown or Bust. (1912).

[38]ibid.

[39]ibid.

[40]ibid.

[41]B. J. Widlick, "End of a Dream," *Nation,* January 6, 1964. What caused Studebaker's decline? The dream ended in 1963 when Studebaker's plants were closed. Some say that the sporty expensive Avanti was the straw that broke the camel's back. Others maintain that the Studebaker management was too slow in changing with the times.

[42]Woolley.

To me, the gasoline auto is
a clumsy, dangerous, noisy
brute of a vehicle.
People will be killed.
If cars are using
steam, they'll blow up.
If electric, they'll run down.
If using gas, they'll catch on fire.

— JOHN STUDEBAKER

Barry Goldwater

The Goldwaters of Sonora

January 5, 1991.

Barry Goldwater
P. O. Box 1601
Scottsdale, Arizona

Mr. Carlo De Ferrari
Tuolumne County Historical Society
Bradford St., Sonora

Dear Mr. De Ferrari

After spending 82 years of my life hearing the stories about Sonora, and how it was when my grandfather settled there in 1850, with the first business he ran in the U.S., it naturally created in me a desire to visit there.

I did visit there, the weekend after Christmas. I visited the City Hall, and received the most courteous treatment from the two ladies who took care of me. My interest in going there, was to see if there was any recorded deed, on land or buildings owned by my grandfather in or around 1850. His name was Michel Goldwater and he arrived from England into San Francisco.

Sincerely,

Barry Goldwater

Michel Goldwater

Even presidential candidates have problems trying to fill gaps in their family's genealogy. Barry Goldwater, the man who made an unsuccessful bid for the White House in 1964, reveals rather clearly in this letter how few people know about Sonora's famous men and women, not even their own families.

One of those families that would reach for the American dream were Barry's grandparents, the Goldwassers from Konin, Poland. Hirsch and Elizabeth were innkeepers and shopkeepers.[2] The Goldwassers raised twenty-two children, two of whom, Michel and Joseph would take the first bold steps toward creating a new life in the United States.

As early as 1412, a Jewish settlement had existed in the small community of Konin, Poland. Life there had been difficult. Jews had been systematically denied educational opportunities, their right to own land or prepare for a profession. Employment restrictions and the fear of being conscripted into the military necessitated a change.[3] As the eldest, Michel was already on his own at fifteen, first going to Germany, then settling in Paris.

There, he learned to speak French fluently and also picked up an important skill, tailoring. He remained in Paris for eleven years. Unfortunately, once again, political upheaval resulted in the revolution of 1848. To escape the inevitable persecution, Michel left for London, England. Just two years later, in 1850, he met and married Sarah Nathan.[4] She came from a prosperous

MICHEL GOLDWATER

family, established as tailors.

Joseph, thirteen years younger than Michel, had always been very close to his older brother. He looked up to Michel, and there was reason to do so. Michel was 6' 3". As a result, the name Big Mike was appended to Michel, as was the name Little Joe, to Joseph. Like his brother, Joseph too, left Poland and joined Michel and Sarah in London.

In yet another giant leap of faith, perhaps an idea generated by the still single Joseph, the brothers made the decision to embark for America.[5] Having heard the stories filtering through the European papers, Joseph painted a rather glorious picture of wealth and prosperity that could be found there. After all, the pilgrims headed for America for religious freedom. All immigrants wanted political opportunity. How many times did they say under their breath, "Who knows, perhaps someday my son or grandson will be president"?[6] There were no pogroms against the Jews in the New World, Joe told his brother. "California has room for everyone and they don't harm Jews there."[7] All they would be leaving behind was bigotry and animosity.

This was an enormous gamble for the family to undertake, and, no doubt, Sarah had misgivings. Leaving a well established business in London was not a choice she would have made alone. Judging from her conservatism later in the rough and tumble wasteland of California, Sarah was a city girl, used to the amenities of city life. She also had the children to think of. With a great deal of discussion around the family dinner table, it was decided that Michel and Joe would leave first for America, travel to California and when a home and business was established, Michel would send for his family.

The two Goldwater brothers, who had by this time anglicized their name, left Europe and landed not in New York, but in Philadelphia, Boston or Baltimore.[8]

In late 1852, they boarded a steamer via the Isthmus and headed immediately for San Francisco and the Southern Mines. They may have stayed in San Francisco, a booming city at the height of the Gold Rush, to put together enough money to open a store in Sonora.[9]

The Sonora that the Goldwaters encountered in 1852, was much changed from the turbulent Gold Rush Era of just three years before. Sonora had no less than twenty-five physicians and surgeons in 1851.[10] Each year, however, several fires swept through the tent city. In June 1852, a fire had burned nearly every building along Washington Street, the main thoroughfare.[11] The town, nevertheless, revived and rebuilt and continued to grow. Gone were the tents, the shanties and hovels. Stagecoaches ran weekly, furnished hotels had been established, large tracts of land reclaimed and much of this land was put under cultivation.[12] A boom period followed the 1852 fire. There were three bookstores in town. Plump's Coffeehouse served ice cream. There were six banking facilities and the Phoenix Theater opened in 1853.[13]

Michel first entered into business as a fruit dealer in Sonora, but this proved unprofitable.[14] The miner's tax of 1850 may have prevented the Goldwaters from mining.[15] Sometime thereafter, the brothers were engaged in the saloon business in Sonora. The problem of getting started in business was the availability of cash. A general merchandise store would be a better long-term investment, but there was simply not enough money to make that kind of initial outlay. A saloon, on the other hand, was less expensive. For a few hundred dollars, one could put up a rough bar, buy enough liquor to get underway and returns were rapid. The decision was made. Their bar consisted of rough pine planks, no fancy mirrors, no portraits and only a few tables. Joe slept on a cot in the rear of the saloon.[16] The building they rented also contained a brothel upstairs. The brothers found the situation advantageous financially, but morally repugnant.

The business thrived and in 1854, Michel and Joe were doing so well, they decided to send for Sarah and the children. Sarah left London and sailed for the United States on July 2, 1854.[17] The *Alta California* noted the arrival of a steamer, *The Sierra Nevada*. In the list of cabin passengers was the name,

Mrs. Goldwater and her children, Morris and Carrie. Also traveling with Sarah was a sister, Esther Tash.[18] Michel went to San Francisco to meet them. On July 13th, they reached Sonora on the Pioneer Stage.[19]

After seeing San Francisco, Sarah must have been disappointed in the little town of Sonora. By this time, San Francisco was a fashionable and sophisticated city well on its way to establishing a cultural tradition on the West Coast.[20] There were marble, granite and brick buildings, a harbor full of ships and a society aware of its unique position in California. Also, unmistakably, wives of professional and prosperous men lived in San Francisco, Stockton or Sacramento. They did not live in the gold fields. The parallels were difficult to ignore. The women of ill repute were more conspicuous in the mining camps like Sonora, the respectable women, rarer. It was still a male society with, as yet, few wives accompanying their husbands.[21]

Jewish families tended to live in large cities where the traditional trades of clerks, salesmen, managers, owners and operators of retail stores could be pursued. In the little town of Sonora, the Goldwaters were on the edge of civilization. Joe and Michel were close, but with Sarah and the children to think about, changes had to occur. Michel had rented a clapboard house for Sarah and the children while Joe continued to sleep in the rear of the saloon. It was not an altogether ideal situation. At some point, Joe left Sonora and established a store in nearby Shaws Flat.[22]

Sarah was not happy in the small mining town. There were few women she could talk to and the presence of society's "tarnished" females was a constant source of worry. The problem of living in close proximity to a brothel was also a daily reminder of the conditions she had to endure. This was made noticeably apparent when Big Anne, a lady of doubtful morals, had, according to some sources, insulted a decent woman in Columbia. A group of five boys who ran the fire engines down the street headed for Big Anne's shack. There, they turned on their hoses and literally ran her out of bed into the middle of the street.[23]

In early February, Sarah declared that she would run a business in her own name. Perhaps, this was in response to her husband's growing business problems. She had, after all, been in business in London, having assumed ownership of the fur shop, which her parents operated until the time of their death.[24] The first license she requested was in tailoring and merchandising from December 1854 to January 1855. The second, in merchandising goods, groceries, and fruit was filed July 1, 1855.[25] Also in 1855, in the license collected by the county treasurer, Michel is shown to have paid $15 for a liquor license. That same year, Michel was listed as a member for the first time as Master Mason of the local lodge.[26]

In *Records of a California Family*, Dr. Gunn states that as of November 1855, business was good in Sonora and the mines were yielding well.[27] However, according to other sources, the Goldwater store was closed in Sonora and Mike went back to San Francisco, spending three years taking odd jobs to pay off creditors.[28]

In 1856, both brothers were again united in Sonora and were issued a liquor license. The *Sonora Herald* ran the following ad.

Union Saloon

Michel Goldwater respectfully informs the public and citizens of Sonora that he has taken the saloon in G. S. Evans brick buildings on Washington St.[29]

Also, in 1856, in the *Miners Businessmen's Directory* Goldwater's name appears as a charter member of the Hebrew Benevolent Society.[30] The Hebrew Benevolent Society of Sonora was a charitable and burial society. It also functioned as a congregation. Michel was listed as a vice-president.

From the *Union Democrat*, the following story appeared.

RIOTING AND SHOOTING IN COLUMBIA

Prizefight near town followed by destruction of an ice cream saloon and then an assault upon a Frenchman in his own store. He promptly gave them the contents of a double-barrel shotgun, wounding 2 or 3 of the party and a gentleman of this city Mr. Goldwater who was passing the store at the same time and was wounded very severely but will recover.[31]

In 1857 and 1858, business in Sonora suffered a downturn. Joe, who had tried to establish business elsewhere, filed for bankruptcy.[32] Soon thereafter, he left Sonora for good and headed south, to Los Angeles. Throughout this same time, Michel continued to run his store, selling cigars and other items. The 1858 assessment roles show Michel as owning real estate and personal property.[33] Where this property was located may be indicated by an article that appeared years later in the *Union Democrat* of 1948.

"Following Stanislaus downward from Pine Log we passed localities once populated and known as Goldwater and Texas Bar. But no trace of them are left."[34]

By 1858, the Goldwaters could no longer ignore their deepening financial difficulties. There were many reasons for the economic downturn. A depression had hit the mines and there was the failure of the Adams and Company Express, which caused a ripple effect throughout the Southern Mines.[35] There was, on April 16, 1857 a writ of attachment issued against Joe Goldwater and Company alleging that the Goldwaters were merchants and partners, and were indebted in the sum of $604.[33] The Plaintiffs were awarded that sum. In addition to their financial woes, Michel's encounter with ruffians added to Sarah's general dislike of the frontier community. The Goldwaters had tried, but they could not wage war against economic impossibilities. They decided to move to Los Angeles.

In the City of the Angels, there were advantages. Granted, it was not a city like San Francisco—fashionable, culturally mature or sophisticated. But it was a city with enormous optimism in its future. It was also fortunate in having a few intensely motivated men who believed the small community that began as a Spanish Pueblo would one day become a great metropolis, long before there were any indications that this could ever be a possibility. There were men like Phineas Banning, who looked beyond the natural disadvantages of Los Angeles. Banning would set in motion the gears necessary to build a major harbor. He would convince Angelinos to become indebted to the tune of $640,000 in order to insure the arrival of the Southern Pacific Railroad directly into the city. He pioneered the early stages and invested in oil. By the time the improbable city began to blossom at the turn of the century, it was due in large part to Banning's drive.[36]

Los Angeles also had a viable Jewish community. Men like Harris Newmark, Bernard Cohn and others had well-established businesses. There was a faithful congregation of Jewish men and women who could worship in several synagogues with full-time Rabbis.[37] Here again, as in Sonora, Michel assumed leadership in Jewish communal life. The original incorporation papers of the Congregation B'nai B'rith temple, now located on Wilshire Boulevard, show that Michel served as vice president.[38] The members often helped out failing debtors in the area.

The brothers opened a General Merchandise Store in the famous Bella Union Hotel in the downtown plaza. Calling themselves the Goldwater Brothers, the business was put in Joseph's name, perhaps because of the fact that Michel's credit from Sonora made it difficult for him to get a line of credit in Los Angeles. They sold cigars, tobacco, pipes, perfumes, candies, and sundries. They also imported from San Francisco a wide variety of fruit. In the *Los Angeles Star*, the following ad ran.

J. Goldwater

Wholesale and retail dealer in Cigars, Tobacco, Pipes,

Yankee notions, cutlery, perfumes, candies, furnishing goods, etc. Bella Union Hotel, L. A.[39]

Their store was located at Main and Commercial Streets, a busy thoroughfare. The Bella Union Hotel was also a terminus for the stage line. When the Butterfield Stage Line inaugurated its maiden 2,750 mile twenty-five day trip from Missouri to San Francisco, the stage stopped at the famous Bella Union.[40]

The brothers enlarged their shop by adding a billiard parlor and a saloon. They opened two other stores, one in a building next door and one on a nearby corner.[41] After the new store opened in the Bella Union, they bought, in 1860, a Spring Wagon and four-mule team.[42]

In the Los Angeles census, June 18, 1860, Joseph Goldwater, twenty-five, is listed as a tobacco merchant, born in Poland. Michel, thirty-eight, and his family were listed as shopkeepers. The children were: Carolyn nine, Morris eight, Elizabeth (Beth) five, Samuel three, Manny (Henry) two and Leonora (Annie) under one year. Yet to be born was Benjamin in 1862 and Baron in 1866, the future presidential candidate's father.[43]

Sarah had her hands full. Not only did she tend to the large family, but she had to make sure the children's schooling was properly attended to. In predominately Catholic Los Angeles, many of the children of Jewish parentage attended La Escuela Parroquilde, a private Spanish language Catholic school.[44]

In 1861, Michel and Joseph received their naturalization papers and again, as in Sonora, the brothers, having been Masons, transferred their membership to Los Angeles, Lodge No. 42.

In 1862 and 1863, news of a gold strike caused a flurry of activity in the Arizona Territory. Much like the 1849 gold discoveries of the Mother Lode, this held out the promise for those in the west to become rich. Like other businesses, the Goldwaters had purchased goods on an open note basis. When times turned sour, creditors demanded payment. In 1860, the

Los Angeles Star listed the Goldwaters as bankrupt.[45] Soon thereafter, the newspaper ran the following ad:

> *La Paz Placers—We saw a parcel of gold weighing 150 ounces at the office of Wells Fargo and Co. which a couple of miners had just brought from the placer mine at La Paz on the Colorado River.*[46]

This good news, however, coincided with the worst drought to hit southern California in recorded history. It was followed by torrential rains. Thousands of cattle, known to the rancheros as California "bank notes" lay floating in the swollen rampaging rivers. Crops failed.

The Goldwaters were again facing dire financial problems. This time they turned to Bernard Cohn.[47] Cohn had become successful in the area by investing, banking and loaning money to other businessmen. With the obvious disastrous business downturn in Los Angeles, Cohn and the Goldwaters decided to pool their resources and work together for a chance at making a strike in Arizona. In December 1863, Bernard Cohn traveled to La Paz. He set up a general merchandise store which the brothers Mike and Joe would manage.[48]

Once more, the Goldwaters were on the move. But La Paz was an outpost, a mosquito ridden, desperado country. Several Apache tribes were raiding because of the intrusion of settlers. Among them was the famed Apache war chief, Cochise.[49] This time, Sarah refused to go. Sonora was one thing, but Arizona, quite another. She returned to San Francisco. There she would remain for over twenty years, while her husband and brother-in-law worked to establish their business. Michel would visit her and the children. Not until he had reached complete financial independence, however, did he move permanently to the City by the Bay and live permanently with Sarah.[50]

Michel found La Paz a boom town when he arrived. After the Gadsden Purchase of 1853, Arizona was opening up to settlers. In 1863, President Lincoln proclaimed Arizona a territory.[51]

Shortly after La Paz got underway, an act of nature changed the river's course. La Paz was left high and dry. The brothers moved to Ehrenberg, named after a friend, Herman Ehrenberg. There, a large store was built.[52] Both Mike and Joe became involved in the affairs of the town and both were appointed postmasters. Joe became a member of the first school board.[53]

Finally, after ten years of struggling in business, a reversal of fortune took place. One of Cohn's creditors was the Vulture Mine. The owners became indebted to Cohn for supplies. In order to continue to buy goods, they turned the mine over to Cohn, as the chief creditor. Soon thereafter, the unproductive mine hit a huge pocket of gold. Cohn benefited and so too, did the Goldwaters. Eventually they bought out Cohn and in 1867, renamed the store, J. Goldwater and Brother. [54]

The Goldwaters became freight handlers, joining with Phineas Banning of Los Angeles. In effect, they were laying the groundwork for the opening not only of Arizona, but mountain-ringed Los Angeles. They made several trips to Los Angeles and San Francisco. The brothers must have felt at long last some pride in being able to display their newfound wealth to their former creditors. The *Los Angeles Semi-Weekly* ran the good news.

> *We were shown by Michel Goldwater, who arrived in this city a few days ago from Arizona, about 500 ounces of gold dust. Mr. Goldwater gives good accounts from the mines of Arizona.*[55]

There were problems of course. The Indians, this time led by Geronimo, did not cease attacking freight wagons until the 1880's. Business, they learned, could be hazardous, as they were to experience firsthand when returning in 1872 from Prescott. Just south of town, Yavapai Indians attacked their wagon. Bullets whizzed past them. Joe was wounded in the back and shoulder. In another incident, he was doing business in Tombstone when Wyatt Earp and Doc Holliday took on the

Clanton brothers in the famous shoot out at the O.K. Corral on October 26, 1881. Because of this, the search began for yet another location closer to interior towns and the safety of military forts. The Goldwaters established a store in Prescott, Arizona. It was an immediate success, and shortly thereafter, they opened a store in Phoenix.[56]

The Goldwater brothers were finally able to branch out into finer merchandise. What eventually became the fashionable Goldwater store in Scottsdale, Arizona, set a high standard for women's apparel, unequaled in the west. The Goldwaters were not just pioneer merchants of the west. They gave enormously to the communities in which they lived, not only financially, but also in establishing many firsts in Arizona's raw frontier towns. Services needed to be brought to the aspiring towns and schools, firefighting, post offices and politics were areas in which the family would contribute their skills. "He (Michel) gave financial backing to countless public officials." [57]

In Sonora, the brothers had belonged to the first Hebrew Benevolent Society. An old Jewish adage believed that you perpetuate poverty by giving a man a handout, but if you grubstake a man, then he can make it on his own. For Michel this sometimes resulted in criticism. He pioneered many modern welfare practices, so much so, he was accused of giving too generously. He was very active in the Jewish Benevolent Society in Arizona.

During Big Mike's many years in Arizona, Sarah visited just once. In spite of their long separations, the family unity prevailed. When Michel returned to San Francisco permanently, he assumed for the third time what was dearest to his heart—participation in a temple congregation. He held the vice-presidency for eight terms, finally becoming its president in 1897.

His youngest son, Baron, was born in Los Angeles in 1866, but he would celebrate his Bar Mitzvah in San Francisco in 1879. He then moved to Arizona in 1882, clerking in the Prescott store and later becoming a full partner. Phoenix was growing and the railroads were making it an important hub. In

1907, Baron married Josephine Williams, a nurse. Two years later, Barry Goldwater was born.[58]

The Goldwaters tried and failed at many business enterprises, but they made a solid success in retailing, in one of the most unlikely of western towns, Phoenix. When Baron died in 1929, Barry, then only twenty, went to work in the main store as a ribbon clerk, earning twenty dollars a week. He went on to become president of the company in 1937 and in 1953, chairman of the Goldwater stores.[59]

As a presidential candidate in 1964, Barry Goldwater often recalled the stories he had learned from his family. Standing before the Republican Party's convention to accept their nomination for President of the United States, he recalled his personal beliefs which were formed, in no small part, by his family's history, the stories he had heard of a young American West—of Sonora, of Los Angeles and Arizona.

Footnotes

[1]Letter from Barry Goldwater, July 5, 1991. Courtesy of the Tuolumne County Historical Society.

[2]William Kramer and Norton Stern, "Early California Associations of Michel Goldwater and his family." *Western States Jewish Historical Quarterly*, July 1972, p. 174. An even earlier spelling of the name was GILTWASSER, the name of a brandy produced in Northern Poland. Earlier European officials had been known to give the names of locally manufactured products when registering them for a census. Dean Smith, The Goldwaters of Arizona, (1986).

[3]ibid. There also is a possibility that Michel may have been active politically. According to Barry Goldwater, there were student revolts against the oppressive oligarchy of the Czars. "One family story says that Big Mike left home and family just before the political police arrived." Barry M. Goldwater, "Three Generations of Pants and Politics," *The Journal of Arizona History,* p. 144.

[4]Stern and Kramer, p. 174. From Sarah and Michel's Ketubah, it shows that Michel's Hebrew name was Jehiel ven Zvi Hirsch and that Sarah was the daughter of Moses Nathan.

[5]Lu Gandolfo, "Barry's Nomination Recalls Granddad's Early Days in Sonora," *Modesto Bee*, August 16, 1964.

[6]Dean Smith, The Goldwaters of Arizona, (1986).

[7]*Western Jewish History Quarterly*. While still living in London, they anglicized their name.The Goldwater family maintained that they landed in New York. However, official lists do not mention them among the passengers. E. McDowell, Barry Goldwater: Portrait of an Arizonian, (1964), p.32.

[8]"Years ago when Barry was running for president, some persons talked to me at the courthouse and expressed the opinion that the name had never been "Goldwasser." However there may have been some connection of a political nature I didn't understand." Carlo De Ferrari, Letter, April, 2000.
Sonora was an outstanding example of early Jewish settlement. Mayer Baer owned and operated what became the oldest merchant store in California. It survived an incredible 144 years! Irena Narell, Our City: The Jews of San Francisco, (1977), p. 52.

[9]Edna Buckbee, Saga of Old Tuolumne. (1935).
Carlo De Ferrari believed that their first store was near Springfield. Conversation, April 2000.

[10]B. F. Alley, History of Tuolumne County, (1882).

[11]William Perkins, Journal of Life in Sonora 1849-1852, (1964).

[12]Alley.

[13]Fred and Harriett Rocklin, Pioneer Jews: A New Life in the Far West, (1984).

[14]Lee M. Friedman, "A Forty-Niner," *Jewish Pioneers and Patriots*. Philadelphia: Jewish Publication Society, 1942. The California legislature had passed a statute commonly known as the "Anti-Greaser Law," which levied a twenty dollar per month tax on foreign miners. It was aimed primarily at miners from Mexico and South America and was intended to drive them out of their mining claims. The 1850 tax was repealed in 1851. Carlo De Ferrari, April 2000.

[15]Stephen Shadegg, Barry Goldwater: Freedom is His Flight Plan, New York. (1964).

[16]*Arizona Historical Foundation*. Research Report from Mrs. W. Simpson, San Francisco, July 12, 1956.

[17]*Daily Herald*, July 2, 1854.

[18]The fare was $12, their stagedriver's name, Dick. From an account book of the Pioneer Stage Line. *Arizona Historical Society.*

[19]William Perkins, Three years in California A Journal of Life in Sonora 1849-1852. (1964).

[20]Robert E. Levinson, The Jews in the California Gold Rush, (1978).

[21]ibid.

[22]Floyd Fierman, Some Jewish Settlers on the Southwestern Frontier, El Paso Press, (1960). p. 13-14.

[23]Stern Kramer, *Western States Jewish Historical Quarterly.*

[24]*Union Democrat,* February 10,1855. Also July 1855.

[25]From *Arizona Historical Foundation*. Files of Goldwater family. Letter, July 14, 1997.

[26]Dr. Gunn, Records of a California Family. (1928).

[27]*The Pony Express Monthly* printed that Michel Goldwater operated a push cart and as part of his merchandise carried liquor. Community and Valley. August 16, 1964.

[28]*The Sonora Herald*, February 6, 1858. This building was located adjacent to the current *Union Democrat* on Washington Street. G. S. Evans was later General George S. Evans during the American Civil War. Carlo De Ferrari. Conversation, April 2000.

[29]John Heckendorn, *Miners and Businessmen's Directory*, Columbia, 1856.

[30]*Weekly Columbian*, August 16, 1856.

[31]*Arizona Historical Society*, Papers.

[32]Assessment Roll, 1856. County of Tuolumne.

[33]*Union Democrat*, 1948.

[34]Edwin McDowell, Barry Goldwater: Portrait of An Arizonian, (1964).

[35]David Clark, Los Angeles, A City Apart, (1981).

[36]Newmark, Sixty Years in Southern California, (1984).

[37]ibid.

[38]*Los Angeles Star*, May 3, 1862.

[39]Newmark, Sixty Years in Southern California, p. 234.

[40]ibid.

[41]McDowell, Barry Goldwater: Portrait of An Arizonian.

[42]ibid. Note: the spelling of Michel's name is often written as Michael. In order to be consistent, I maintained the original spelling of Michel throughout. (Author).

[43]*El Clamor Publico*, Los Angeles, July 30, 1859.

[44]*Los Angeles Star*, December 17, 1860.

[45]ibid. January 24, 1863.

[46]J.A. Graves, My Seventy Years in California. (1927). p. 286. The Cohns often helped out failing debtors in Los Angeles.

[47]*Los Angeles Evening Express*, November 2, 1889.

[48]Fred, Harriett Rocklin, Pioneer Jews: A New Life in the Far West.

[49]ibid.

[50]Paul N. Garber, The Gadsden Treaty, (1923).

[51]Sam Drackman, "Arizona Pioneers and Apaches: 1885," *Arizona Historical Society,* Library.

[52]ibid.

[53]Barry Goldwater, "Three Generations of Pants and Politics," *Journal of Arizona History*, Vol. 13, Autumn 1972. pp. 141-158.

[54]*Los Angeles Semi Weekly*, 1866.

[55]"Barry and the Boys," *New West*, April 11, 1979.

[56]Barry Goldwater, Freedom Is His Flight Plan.

[57]Barry and the Boys," *New West*, p.135. April 11, 1979.

[58]There were five Goldwater stores in the valley, two in Tuscon and Las Vegas and Albuquerque. In 1962, the stores were purchased by Associated Dry Goods Corp. and in 1989, the Goldwater name disappeared when May Company Department stories merged with ADG. Charles Kelly. "Family legacy: Business, politics." *The Arizona Republic,* May 31, 1998. The company survived for 128 years, quite a record in the Southwest.

[59]ibid.

The Murphy Bed
William Lawrence Murphy
Gladys
WD

William Lawrence Murphy

Charlie Chaplin had great fun playing with a Murphy Bed in the 1916 film, *One A.M.* In typical slapstick comedy, Chaplin wrestled with the mischievous bed until, finally, it flipped him into a closet.[1]

William Lawrence Murphy, inventor of Charlie Chaplin's nemesis, was not amused. He had labored long and hard over the original concept of a bed-in-a-closet and did not relish seeing his invention wreck havoc on innocent people.[2] Of course, it was all in fun. The film immortalized the name Murphy Bed and placed it forever in the nation's popular vernacular. However, it was a long way from the Hollywood of the Chaplin era back to the simple beginnings of William Murphy.

For that, one would have to begin in the Ireland of the 1840's, more specifically, in Tipperary, a town and urban district of County Tipperary, 112 miles southwest of Dublin. Like the rest of the country in the 1840's, it was on the brink of immense change. By 1841, there were approximately eight million people in Ireland and the increase had been chiefly in the overcrowded and infertile counties of the west. Destitution had become so prevalent that landowners were already doing their utmost to encourage emigration and to reduce the number of holdings. Unable to pay rent to their English landlords, entire families took to the roads of Ireland.[3]

The potato crop, for many their sole source of food, suddenly declined because of a devastating blight. Emigration, then, became the only hope of escape and the population declined from eight million to six million. Help came too late and farms and homes were deserted. With nowhere to turn, emigration seemed the only way out.

The Murphy family, like their neighbors, fell on hard times. Young Bernard Emmett Murphy, father of the future inventor, was barely in his early teens, but old enough to shoulder a huge responsibility. He must leave the only home he had ever known and make a new life for himself in an alien land.

The potato famine in Ireland created an Irish Diaspora to America. When they arrived, the largest number of Irish tended to settle in urban centers, particularly New York, Boston and Philadelphia.[4] Bernard said good-bye to his loved ones and left Ireland forever in 1844. It is possible that he left with one or more of his siblings.[5] "Unlike long-time inhabitants of the United States, in industrial areas of England, Irish people lived in a society where one was respected for his co-operative spirit rather than for the degree to which he economically dominated others."[6]

Seeking work, Bernard found employment digging the Erie canal in New York.[7] The Canal was begun in 1817 and was opened to commerce in 1834. Tradition has it that Irish immigrants built the Erie Canal and many sons of Erin were included in the labor force.[8] Henry O'Reilly, led the canal forces of the West New York region, certainly an incentive for other Irishmen. In 1836, contracts were let for double locks along the eastern section of the canal and in 1838, millions of dollars were expended on enlargements. In 1839, there was a rush program of construction. Of the more than one million newcomers from abroad that landed in New York in three decades from 1820 to 1852, records attest to the many fellow Irishmen who worked on the canal.

Then, in 1848-49, came the news of the California gold strike. The "Western Frontier proved to be incredibly liberating for Irish immigrants and it was the impact of this social and economic fluidity of the west upon Irish immigration that distinguished them from their eastern counterparts, creating an innovative and enterprising spirit."[9]

Heading for the gold fields, Bernard arrived in Springfield, California.[10] The small community in the hills north of Sonora already had a colorful history. Sometime before 1851, Dona Josefa Valmasada had arrived from Mexico at what was then called Tim's Springs. By the fall of 1851, a town had started. It received its name from the abundant springs gushing from limestone boulders.[11]

A large number of Irish settled in the South-Central Mother Lode counties during the first twenty-five years of their history.[12] By 1869, the Irish constituted 28% of the Assessment rolls.[13] Their membership in various Irish Societies corroborates this as well. The Hibernian Benevolent Society was a popular and well-supported nationalistic organization which included several communities in the Mother Lode.[14]

The Fenian Society was a secret organization which had its roots in Ireland, brought about in no small part by the potato famine. Organized in 1858, it hoped to achieve Irish separation from England by force of arms. It found its way into the Mother Lode in 1864.[15]

In 1857, residents of Columbia, (formerly Springfield) organized a chapter of the Hibernian Benevolent Society. This was a group which Bernard Murphy joined and supported.[16] Their goal was fraternal, to offer material support to their members and families during times of bereavement. It is doubtful that Bernard would have belonged to the more politically revolutionary and secret Fenian group, since the Catholic Church had voiced strong objections to it. Bernard remained a faithful Catholic his entire life and was buried in the cemetery of St. Anne Catholic Church, Columbia.[17]

Soon after arriving in the small community, Bernard settled down to farming, but he was also active in mining.[18] In the 1860 United States Census, Bernard Murphy was listed as residing in Tuolumne County, having been born in Ireland. His occupation was that of a miner. In 1867, he became a naturalized citizen in Sonora.

In 1875, Bernard was forty-five years old and single. That was about to change. A very attractive young woman of nineteen, Ellen Luddy, caught Bernard's attention and heart. She was the daughter of William Thomas Luddy, a close and dear friend of Bernard. The Luddys, like the Murphy's came originally from Tipperary, Ireland.[19] William Luddy had come to California in 1853 and mined in the Springfield area from 1857 to 1859. His home was also in Columbia on Yankee Hill Road. He and others organized the first Catholic Church of Columbia.[20]

By the light of a California moon and perhaps an Irish ballad, Bernard proposed to Ellen. The festive wedding which followed took place in Sonora with Joel Shine of Columbia, serving as a witness and Father Thomas Phillips, officiating as the priest.[21] Soon thereafter, Bernard and Ellen began life on a ranch, thereafter known as The Murphy Ranch in Columbia. The 213 acre ranch was purchased by Bernard's sister, Joanna from Colby and Stone in 1875.[22] There was a house and two barns and the property was eventually stocked with horses and cows and all the equipment necessary to operate a prosperous farm.

The land around Springfield was, before mining, rather level. Miners cut down the beautiful old oak trees to reach the bonanza which lay beneath the topsoil. Prior to that, it was a peaceful community, an idealistic small town, much like the Currier and Ives picture postcards of an earlier America. Children got into mischief, but it was harmless. Pranks, such as stealing the custard out of a neighbor's pie or catching flies to put in a young child's ear, were the extent of their trouble making.

Here, Bernard and Ellen settled down to raise their family. Six children would be born: William Lawrence, Mamie, Katie, Emmet, Anne and Joe.[23]

What mining Bernard engaged in is not clear. He owned the Majestic Mine, which was in the vicinity of the Murphy Ranch. The mine had been active in the 1850's and had, according to oral accounts, yielded a rich gold reward.[24]

The Murphy children attended the Springfield school which

was situated two miles from their home. The children had to walk, so they carried their lunches with them.[25] Will, an excellent student, appeared on the roll of honor February 18, 1889.[26]

Then came the event that would devastate the family. Will's young mother, Ellen, only thirty-nine at the time, died suddenly from heart failure on March 7, 1893. If this event were not tragic enough, less than a month later, on April 3, Bernard also died. The physicians diagnosed heart failure as the cause of death. More likely, I suspect that while Ellen's malady was physical, Bernard's was from the loss of his wife, whom he deeply loved.[27]

Only sixteen years old at the time, young William, like his father before him, had to shoulder enormous responsibilities. A relative, Mary Robles, in a 1992 letter, states that Will lived in Tuolumne City with his aunt Alice Wilson after his parents died.[28] The Murphy clan stayed intact and members of the family testify fondly that it was Will who held them all together.[29]

During these early years of boyhood, Will worked at a variety of odd jobs. He became a stage coach driver, horse trainer, a constable and when time allowed, he worked on his own ranch. He assumed the role of both a mother and father to his younger brothers and sisters.

In 1907, in a record of distribution of the Murphy Ranch, John Luddy acted as the administrator of the estate which was then divided among the six Murphy children.[30] With this money, William and his Uncle Joe Luddy bought a livery stable in Tuolumne. Will wanted to make an investment in his future. Without knowing it at the time, his "future" was about to happen.

At the old Turnback Inn, so the story goes, Will was leading a pack trip to the high Sierras.[31] On one of these trips, up and over a narrow path, his eye could not help but be turned to a young and lively woman, Gladys Kaighin. She and her mother had come up to the Inn to get away from San Francisco.[32] Sparks flew.

Will possessed a decidedly "colorful" personality.

According to relatives, he was simply a character. The story goes that during a family card party, one of the guests had a little too much to drink. When he retired to sleep it off, Will put him in a hearse, glass enclosed and, with flowers, vegetables and whatever else the mischievous Will could find, drove him around town.[33]

His personality was infectious. No doubt, young Gladys thought so, too. She was well known in San Francisco musical circles for her charming soprano voice and had performed concert work. She figured prominently in The California Club and other well-known organizations. She was one of the best-known dramatic sopranos in non-professional circles.[34] Gladys' father was an engineer engaged in the construction of railroads and was instrumental in building San Francisco's enduring cable cars. While the differences in the two young sweethearts may have caused some concern initially, it was obvious in time that Will had won everyone over, including Gladys.

Soon, the young couple were spending a great deal of time in the Sierras and Will was making a number of trips to San Francisco. After several of these visits, the conversation wound around to the impropriety of being in a hotel room with a bed! Faces turned red. In spite of the fact that Mrs. Kaighin accompanied the young couple and chaperoned them carefully, Will was having problems finding places to sit down and talk to Gladys in private. Ah, the trials of the young at heart! One discussion led to another and an idea was born. Necessity, after all is the mother of invention. This particular problem would give birth to a famous invention. Will asked, or perhaps it was Gladys who asked. Why couldn't a room be a bedroom at night and a living room by day?[35] After discussing the concept with Charles Kaighin, the formula for success was finally worked out. Will figured out a way the bed could fit into a normal size door and also swing or pivot around to fit behind the wall next to the door. It was a sensational idea!

With the help of the Kaighins and Mr. Fred Simmons, manufacturer of the famous Simmons Mattress, Will's fledgling company took off.[36] Later, a well-known San Francisco patent attorney, William K. White, did the legal work in getting a patent and took shares in the new company for his services.

Will and Gladys were married in San Francisco in 1913. From the *San Francisco Examiner's* society page, their wedding announcement read as follows:

DOINGS OF SMART SET IN CITY AND COUNTRY

The wedding of Miss Gladys Kaighin and William L. Murphy, both of this city, was an event of last Wednesday evening. The ceremony took place at the home of the bride's uncle and aunt, Mr. and Mrs. Morton S. Price on Divisadero Street. The bride is the daughter of the late Mr. Charles Kaighin, for many years, a well-known railroad official in San Francisco. Mrs. Kaighin is prominently identified with the club life of this city. About 75 guests witnessed the service. The groom was served by William K. White as best man.[37]

Will continued to perfect other ideas as well, principally an important step which led to the first compact kitchen, called the Murphy Cabrinette. In 1928, the Murphy Door Bed Company began manufacturing compact kitchens which are still in production today.

During the 1920's and 1930's, the popularity of both the Murphy Bed and the kitchens ran high. In 1925, the company moved its corporate headquarters to New York City. During The Depression, Will kept every employee on salary, reduced his own salary and almost depleted his entire bank account. "That was the kind of man he was."[38] Production stopped during World War II, because of the shortages of steel. After the war, Will and Gladys' son, William, took over as president of the company. Will senior passed away in Belle Vista Beach, Florida.[39] He was eighty-one years old. The Murphy Bed Company continues to flourish, and is run today by Will's grandson, Glenn Murphy.[40]

Footnotes

[1]Charlie Chaplin, *One A.M.* Film made at the Chaplin Studios in 1916. *Time Magazine*, June 3, 1957.

[2]Ann Rooney, Tuolumne County Genealogical files, "Murphy." "Unless I am mistaken, Will Murphy was not the originator of the wall bed. The early wall-bed was a rather cumbersome bed, used for emergencies, or unexpected guests."

[3]Frances L. Rohrbacher, *The Finian Brotherhood in Tuolumne County 1864-1870.*

[4]Timothy Ed Scarbaughand, The Irish In the West, (1992).

[5]From biographical files at the Tuolumne County Genealogical Society in Sonora. There are many conflicting facts on the Murphy family, apparently submitted from a number of family members who have heard stories passed down over the years.

[6]Scarbaughand. In 1850, only 4% of the 9,000 Irish-born immigrants resided in the West and 75% in the East.

[7]Mary Dythe-Egleston, "Fifteen Miles on the Erie Canal" *Golden Roots,* Tuolumne Genealogical Society publication, p. 22. Apparently, other residents of Springfield also worked on the canal.

[8]Ronald Shaw, Erie Canal West: A History of the Erie Canal 1792-1854, (1966). The canal was completed in 1825, but millions of dollars were spent in the late 1830's on locks and enlargements. Work was completed in 1862.

[9]Timothy Scarbaughand, The Irish in the West, (1992).

[10]Louise Echel Gibbens, "Springfield Remembered," *Chispa*, Vol. 18. No. 1, July-Sept. 1978. "The road to the right passed the old Colby place, later known as the Murphy Ranch." p. 607.

[11]J. W. Heckendorn and A. Wilson, "Springfield," *Miners and Businessmen's Directory.* The *Sonora Herald* mentioned the name Springfield in 1859.

[12]*Golden Roots of the Mother Lode,* Vol. 13, No. 3, Summer 1993. Springfield was only mining camp where a church was established before the first gambling house opened.

[13]*Golden Roots of the Mother Lode,* "Great Register," pp. 18-21.

[14]Louis Bisceglia, "Irish Identity in the Mother Lode," *Chispa*, Vol. 25, No. 2, p. 837-8.

[15]Frances L. Rohrbacher, p. 2.

[16]He paid dues regularly. Tuolumne County Genealogical Society, Clippings file.

[17]ibid.

[18]Erwin G. Gudde, California Gold Camps, (1975). p. 331. Murphy papers, Tuolumne County Genealogical Society. The Majestic Placer Mine consisted of 213 acres on Table Mountain West in Springfield. Apparently placers were notoriously rich. The Springfield flat alone yielded $55 million dollars.

[19]Name: O'Luddy. File at Tuolumne County Genealogical Society. O'Luddy was eventually changed to Luddy.

[20]First church built in Columbia.

[21]Joel Shine went to the legislature and introduced a bill which brought roads into Yosemite. Tuolumne County Genealogical Society files.

[22]I found only property from Colby and Stone in 1875 listed by a Joanne Murphy. Genealogical files, "Murphy."

[23]Tuolumne County Genealogical Society files.

[24]The Majestic Mine was worked by Bernard and his sons until his death. Also, they broke through to an underground river and the mine was flooded, hence no longer possible to work. Letter, April 27,1992.

[25]Gibbens, "Springfield Remembered," *Chispa*, p. 608.

[26]*Golden Roots, Roll of Honor,* February 18, 1889, p. 17.

[27]County Recorder's Office, Sonora. Ellen died at 39, March 7,1895. Bernard, on April 3, 1895.

[28]Kay Murphy, Letter, Sept. 27, 1998.

[29]Decree for distribution of Estate, December 12, 1907. Tuolumne County Superior Court. Probate in matter of the estate of B. Murphy, deceased.

[30]The Turnback Inn was built by Thomas Bullock, of the Sierra Railroad in 1902, on the present site of the Tuolumne Veterans' Memorial building. The beautiful two story Inn provided tourists an overnight stay before embarking to Yosemite.

[31]Ann Rooney. Conversation Nov. 23, 1998.

[32]Mr. Kaighin knew Thomas Bullock, both being railroad men, hence, The Turnback Inn would have been a favorite place to get away from the city.

[33]Ford Clark, *"Murphy Bed was Romance Venture,"* December 1977, Iowa City.

[34]Riggs, "Disappearing Act," *Dunn and Bradstreet Register,* March/April 1992, p. 34.

[35]Joan O'Sullivan, "A Bedroom Story that Reads like a Novel," *The Irish Echo,* July 1, 1989.

[36]"A Brief History of the Murphy Bed Company." Murphy Bed Company, Inc. Sept. 11, 1998.

[37]*"Doings of Smart Set in City and Country,"* Society page, *San Francisco Examiner*, 1913.

[38]Kay Murphy, letter, September. 27, 1998.

[39]"W. L. Murphy Dies. Devised Door Bed," *New York Times,* May 24, 1957.

[40]Carolyn Jones, "Murphy Bed Makes Comeback," *Marin Independent Journal,* October 21, 1975. The Murphy Bed Company sold over 200,000 beds a year during its heyday in the 1920's and 1930's. About 14% of hotel and motel rooms in the Marriott, Hyatt, Hilton and Sheraton hotels currently have concealed beds.

"I think a lot more decisions are made on serendipity than people think."

— JAY LORSCH
Harvard Business School

Sonora's Cleopatra

Women have sometimes been called chameleons, changing their spots and their minds with whimsical nonchalance. That attitude supposedly went out of style with the women's movement of the 1960's, with the insight of feminists like Betty Friedan and Gloria Steinman. We have come to understand that much of what was said about women, particularly in the early press, was very biased. A case in point, was a story I ran across in the files of the *Union Democrat* of 1903. I couldn't help but wonder how the same story would have been written by a contemporary reporter.

Whether Mag Johnson was indeed a "scarlet" lady, or a woman trying to earn a living in a society where women's employment was limited, she was by any standard, a very colorful character. She began her working career in one profession and ended up in quite another. Why, we shall perhaps never know.

On August 22, 1903, the following story appeared.

HER BEAUTY WAS FATAL

Recently death by accident in London (claimed) Mrs. Margaret Vandever, an eccentric and wealthy American lady. Apparently she had spent a great deal of money bringing women back to the path of rectitude. But—when some of the old timers were told that Mag Johnson and Mrs. Margaret Vandever were [one and] the same person, then you can expect a, "Well, I'll be darned!"

Mag Johnson first appeared in Sonora in the early days of El Dorado's placer mining. Men raved over her beauty, while women merely noted that she was "good-looking."

And in those early days she did not travel the straight and narrow path. In fact, the "road to ruin" was her chosen thoroughfare. She proved it by spending one night in a hotel, [and] the following day finding her an inmate of the "Palace," Sonora's edition Deluxe in the way of glittering gorgeous brothels and the most notorious resort in the Southern Mines tenderloin. In less than a week, a dozen lucky miners had tossed gold buckskin bags of yellow nuggets into her lap for a temporary favor.

Jack Valentine, a young Kentuckian, madly infatuated with her, proposed marriage and was told to drop around again when he was a millionaire. Instead, he dropped dead with a bullet in his love-grazed brain at Mag's lovely feet, apparently due to rejection. With scarcely a change of color she ordered the body removed and deplored the crimson stain on her carpet. Nerves of steel and a heart of iron were in that gloriously lovely person.

The next day, she went to the funeral [parlor], placed a $50 gold piece into the minister's hand, settled with the undertaker and having dismissed this little tragedy, went back to the palace, wondering whether the next victim would be fool enough to shoot a hole in himself and spoil more carpets.

Mag was fairly tall, face fair as a lily, clean cut as a cameo and as delicately tinted as a sea shell. [Her] eyes varied from deep violet to sea green. [She had] black eyelashes, gold hair, which fell almost to her feet. To these [add] the form of a Venus and you have a fair picture of a woman who lived in the half world.

No one knew where she came from. Apparently she told people something different—that she was American, French, Irish-American, Spanish-American and any other hyphenated American that the liberal use of a world's map might justify.

Mag didn't stay long in Sonora. The last night, she went into the Long Tom Saloon and gambling house, now the J.B.

Ventri block and beat Cherokee's Monte game out of $5,000 in less than an hour, ordered champagne for everyone and suddenly kissed proprietor Murphy good night and was gone.

Next, she was on the stage bound for Sacramento. Three months of Sonora had been enough. The express company had carried out her $60,000 to be deposited to her credit with Moffitt and Company, Sacramento bankers.

A month later, news surfaced that a woman who alternated between Sacramento and San Francisco, whose beauty was said to exceed that of Lolà Montez, was called, The California Cleopatra. Obviously, our Mag had surfaced once again.

In San Francisco, the manager of a Pine Street variety theater, then known as melodious, was said to have offered her $1,000 a week to do plastique poses at his amusement house. She responded, "Mag Johnson isn't cheap and also has a little self respect left."

And life for those in the City by the Bay who fell slaves to her magic was just as tempestuous and as uncertain as it had been in Sacramento or Sonora.

Louis Egrix, a young Frenchman, who had cleaned up a big pile from a rich claim in Columbia, went to San Francisco to enjoy himself. There, he met Mag and added more brilliance to her already heavily diamond-laden person. In less than a week, she had his last dollar and ordered him to go back to the mine and dig for more. Instead, he jumped into the bay. His body was fished out the next morning and as usual Mag paid cheerfully the expenses and was on hand for the funeral.

Bob Ray, pioneer river boat captain and George Van Ness also paid with their lives through the penalty of loving Mag. On Christmas night, the Overland Gambling House was crowded. Every game was bombarded with money and gold dust, while Mag, in full evening dress was dealing Faro at $1,500 a week, a rather high salary, but cheap at that.

Henry Weber, her brand new lover and one of the proprietors of the establishment was standing beside her chair, when John Lyons, a dandy of the period entered. He and Weber were bitter enemies and Mag was the cause. Both were desperate men. Two pistol shots rang out. Both men were buried side by side, Mag acting as principle mourner. She put a wreath on each grave, settled the postmortem bills and left.

Then, if this were not enough, Henry Weatherbee, a promising young attorney of New York followed the human tidal wave westward and settled in Jamestown, pitching his tent on ground occupied by Preston's Livery stable. Soon tiring of life as a miner, he went to San Francisco, hung out a shingle and was soon recognized as one of the brightest members of the local bar.

But, he bowed before the fatal beauty of Mag and all else—ambition, honor, everything was forgotten. His passion for her was a mania. Hers for him was merely mercenary. One day she told him so. Quick as a flash he whipped out a dagger and drove it to the hilt into her breast. He took the blade out and plunged it into his own heart. He died but Mag lived, hovering for a week between life and death. However, Weatherbee had a young sweetheart, a Mexican girl whom he loved before falling under the spell of Mag. She vowed to wreak vengeance on the destroyer of her happiness.

Mag was gaining strength. One day, a visitor came to call. It was Weatherbee's sweetheart. She had come to see the poor American lady and to offer her a present. It was only a cup of Jelly. Mag raised an elbow and got the cup's contents right in her face.

Mag's popularity departed with her beauty. She went to Europe and never came back. For over forty years she labored in the slums of London's White Chapel helping women, who, like herself, had at one time entered the wrong profession. She was run down by a train at Charing Cross, rather an unroyal death for a one time queen, Sonora's Cleopatra.

"I always say,
beauty is only sin deep."

— SAKI

The Union Democrat
Albert
Francisco
OFFICE
WD

Albert Newman Francisco

What makes a good newspaper man? Is it a passion for his work, a dedication to an unbiased point of view? If these qualities were necessary requirements to succeed in this field, Albert Francisco, the founder of the *Union Democrat*, would have failed miserably. Were it not for the fact that twenty-six of Albert's letters written from the gold fields in the 1850's, have only recently surfaced, we would not be able to ascertain the persona of this multi-faceted pioneer newsman's personality. We would be lacking the significant events in his life that led inevitably to a decision that would have enormous consequences for Albert and for those of us who live in the Mother Lode today.

When I initially decided to undertake research on Albert, all that I could find on his background was a brief sketch of his life taken from his obituary which was written by the newspaper on March 9,1867.[1] Aside from the obituary and Albert's tombstone marker located in the Masonic Lodge Cemetery above Sonora, information on Albert was sparse and often redundant. The imposing Francisco Building, named in his honor was built over the site where Albert first began publication of the paper July 1, 1854. While the imposing four-story building commemorates this early newspaper man, not even a picture of Albert exists among those of the paper's publishers.[2]

Here, I admit to serendipity and luck. It is ironic how often these factors weave their magic spells during the course of research. Through nothing more than a chance encounter one day at the local library, I happened to glance at a newly published book on the Gold Rush. Curiously I thumbed through it and Albert's name loomed before me. Surely, I thought, this must be another Francisco. I could not believe my good fortune when I discovered that the author's reference listed the Huntington Library and Albert's letters he had written from the gold fields.[3] If this "find" were not enough, quickly upon the heels of that chance discovery came yet another. The genealogical society informed me of an inquiry they had recently received from one of Albert's relatives in Wisconsin, asking about Albert's activities on the West Coast. Writing this relative opened the proverbial flood gates and suddenly Pandora's box yielded a researcher's dream.[4] Albert's life began to take shape before me and I was able to piece together the dreams and aspirations of a young man escaping from his past, seeking a new life in the gold fields of Sonora.

Albert's genealogy was unique. His great-great grandfather was Atome Francisco, born in France in the 16th century.[5] A French Huguenot, he lived in a time of enormous turmoil and animosity, fired by religious persecution. Protestants in France had, since Martin Luther posted his famous ninety-five theses in 1517, suffered a reign of terror.[6] The theses were widely read, and men and women everywhere began to question many of the Catholic Church's practices, leading to the Great Schism, the birth of Lutheranism and, ultimately, Protestantism.

By the late 16th century, Atome Francisco had fled with his family to Amsterdam, Holland.[7] There he married a Dutch woman and returned with her to France. It was here that Henry Francisco was born in Essex, May 31, 1686. However, religious persecution reared its ugly head and once again the family was forced to flee. This time, they went to England.[8]

Henry's parents later immigrated to America, settling in New York, at Whitehall.[9] Here, Albert's great grandfather, Henry, married Ruth Fuller and had twenty-one children. He served his country in the American War of Independence and was a private under Captain Jeremiah Burroughs, 1777.[10]

What is unusual is that Henry must have been at least ninety years of age when he enlisted in the American War of Independence. He died October 25, 1829. If one believes these dates, he was 134 at the time of his death![11]

Solomon Francisco, Henry's son and Albert's grandfather, was born on October 2, 1768, in Albany, New York. At just nineteen, he married Mary Freeman, in Skenesborough/ Whitehall. One of their sons, Henry, moved to Cincinnati sometime before 1808.[12] This was a vast new area, which came into being after the French and Indian wars, known as the Northwest Territories. A grant of approximately 250,000 acres between the Great Miami and Little Miami Rivers was destined to become one of the most important new settlements in the United States. Named Cincinnati, it was to be the home of the Francisco family for many years to come.[13]

Solomon and his family moved to Pittsburgh around 1810. There, they built a flatboat and embarked on a journey down the Ohio River. They arrived at Cincinnati around the end of October, 1811.[14] By 1812, he had set up a farm in an area today known as Central Avenue, leased a piece of land on the bank of the Ohio River and acquired a lot in what is now downtown Cincinnati.[15] In 1827, Mary died of consumption. Solomon then married his second wife, Eunice Johnson. By this time, only two of Solomon and Mary's children were still living in Cincinnati.[16]

David Francisco, son of Solomon and Mary and father of Albert, died young, in 1826, just short of his thirtieth birthday. He had married Elizabeth Norris in Hamilton County, Ohio and produced five children: Helen Louisa, Albert Newman, Andrew Wiggins, Albinus James, and David Francisco.[17] Albert's mother was left a widow with four small children and one on the way. In order to support her five children she set herself up as a tailor.[18]

Young Albert was brought up by his mother and, as a result, was probably closer to his mother's numerous Norris relatives than to the Francisco's.[19] Judging from the letters Albert wrote to his mother from the gold fields, he was well-educated, probably self-taught, extremely sensitive and very close to her.[20]

Albert's choice of the field of newspaper work was, perhaps, based on his brother's influence and secondly, on Franklin County. His second youngest brother, Andrew, went into printing and subsequently became part owner and business manager of *The Cincinnati Times*.[21] Andrew was also part owner of the *Ohio State Journal* in Columbus, the oldest newspaper in Franklin County. Later, he and his family moved to Los Angeles where he briefly owned shares in the *Los Angeles Times*.[22] Secondly, Franklin County was prolific in newspaper publication. Since the beginning of the county, no less than sixty-four newspapers had been created.[23]

Sometime before 1840, Albert made his way to Columbus to serve as an apprentice to a printer on *The Ohio Statesman*. The paper had earned a reputation which strongly advocated democracy, a belief that would become passionately engraved in Albert's moral and ethical principles.[24]

Generally, the American Press had maintained, since 1790, an intensely political character and newspapers were powerful factors in controlling the politics of the state. So too, *The Ohio Statesman*, helped form political viewpoints in its area of the country, which molded the political councils of its respective parties.[25] At the very crossroads of commerce and information, Columbus must have offered the young Albert a stimulating and dynamic cross-section of the times.

On December 16, 1844, in Cincinnati, Albert married Minerva T. Covert.[26] They traveled down the Mississippi Valley, arriving at New Orleans. Albert went to work as a foreman in the composing room of *The New Orleans Picayune* newspaper.[27] He worked there until his departure for California.

Then came the news that would shake the nation to the core: Gold! On January 24, 1848, James Marshall picked up a few nuggets of gold from the bank of the American River. However, the biggest story of the decade, was not immediately printed.[28]

In California, Marshall's discovery did not break in *The Californian* until March 15th.[29] Conservative owner, B.R.

Buckelew, placed the story on page 2, column 3.

GOLD MINE FOUND

In the newly made raceway of the sawmill recently erected by Capt. Sutter on the American Fork, gold has been found in considerable quantities.[30]

April 1,1848, an issue of *The Star* finally reached the east and was picked up in the August 19th edition of *The New York Herald*. By October 1848, the first steamers out of New York headed for the gold fields.[31]

The flurry of stories, however, forced the United States Government to quickly authenticate the news before panic broke out. It took eleven months from Marshall's discovery, for official sources with the best proficiency tests available to place an official approval on the gold discovery.[32]

To try to authenticate the stories, California's military governor, Richard Mason, sent two messengers, Lucien Losier and David Carter, with letters to Washington, after he had personally toured the gold fields.[33] Carter gave an interview to *The Picayune* and it would seem likely that Albert may have been present. As an editor-printer of the paper, Albert was sitting on top of a newsman's dream. However, *The Picayune* was hesitant about releasing the news. In spite of the fact that stories were filtering back through the various news sources and men were returning from the gold fields with news of their finds, the gold stories were consistently put on the back pages. Why? It may be that at the very heart of the discovery of gold was a reality that flew in the face of American ethics and morality.[34] At *The Picayune* for example, one individual's story of success in the gold fields ended with a protest from the editors.

We protest setting up the career of such a scoundrel as a monument of Yankee enterprise.[35]

On August 17, 1848, when Govenor Mason's report had

reached officials in Washington D.C., the situation was beginning to change rapidly. By the time President Polk gave his State of the Union Address on December 5, 1848, the flood gates were open.[36]

Albert's decision to leave for California was prompted, at least in part, by a marriage that was falling apart. From New Orleans, June 17, 1849, he wrote to his mother.

Dear Mother

Absent, though not forgotten... If you can appreciate my position you will not wonder at my long silence. You are the only being I feel any regrets in leaving behind... And another thing prevents me... I expect to get the foremanship of the office in case the present foreman leaves... There is no knowing what I will do with myself yet. I am extremely unsettled, and only waiting for a favorable opportunity to strike a blow that will either make me or break me. I would rather get out of the place if possible.[37]

In the same letter, Albert added,

"Were I a single man and could retain my present moral and industrious habits, it would not be long before I could leave a business which I feel is taking me off by inches."[38]

Yet almost a year passed before Albert struck the blow.

San Francisco, May, 1850

Dear Mother

...Left New Orleans as you are aware on the 28th of February, reached Chagres on the 10th of March, left Chagres in a canoe on Monday, reached Gorgona, the head of navigation. Staid all night on the 14th, took mules in the morning for Panama... The business of the place is principally conducted by Americans and there is gambling and whiskey shops in abundance. They wanted me to start

a paper there and made me a good offer, but as I left New Orleans to get out of the business, I declined.[39]

Albert did not write in detail about San Francisco except to mention the enormous rents. "Two or three rooms will rent from $600 to $1,000 a month!"[40] The new world that greeted Albert upon his arrival was, in some respects, similar to that of New Orleans—a thriving seaport, a cosmopolitan community filled with the unfamiliar sounds of strange languages and a gateway to the surrounding wilderness. There the similarities ended. At the time Albert first laid eyes on the burgeoning new city, San Francisco's hills were still surrounded by tents and adobe huts.

Albert made his way inland to Sonora. Situated in a valley sheltered under the western rim of the Sierras, Sonora was populated by people from every nation in all varieties of dress, with the sounds of dozens of languages.[41] He settled in Brown's Flat north of Sonora. The community was flanked by Squabbletown, and to the east, Bald Mountain.[42] Here, he met Dr. Franklin, a man who would handle Albert's many aches and pains and who would later testify to the insurance company that denied Albert's widow's claim.[43] On July 27, 1851, Albert wrote to his mother.

My Dear Mother,

...I have become almost reckless of myself as regards a fortune though I think I have it now within my reach....I can get no letter from Minerva, though I have written fifty... I feel as though Minerva had deserted me...else why could she remain quiet so long, and me so constantly writing. [44]

On December 25th, Christmas day, Albert wrote:

Dear Mother,

...I thought last fall I should have plenty of money by this time, as I was then quartz mining, but after

spending considerable money on the concern, I was obliged to abandon it for want of funds...I was offered $1,000 for my share before I had done my work upon it. Now I could [not] get a thousand cents. Luck is the fortune of miners.[45] *I have been thinking of going to San Francisco this winter to work at my trade."*[46]

In 1852, Albert wrote his brother Andy.

"My success in mining has been poor, poor indeed. I endeavor to wear a face of sunshine...but the effort is sometimes a desperate one."[47]

Judging from this letter, it almost seems as if Albert has concluded that mining was not going to yield the bonanza he had hoped. The newspaper business seemed a better choice.

In June, 1852, he wrote his mother.

"I am getting very old mother; you would hardly know me. My hair is quite grey."[48]

Perhaps suffering from melancholia he wrote a poem.

The Miner's Lament

This to me's a dreary calling.
Full of sadness—full of pain—
And I'm longing—I am pinning
For my own dear home again.
The time I've lost in useless efforts
To obtain the shining ore,
And expending fast as getting—
Oh! That I could sin no more!
Had it been devoted solely
To the quiet cares of life—
In the midst of friends and
With a fine and cherished wife—

I had been a happier being—
Filled with joy and love for all,
Never dreaming—never dreaming
Such a fate could man befall.[49]

On December 22, 1852, he wrote. "There is no society, no nothing that is commendable and were it not for the exciting life of a miner, I really believe I should die of ennui."[50]

In May 1853, he told his mother. "The miners, generally speaking, are doing better than they have for the two years past. The shipments of gold dust will exceed that of any similar period since the discovery of the placers."[51]

On June 9, 1853, he bragged to his brother. "My house [*is*] the reading room for the neighborhood, and I stand very high in the estimation of all."[52]

Albert's letters are also full of up-coming elections. In the same letter, he writes. "I have been electioneering for an old friend of mine, who is a candidate for the office of sheriff. The convention to nominate candidates comes off next Wednesday."[53]

In July, he told his brother that he had been offered a situation as deputy, "which is worth four or five thousand dollars a year."[54] He also became an amateur archeologist, unearthing a tusk "ten or twelve feet long and twenty-eight inches in circumference."[55]

In October, he traveled back to New Orleans for a family reunion. Having returned from that happy occasion, he wrote Andy on April 13, 1854 from Sonora. He seemed closer now to the decision to get involved in a newspaper.

Dear Andy

I am halting between two considerations—one the deputies place, and the other, the publishing of a paper. I shall know shortly what I will do.[56]

On April 24, just three months before beginning the first issue of the *Union Democrat*, he wrote.

Dear Mother

...Were it not for your sake, I would select some quiet place in the mountains far away from the hectic and humdrum of society and there end my days in solitude and silence. Were I untrammeled by the divorce of last fall, I should look forward to the future, not my distant past... I have not entered upon my business as yet... I would have taken the deputy sheriff's place ere this, were it not for the fact that my friends wish me to publish a newspaper. But as they have not yet furnished me with an office, I can do nothing.[57]

On July 1, 1854, *Union Democrat* began publication.[58] From that time to the first day of March 1867, the day of Albert's death, not a single issue of the paper was missed. Indeed, 147 years later, the paper can still make that statement.

Albert did not have the necessary funds available to begin a paper himself, or, as these letters reveal, the incentive to do so. But Albert was passionate about politics. He believed in states rights and often quoted The Kentucky and Virginia Resolutions of 1798. Harking back to the controversy between a strong Federal Government and states rights, the resolution resolved that the "several states composing the United States of America are not united on the principle of unlimited submission to their general government."[59]

The newspaper's editorials were flowery and bombastic. It is obvious that the early paper was chosen as a platform to air certain political views. He wrote:

...this generation has dug the grave of liberty and are now striving to rear a monument of crime and expression upon its sacred tomb.[60]

Albert finally found a woman who could share his life. She was Dolores Carillo, the foster daughter of Abelina Carillo.

They were married September 4, 1866.[61] Unhappily, their married life was short. On March 1, 1867, Albert passed away. Some say he was forever disillusioned by the events and outcome of the Civil War. Some say the death of his mother in 1865 was unbearable. His son, Alberti, was born just months after his death.

Unfortunately, a legal controversy ensued regarding Albert's life insurance. The $2,000 policy which would have helped defray the expenses of his widow was denied by the insurance company. Dolores sued, and eventually the case was heard before the United States Supreme Court. In Manhattan Life Insurance Company vs. Dolores Francisco, the jurors ruled for the insurance company, basing their decision on the company's claims of bench errors in the circuit court trial.[62]

Young Alberti visited his father's relatives sometime thereafter. In 1873, a guardianship case document in Hamilton County, Ohio, lists James Albert Francisco (Albinus James), Albert's younger brother, as being awarded guardianship of six year old Alberti.[63] Perhaps James had visited Dolores and asked his sister-in-law to take Alberti to Ohio where the family could provide more advantages for the boy. According to the 1880 census, however, young Alberti was back in California.[64]

We do know that the twenty-six letters Albert wrote from the gold fields made their way back east. Eventually they turned up in an Ohio bookstore and in 1960 were sold to The Huntington Library in San Marino.[65] Today, copies of the letters are filed at The Tuolumne County Museum, safely located in the community that inspired a young man to come west to pursue his fortune. The fortune eluded him, but his creation the *Union Democrat* survived.[66]

Footnotes

[1]The information in this obituary, plus a paper written by Kathy Herrick in 1960, comprise the sum and substance of information available in Sonora prior to the knowledge and examination of the Huntington Library letters and the research by Eleanor Davis.

[2]The first home of the *Union Democrat* was a small wooden building on Yaney Street, opposite the old courthouse. It was built in 1855. On August 7, 1861, fire destroyed the offices and the paper moved temporarily to Washington and Elkin streets. In October 1861, the paper returned to Yaney and Green Streets. In 1954 it moved to 21 South Washington Street. In 1964, it was relocated to 59-61 North Washington Street. In 1969, the paper moved to its present location at 84 South Washington Street. Originally the paper was four pages long.

[3]Malcolm Rohrbough, Days of Gold, The California Gold Rush and the American Nation, (1997), p. 306.

[4]Eleanor Davis, great-great granddaughter of Calvin Francisco, David's (Albert's father) younger brother, and Albert's uncle.

[5]Mormon Archives. Francisco/Sisco. 1680-1820. Oct. 19, 1997. Family History Center, Sonora.

[6]Under Henry IV of France, the Edict of Nantes granted a measure of freedom to his Protestant subjects. However, during another wave of persecution, Louis XIV revoked the Edict in 1685, and Protestants were driven into exile. Encyclopedia Britannia, Vol. 15, p. 1169. (1972).

[7]Eleanor Davis, Letter, November 17, 1998.

[8]ibid.

[9]ibid.

[10]ibid.

[11]This unusual bit of information appeared in *Ripley's Believe It or Not*. February 17, 1939. Eleanor Davis said: "The story of Henry Francisco is filled with ambiguity." In 1819, a Yale professor, Dr. Benjamin Stillman, interviewed Henry, but his age was not clarified. While I was unable to obtain the book, much of the Mormon Archive information was based on Ross Francisco, A Brief Account of The Francisco Family, (1921).

[12]Eleanor Davis, Letter, November 17, 1998.

[13]E. H. Rosenbloom and F. P. Weisenburger, History of Ohio, (1943). The name Cincinnati was originally derived from a Roman citizen soldier Lucius Quintius Cincinnatus. Officers of the American Revolutionary Army formed a fraternal group in 1783, giving it that

name. George Washington was a member.

[14]Eleanor Davis, Letter, November 17, 1998.

[15]ibid.

[16]ibid.

[17]ibid.

[18]ibid.

[19]Of the twenty-six letters which the Huntington Library owns, most were written to his mother.

[20]*Union Democrat*, March 9, 1876. "He did not, as is supposed, possess the advantages of an early education and never (owing to circumstances beyond his control) did he acquire a finished one."

[21]Opra Moore, *History of Franklin County, Ohio*, 1939. Andy worked at the *Western Intelligencer*, the first newspaper published in Franklin county, Ohio, 1811. The newspaper then moved to Columbus, Ohio in 1814, becoming the *Ohio State Journal.*

[22]Eleanor Davis, Letter, November 17, 1998.

[23]Moore.

[24]To define the significance of the term "Democracy' to those living in Albert's era would not yield the same connotation as today. Suffice it to say, it meant a great deal to Albert. He stated repeatedly, if somewhat ornately, what his principles were. (Author).

[25]The literature of journalism was strongly based on social responsibility and that rested within the framework of how political demarcations were drawn. As a result, papers were spokespersons for specific parties, strongly regional and were often sounding boards for editors' opinions. (Author).

[26]For whatever reason, this was not a match made in heaven. While Albert does not specifically state the reasons for the break-up, it seemed to result in a confining strangle-hold over him. Minerva was born in 1824 in Ohio, and lived in the household of James Freeman Francisco, Albert's uncle. Eleanor Davis, Letter, November 17, 1998. Also, in the marriage license to Dolores Carillo, which was written in Latin, he is defined as an "infidel." *St. Patrick's Register*. September 1867. Eleanor Davis states that Albert was not Catholic but Minerva most likely was. Letter of April 10, 1998.

[27]*The Picayune* is still in business. (Author).

[28]Ralph P. Bieber, "California Gold Mania." *Mississippi Valley Historical Association*, April 22, 1948. No one believed the stories. Some newspapers printed stories suggesting they had found pyrite, not gold.

[29]*The Star* was published in Yerba Buena before San Francisco had a name.

[30]John Bruce, The Story of San Francisco's 100 Years of Robust Journalism, (1948). *The Californian* began publishing in Monterey, August 15, 1846. In 1847, Robert Semple took the newspaper to San Francisco and sold it to B.R. Buckelew.

[31]Rohrbough, Days of Gold, p. 23. The steamship *California* sailed on her maiden voyage to San Francisco from New York on Oct. 6, 1848. She had staterooms for sixty passengers and steerage for 160, yet there were only sixty paying travelers. Within three months, riots broke out over these same accommodations.

[32]ibid, p. 25.

[33]ibid, p. 24.

[34]William Benton, *The Annals of America 1841-1849*, Vol. 7. David Thoreau said "the rush to the gold fields reflected a disgrace on America."

[35]*The Picayune*, 1949.

[36]"The accounts of the abundance of gold in that territory are of such an extraordinary character as would scarcely command belief." December 6, 1849.

[37]Albert Francisco to his mother, June 17, 1849. Henry E. Huntington Library (HEH) in San Marino, California.

[38]ibid.

[39]Albert Francisco to his mother, May 1850. HEH.

[40]ibid.

[41]William Perkins, Journal of Life in Sonora 1849-1852, (1964).

[42]B.F. Alley, History of Tuolumne County, (1882).

[43]Tuolumne County Genealogical Society files. Anne Williams. Dr. Franklin was Albert's physician since 1866. His diseases were diagnosed as indigestion, liver and colic problems. Also, Eleanor Davis, Letter May 5, 1998. Dr. Franklin arrived in California in 1849. *Chispa*, Vol. 3 No. 3. He died in 1876.

[44]Albert Francisco to his mother, July 27, 1851. HEH.

[45]Albert Francisco to his mother, December 25, 1851. HEH.

[46]ibid.

[47]Albert Francisco to his brother, February 12, 1852. HEH.

[48]Albert Francisco to his mother, June 9, 1852. HEH.

[49]ibid.

[50]Albert Francisco to his mother, December 22, 1852. HEH.

[51]Albert Francisco to his mother, May 16, 1853. HEH.

[52]Albert Francisco to his brother, June 9, 1853. HEH.

[53]ibid.

[54]Albert Francisco to his brother, July 6, 1853. HEH.

[55]ibid.

[56]Albert Francisco to his brother, April 13, 1854. HEH.

[57]Albert Francisco to his mother, April 24, 1854. HEH.

[58]Chris Bateman, *Union Democrat* reporter, interview May 15, 2002. The *Union Democrat* name was changed on Dec. 6, 1961 to *The Daily Union Democrat* by the Editor/Publisher, Harvey McGee. The name was changed back to the *Union Democrat* on February 2, 1981 to avoid the common reference to the paper as the "DUD."

[59]*Annals*, Vol. 4. pp. 62-67. "It was his delight to nail to the cross, to hang, draw and quarter the advocates of a strong centralism which can only be built upon the ruin of the States." *Union Democrat*, March 1, 1867. The *Union Democrat* was "started as a newspaper sympathetic to the Confederacy. Not until after Lincoln's assassination did the paper change its views." *Tuolumne Prospector*, July 14, 1957. Albert was elected as a delegate to the Democratic National Convention. *Union Democrat*, January 28, 1860.

[60]*Union Democrat*, September 1866.

[61]Eleanor Davis, Letter, April 10, 1998.

[62]Eleanor Davis, Letter, April 10, 1998. " The insurance company refused to honor the policy because Dolores had paid only about a third of the first of ten years of premiums. They also suspected fraud on the part of Dolores and Albert." In addition, Albert had not had the policy in force very long before he died. In several letters he mentions having problems with his kidneys. Letter, February 24, 1853. HEH.

[63]Hamilton Co. Ohio court in Cincinnati: *Guardianship*, Vol. 8, p 399. #17575. 1873. September 1. Min.121. Eleanor Davis, Letter, April 19, 1998.

[64]ibid. Mrs. Dolores Francisco died in Sonora January 30, 1898. *Mother Lode Magnet.*

[65]Ohio Book Store, 726 Main St. Columbus, Ohio.

[66]After Albert's death, the paper was owned and managed by a succession of colorful and brilliant editors and writers. Among them the famous Prentice Mulford, who for years wrote under the by-line, *"Dogberry." Tuolumne Prospector.* The newspaper is the third oldest newspaper in the state of California and the second oldest daily in continuous operation in the state. The oldest newspaper consecutively published is the *Placer Herald,* Auburn, 1852. *The Sacramento Union* is the oldest daily newspaper, started in 1852.

Captain William and Delia Nevills

Captain William Alexander Nevills

He was acerbic, irascible and just plain difficult to get along with. In today's vernacular, we would classify him as a type A personality—someone who shoots from the hip. He sued almost everyone with whom he did business and he shed wives and acquired mistresses with charm and aplomb. His scandalous behavior must have been a newspaper man's dream. But for all the notoriety, Mr. Alexander Nevills remains, to this day, an enduring memory of Mother Lode history.

He was born in 1842, on the Canadian side of the river near Niagara Falls, but at an early age moved with his parents to a farm near the town of Hamilton.[1] For seventeen years he went to school and worked on what he described as the coldest farm in the world. Leaving home, he arrived in Buffalo, New York. Here, he shipped out as a sailor on *The Baltic*, sailing between Buffalo and Chicago. On Thunder Bay, a small cove on the Manitoba coast, young Nevills witnessed an unforgettable sight. Looming before him in the bay, rose an Island which just happened to be one of the richest silver mines in the world.[2] When Nevills discharged his supplies, it seemed to him that the area was permeated with an unforgettable charm. Compared to the world of ships and the sea, Nevills knew he had to change careers.

Working as a miner, he eventually found a partner to share his findings. They were able to uncover a magnificent property and open it up for development. When they sold out, young Nevills split $210,000—a fortune in that day.[3]

In the summer of 1869, flush with more wealth than he ever imagined, he went to Chicago. Wined and dined and perhaps somewhat awed by the big city, he was elected to the prestigious but expensive Chicago Board of Trade. He could not keep up the pretense, however. He later told the story that his $100,000 lasted him about as long as a snowball in Hades, or candy in an orphanage.

With just $2,800 left, he made the decision in 1870, to head for Cheyenne, Wyoming. But the greenhorn from the east was confronted with a whole new set of rules. Mining, he discovered, was an uphill adventure. Stages were robbed regularly and hostile Indians raided the camp. Murders were routine.[4]

California beckoned, and in 1872 he began prospecting in the Kern Mountains. He learned to sleep in the open, night after night, and prospect during the day. He moved north to El Dorado County and from there to Amador County in the Mother Lode region.

Nevills, had, by this time, acquired the title "Captain."[5] About the same time, he had met two Germans who owned what was known as the Old Spanish Mine. They were not having much luck with it, in spite of its reputation. Discouraged and too poor to work the mine, they offered a one-half interest to the young entrepreneur, provided he would put up a ten-stamp mill on the property. This he secured for $1,200. Still, the mine did not pay off. The owners upped their offer, and for $1,700, Nevills became the sole owner. For seven years he worked the mine, stubbornly refusing to give up. His meager funds, however, were running out. In order to make money, he accepted an offer from the owners of a company who owned a mine in the Arizona Territory. It was dangerous country. The Mescalero Apaches were constantly on the warpath. There were Gila Monsters and the heat reached 120 degrees in the shade. After several months he decided to return to his Spanish mine. This time his hard work paid off in spades. Within sixty days, with nothing but a hand motor, he hammered out $160,000 of gold. Nevills was learning the tricks of his trade. Immediately he sold a one-half interest in the mine for $250,000! The mine continued to yield a fortune and what seemed a lost cause turned out to be a treasure after all.[6] The lessons these experiences taught Nevills would last for the remainder of his life.

In 1884, he headed for Calaveras County and Angels Camp. Here he purchased and operated the Stickles Mine in conjunction with Senator J. P. Jones of Nevada[7] Five years later he sold the property. The year was 1889 and for Nevills it would be a very good year.

With past events fresh in his mind, he scoured the area for possible investments. He heard about the Rawhide. It was a mine with a terrible reputation. Mark Twain described it in the 1860's when he was living nearby on the Gilles Ranch in Tuttletown. "It [the mine] lived on refuse rock and the pleasure of contemplation. Its running gear was repaired and renovated from time to time with strips of rotten rawhide from which the fence, which enclosed the Rawhide, gave the ranch and the mine their names."[8] Twain took great pleasure in noting the fate of those who tried to work it. Five men had already given up after digging a 120 foot shaft, and had sold their claim. The asking price was $25,000 but since there were no takers, they doubled the price and advertised the mine on the East Coast. There were always naïve investors who could be lured to the enduring hope of a rich strike in the west. From that effort, two men emerged —John Gashwiler and Johnny Skae. However, unbeknown to them, the mine had been sold to someone else within the time limit initially specified. Gashwiler and Skae were forced to transfer the mine to the new owners. Furious over their losses, they sued. When the case was tried in 1866, the court decided against the two men. They left the area sadder, but wiser men.[9]

By the time Nevills entered the picture, the Rawhide was an old and neglected mine, apparently played out and worthless. It was a situation he had encountered before. Upon inspection, he found the mine was not only full of water, but the site had already been worked sporadically for years with no results. Everyone told him, "You put a $1 in and you'll get nothing out." When Nevills bought the mine for the rock bottom price of $16,000, the local townspeople had a big laugh. They referred to Nevills as a city-slicker who had just bought the old Rawhide. What a dud, the newspaper asserted, predicting that the poor sucker was going to loose his shirt. Nevills was not listening. While everyone in the county shook their head in disbelief, he rolled up his sleeves and went to work. $100,000 of hard-earned money disappeared before he ever saw a cent. But when the Rawhide finally gave up its treasure, it proved to be the richest producer in the area or, for that matter, one of the richest mines in California. The Rawhide quartz mine would go on to produce over six million dollars up to 1909. But Nevills was not through yet. In 1893, he followed his hunch to yet another adjacent treasure trove, the App Mine.[10] After that, people ceased laughing. He was acquiring a reputation as a man with the Midas Touch.

Nevills never looked back. He was a man with a mission. He began investing in grape vineyards, a stock farm in Fresno and numerous ranches in the area. He turned his attention to stages, hotels and utility companies. The effect on Tuolumne County was significant. Nevills' luck created a tremendous new era of prosperity. Prior to his arrival, the area was depressed. Mining and employment were at an all time low. His vigor helped reshape and inspire the community.

He was also a man used to the comforts and conveniences of San Francisco and his favorite hotel, The Palace.[11] When he stayed in Tuolumne County on business, he had to "rough" it in poor accommodations that were not up to his taste or standards. Hotels were often crowded to the roof and frequently guests were compelled to seek sleeping rooms in private homes.[12] The story goes that he was so upset one day with the service in a local hotel, he vowed to built a hotel of his own just to get even.

With his typical savvy and energy, Nevills looked around

for a project in which he could direct his enormous energy. The best central location in Sonora was the corner of Washington and Stockton Road. It had been a focal point since 1849, when the first Mexican miners came to town and laid out a central plaza. Later, the Lafayette Restaurant and the American Bath House were built on the site. When fire destroyed Sonora on June 18, 1852, the plaza was eliminated by the city trustees in favor of a uniform, Americanized main street eighty feet wide. It took the name Washington Street. Two years later, Mrs. Mary Bailey established a boarding house on the site. She became the first woman in the region to test a recently-passed state law permitting a married woman to carry on a business in her own name as sole trader. The Bailey House became the American Hotel, and later the Sonora Hotel and in 1858, the Stage Hotel.[13]

In the spring of 1895, Nevills paid $16,500 for the corner, plus two adjacent lots. The hotel that Nevills constructed would be the finest hostelry in the Sierras, befitting the name the town had begun to acquire, "Queen of the Mother Lode." Built of local slate, rock quarried from Tuolumne County's own hills, the walls were extremely thick. The main building was three stories high and contained a large dining room, a saloon, a kitchen, parlors and a total of forty-eight rooms.[14] The basement extended the full length of the building and housed a wine cellar, a bakery, laundries and meat lockers. There was a beautiful court containing flowers and tropical plants. Their delightful fragrance wafted through the premises.

Inside the building, art hung everywhere. Frescoes, paintings, and tintings were in the hands of the well known firm of Blanchard and Shell of Stockton under the direct supervision of Mrs. Nevills. The finest redwoods and mahogany covered the interior walls and stairs. Magnificent gas and electric lights hung from the vaulted ceilings and furnishings were lavish. Menus featured the very best the area could provide. A popular delicacy was "oysters in any style," complemented, of course, with the finest wines and champagnes. Rooms cost 50¢, 75¢ and $1.00 a day on the European plan and five stages roared up to the front door delivering their arrivals with great fanfare and anticipation. Nevills named his new venture, The Hotel Victoria, after the Queen of England. It would cost an astonishing $100,000 to build, but it attracted a wide array of patrons.[15]

The Victoria Hotel was built in 1896 by Phillip Cavalero and G.V. Ventre. After a fire it was remodeled and opened as the Sonora Inn in 1931. Painting by Chris Holman (Photo by Mary Jane Reeb)

Nevills, in effect, was creating a new Sonora, a community perched on the precipice of a new millennium. But jump-starting such a large enterprise resulted in unforeseen problems. The town was small and isolated from the rest of the world. There were growing utility and transportation needs. These, Nevills realized, would have to be addressed if customers were to be properly serviced. Nevills was more than willing to take on the challenges.

Sonora was proud of its new millionaire. His goings and comings were reported in the local papers. When he presented his young and attractive wife with an expensive carriage, the new arrival was lauded as the "swellest and most costly family carriage in interior California."[16] While Delia Nevills was prancing around the county in the $1,200 Henderson rig, her husband was turning his attention to yet another gigantic project—railroads.

Railroads were an important new industry in America. Towns became cities, vital services began and development brought more people. All of this signaled an end to frontier isolation and drew the young country together.

As early as 1865, the first railroad line built east from Stockton in the general direction of Tuolumne was undertaken to serve copper mines. It was a harbinger of things to come. In 1876, in answer to a committee from Tuolumne County, President Stanford of the Southern Pacific extended a unique offer. He stated that if the people of the area would build a line from any point on the railroad, taking bonds in the new company as payment, the Southern Pacific would equip and operate the line and agree to a fair distribution of the earnings. Unfortunately, nothing ever came of either of these plans.[17]

In 1880, the Nevada and California Railroad ran surveys across Sonora Pass for a planned line to Utah. But the line never got past Bryant, east of Richmond in the Bay Area.[18] The San Francisco and San Joaquin Valley Railroad was built south from Stockton and reached Modesto in 1896 and Bakersfield in 1898.[19]

The new captains of the railroad industry arrived in Jamestown in the form of two sets of brothers-in-law: Thomas S. Bullock and Sidney Freshman; Prince André Poniatowski and William Crocker.[20]

In late 1895, with railroad equipment lying in Arizona from an abandoned railroad project, Thomas Bullock looked for a potential investor for his stockpile of idle equipment. He found Albert Stetson, who was involved in building a line in the Yosemite area.[21] Bullock began to spend time in the foothills of the Sierras while awaiting the sale of his equipment. He saw the obvious need for improved transportation in Tuolumne County.

Immediately, Bullock canceled plans to sell his Arizona equipment and formulated instead a plan to build a rail line to the Mother Lode. Remarkably, in just two years, his ideas would come to fruition when the golden spike of the new Sierra Railroad was driven in Jamestown, on November 10, 1897. The occasion was celebrated with a huge crowd of 5,000 people, almost the entire population of Sonora.[22]

Captain Nevills was in the center of the whirlwind of activity. On July 24, 1897, he purchased $50,000 of the bonds of the Sierra Railroad on the condition that the owners guarantee Jamestown as its terminus.[23] Forming the Jamestown Improvement Company, Nevills, Bullock and other members of the Sierra Railroad launched a building program. "A hotel was planned as the most elegant establishment ever built in the county."[24] There were to be lavish gardens surrounding the back of the hotel, while the front opened directly onto a magnificent marbled porch. The view was spectacular. Facing directly onto Table Mountain, visitors could take in the winter landscape, accompanied by stories of Rawhide gold no doubt, swallowed down with sips of ice cold champagne.

The lobby was an imposing room with a huge marble fireplace, supplied from the local quarry at Columbia, and a saloon of mahogany mirrors, and crystal chandeliers. For the architectural style, Nevills chose a flamboyant eye-catching oriental motif designed by Stockton architect George Rushforth.[25] Nothing was too good for the customers. At the bar was John Murphy from the San Francisco Palace Hotel, and a French chef, with Chinese assistants who prepared imported and local delicacies.[26] The hotel's upper balconies were paneled in ponderosa pine from local saw mills, and its sixty rooms were appointed with every luxury. The Hotel Nevills would preside over a new town of 120 acres laid out as a future townsite adjacent to the hotel, part of the plan of the Jamestown Improvement Company.

The year 1897 turned out to be the busiest year of Nevills already overtaxed calendar. Upon the heels of the Sierra Railroad and the hotel, Nevills promoted a new electric power and light company.[27] In December of 1897, the Columbia Marble Works quarry was leased to Prince Poniatowski and T.S. Bullock.[28] "But Nevills," noted the *Union Democrat*, "is the real power behind the throne and furnished the large amount of money necessary to close the deal."[29]

By the end of 1897, however, cracks began to appear. The Sierra Railroad was encountering some stiff and troublesome competition from a woman, Annie Kline Rikert.[30] Like Nevills, she had guts and determination, but the forces lined up against her were to prove overwhelming.[31]

Rikert's Women's Railroad called for an extension line originating at a site near Jamestown, then into Sonora, and finally, the foothills of the small town of Carters, also known as Summerville. The townspeople of Sonora and the local papers backed her plans. But the Sierra Railroad did not dare let Annie get to Sonora or Carters first with her line. Too much was at stake. Over 55,000 acres of rich timberland lay in the mountains, owned by William Crocker. Crocker moved quickly to acquire $515,000 of Sierra Railroad bonds, becoming a member of the Sierra Railroad Board of Directors in 1898.[32] No one, he determined, would reach Carters but the Sierra Railroad. For Nevills, that decision spelled trouble.

Nevills had purchased $50,000 in bonds of Sierra Railroad stock on the condition that Jamestown remain the terminus of the railroad for at least five years.[33] The agreement was ironclad. It was the reason he had built the Hotel Nevills and promoted the new town.

In spite of the agreement, The Sierra Railroad continued its line to Carters. Nevills sued to recover $25,148.50 alleged to have been expended for the hotel at the insistence of, and for the benefit of the defendants.[34]

Nevills was not a man to sit still for long or tolerate what he saw as injustice in business agreements. He would fight back. In his typical fashion, he began his own freight service, which he hoped would cut into the business of the Sierra Railroad. His hauling teams went from Oakdale to Sonora and while it cost him dearly, when Nevills was angry, costs were not a priority.[35]

The toll on Nevills began to show. In July, 1898, he suffered his first heart attack. The biggest problems, however, lay just ahead and had little to do with business. They would be affairs of the heart.

In March, 1898, Nevills brought suit against two men, J. E. Azhderian and M. H. Azhderian for $50,000. Both men worked for him at his vineyard in Fresno. Nevills declared "that a plot had been hatched to get money from him and that his own wife had been used as an instrument to try and ruin him."[36]

In the center of these nasty accusations, was Nevills son, Billy, who had come west to join his father in 1889. Son of his second wife Ruth, he apparently felt estranged from a father who spent more time in his work than with him. Billy had approached his stepmother, Delia, claiming that his father had been unfaithful to her and that if she sued for divorce, she could get all of his property.[37]

From here, the plot thickened. "My wife," Nevills claimed, "was so wrought up over the matter that she became a serious wreck and attempted to take her life. At first she was afraid to tell me the truth, because she feared that I might kill someone."[38]

The trial exposed a certain Mrs. Elsie Williams, who had been given a paper to sign which made her swear that Nevills had been untrue to his wife. For her trouble, Mrs. Williams was to receive $25,000.[39] The story grew daily and appeared on the front pages of the *San Francisco Call* newspaper.

In April, the *Call* stated that Nevills had imprisoned the Azhderian brothers in The Palace Hotel.[40] The charges grew even more outlandish. Behind it all lurked the young and beautiful Mrs. Williams. Nevills, apparently was seduced by her charms. He wrote passionate letters to her and these found their way into the hands of the Azhderian brothers. In trying to recover them, Nevills attempted to imprison the men. Unfortunately, the scheme backfired.

In April, it was charged that a Thomas Dolan had been hired

The Jamestown Hotel — planned as the most elegant establishment ever built in the county

to kill Captain Nevills. Dolan was also an employee at the La Favorita Vineyard in Fresno.[41] The charge stated that Elsie Williams, the *femme fatale* had entered into a conspiracy to have Nevills assassinated while Delia was gone. The plan had been hatched, it was alleged, to take advantage of Nevills explosive temper. An altercation would be staged and in the foray that followed, Nevills would be killed.

On April 23, Dolan was charged with perjury, but getting to the bottom of the mess proved difficult. Nevills claimed there was a conspiracy afoot to blackmail him. John and Myron Azhderian claimed that they had been imprisoned by Nevills against their wills. In the middle of it all was the beautiful Elsie and those incriminating letters.[42]

The imbroglio heated up. On May 14, Myron, Elsie and her sister were arraigned in Court on a second charge of extortion preferred against them by Nevills.[43]

On May 15, as the racy headlines continued, the courtroom filled with curious spectators. This time, another lady entered the picture, a Miss Neal. Miss Neal turned out to be none other than Elsie Williams who was using an assumed name. Why? It seems she had to visit the hospital for an "undisclosed" problem. Flowers had been sent to her room and Nevills had signed a check for $217 for her "treatment."[44]

On May 18th, the headlines read, *"Plotted for Rawhide Gold."*[45] On the 21st of May, Nevills took the stand. He testified that he had known Elsie for four or five years. They met at The Palace Hotel and he had hired the attractive widow to be his housekeeper and bookkeeper at his vineyard in Fresno. A disagreement arose and letters were exchanged. Elsie threatened to see an attorney. The attorneys for the plaintiff asked Nevills, "Did you have an illicit relation with her?" Nevills' attorney objected. The judge sustained the objection.[46]

On June 4th, the Williams vs. Nevills case took yet another turn. Nevills was arrested in The Palace Hotel for sending obscene letters through the U. S. mail. In the meantime, a few of these letters happened to surface. Elsie was willing to part with them—for a price. Elsie would only part with a few, however, holding back the spicier ones.[47]

On June 25th, the *Call's* headlines read: "Rawhide Gold Enlivens the Nevills Case."[48] On October 16th, Captain Nevills caused a sensational scene in court. This time, a Dr. Winslow Anderson was suing Elsie. The claim was for $2,000. Nevills exasperation was evident. He shouted that he would send their attorney and the three of them to the penitentiary. Nevills maintained that Mr. Church, attorney for the three was "just as deep in the scheme to blackmail him as were the others."[49]

On October 18th, Nevills began new proceedings against the illustrious trio. Apparently nothing came of the prior charges. Nevills continued to scream conspiracy and extortion and Elsie continued to charge that Nevills had sent obscene letters to her.[50]

The alleged extortionist trial continued. On November 16th, Judge Cook's court room was filled to capacity. The newspapers described Elsie as petite, painted and in earlier days, no doubt very pretty with doll like features and peculiar gray eyes. Her figure, the paper claimed, was dainty and in silks and sealskins accounted for the fact that she fascinated the wealthy captain. [51]

The prosecution brought out the fact that one of the Azhderian brothers had "shared" a cottage with Elsie overnight in spite of the fact that Nevills had strictly forbidden this. Nevills testified that "he had come down unexpectedly one night and saw John Azhderian flee to his room in the middle of the night."[52]

On November 19th, the trial drew to a close. Billy Nevills testified that he had drawn a confession from Myron Ahzderian in which he had conspired to "dispose" of Nevills and claim his property under forged conveyance."[53] Nevills won the case, and Azhderian was convicted.

If the problems of the trial were not enough, Delia had been a passenger on the Sierra Railroad when one of the coaches in which she was riding crashed. She brought suit against the line for $100,000 in personal injuries.[54]

In December 1899, the Supreme Court reversed the earlier judgments against Elsie Williams and the Azhderian brothers. The charges of extortion were not proved and the court was not satisfied that a crime had been committed.[55] In that same year, Nevills sued his partners in the Rawhide mine, Ballard and Martin. "Captain Nevills, the millionaire mine owner is once again in hot water."[56] This time, Nevills believed he was being eased out of the mine's ownership by his partners who owned 2/3 of the mine to his 1/3.[57]

The lawsuits against the Sierra Railroad continued well into the new century. Nevills revenge against "the boys" as he called them, was by way of increasing his freighting service between Oakdale and Jamestown. Arguing that he had spent over $300,000 on his palatial hotel plus improvements, the hotel had, he maintained become "a white elephant" when the railroad extended its line to Carters.[58]

Nevills battles in the court continued, but they were principally concerned with business. At the end of 1899, he won a suit against the Moore Gold Mining Company.[59]

The controversy with his partners, W. H. Martin and John Ballard and the Rawhide, raged on. In November of that year, Nevills brought suit against them for slander. In 1901, the case took yet another strange turn of events when Nevills sued them for recovery of personal belongings of considerable value. He claimed that rare paintings, wearing apparel, a gold scales and a blacksmith outfit had been taken by the two men.[60]

Also in 1901, Nevills made a trip to southern California and while there, claimed he and Delia peacefully entered the marshal's office to pay taxes. They were somehow placed under arrest without due cause. Nevills sued the marshal for $10,000.[61]

In September of 1901, Nevills again became the sole owner of the Rawhide and App Mines. Jamestown was so thrilled to see their favorite son that "his coming was heralded by the booming of canon and the hurrahs of the people."[62] Once again at the helm of the Rawhide, Nevills, and hundreds of people that relied on him for work in the mine, looked forward to the future with great hope. In a note of caution, however, the local paper wrote, "at his wizard's touch, the Rawhide poured forth a stream of golden wealth and while diminishing process has been in progress the past two years, it is confidently predicted that Captain Nevills will soon be waving his wand over huge deposits of shining gold."[63]

In 1903, Nevills added forty stamps to the mill at Rawhide.[64] and a month later, erected a five-story business block in Fresno.[65] But it would prove to be Nevills last hurrah. His best years were behind him, and his health was waning. Nevills star began to fade just when the fight of his life was about to commence.

In 1906, Nevills was trying to raise $250,000 in order to pay off his former partners and keep the Rawhide Mine afloat. This time however, the tables were turned. His old partners, Ballard and Martin sued him.[66]

Intervening in all of this was the famous San Francisco Earthquake of April 18, 1906. Nevills was in The Palace Hotel when the quake occurred and in attempting to escape, was badly bruised and shaken up.[67] However, he could not rest long. The loan that he incurred in February for $250,000 to pay Ballard and Martin nipped at his heels. He was given ten to twelve days to find the money. Nevills was forced to put many of his assets on the auction block.[68] He sold the Paragon Vineyard in Fresno for $50,000 to the Casparian Brothers. The once famous La Favorita, scene of the much publicized Azhderian and Elsie Williams extortion plot and love triangle, was on the market as well for $100,000.[69]

In 1907, the famous Rawhide Mine was sold, ending almost twenty years of work and memories.[70] Nevills was sixty-five years old and his health was failing. Excitement nevertheless followed the famous couple. In 1910, the Captain and Delia were robbed in Oakland by three thieves. They didn't make off with much because Nevills successfully wrestled one of the would-be robbers to the ground. They fled, however, with a $700 stick pin.[71]

In 1911, still more sensational headlines hit the San Francisco papers, when Nevills and Senator John Jones filed suit against William Fleming. The suit involved a contract between the parties over the purchase price of one-half of the Amador Tunnel, Milling and Mining Company. "And we will prove," Nevills' attorney maintained, "that John Fleming approached Mr. Nevills and said he would kill him."[72]

Two years later, on July 12, 1912, Captain Nevills passed away at the age of sixty-seven. Delia was by his side.[73] The beautiful Nevills Hotel in Jamestown burned to the ground in 1915.[74] For years, newspapers in Stockton, San Francisco and Sonora wrote articles about the Nevills millions and claims against his estate.[75] Apparently, his vast millions had vanished, and all attempts to locate it proved fruitless.

In 1929, the *San Francisco Call* ran the following story:

Mine Millions of Capt. Nevills Missing

All the millions of Capt. W. A. Nevills, one of the best

> *known latter-day miners of The Mother lode and one time owner of the highly productive Rawhide Mine at Jamestown and of the Nevills Hotel, famous as the best hostelry in the entire Bret Harte country, have disappeared. Mrs. Nevills had led a life of mystery following the death of her husband and little is known as to her business affairs.* [76]

Thus ended one of the most flamboyant personalities of the Mother Lode. The Hotel Victoria, now the Sonora Day's Inn, however, remains, a lone but lasting reminder to the man who helped shape a small town of the 1890's into a thriving and bustling community. Senator John Curtin said of Nevills, "No man who ever transacted business in our locality has contributed as much to the general prosperity of the people as did Captain Nevills."[77] And certainly, no man before or since deserves the title of "colorful" more than Nevills.[78]

Footnotes

[1]"Captain W. A. Nevills Dies in San Francisco," *Union Democrat*, July 13,1912. Sources say that Nevills' father was born in Ireland, his mother, Canada. Also, that Nevills came from a titled English family. *San Francisco Call*, 1912. Gaylord Staveley, a distant relative of the Nevills family, told me that Nevills' father was William P. Nevills, born 1808 in Binbrook, Ontario, Canada. Letter, May 9, 1999. (Author).

[2]The *Union Democrat* conducted a series of profiles on outstanding men during 1897.

[3]ibid.

[4]ibid.

[5]One source says that Neville acquired the title "Captain" from his service in the English military. He would however, have been extremely young to have achieved this rank. *San Francisco Call*, July 1912.

[6]*Union Democrat*, June 1897.

[7]David Clark, Los Angeles, A City Apart, (1981). The Stickles Mine in Angels Camp was sold to the Utica Company in 1889 and weeks later he purchased the Rawhide. *Union Democrat*, July, 1912. Mining tycoon and Nevada Senator, John Jones, built a wharf at Santa Monica on the first leg of an effort to carry silver ore from the senator's Owens Valley mines.

[8]"A Scene at Rawhide Ranch" *Chispa*, Vol. 23, No. 3. January-March, 1984, p. 779.

[9]ibid.

[10]ibid, p. 780. Another source said Nevills paid $12,000 for the Rawhide Mine. He did not commence operations until joined by Messrs. Ballard and Martin. Tuolumne County, California. Compiled and issued by The Progressive Association. Sonora, 1901. It must have given Nevills a great deal of pleasure to exhibit a massive block of gold-bearing ore from the Rawhide at the California Midwinter Exposition of 1894. Pat Rhodes, "Don't Throw it Away. Give it to Us," *Chispa,* Vol. 24, No. 4, April-June, 1986, p. 858.

[11]You might say Nevills learned the hotel business indirectly. He lived in suites at The Palace, San Francisco for years. After the San Francisco quake, he moved to the St. Francis Hotel.

[12]*San Francisco Call*, April 13, 1896.

[13]The *Union Democrat,* July 30, 1976.

[14]"What One Man is Doing for Tuolumne County." *The San Francisco Call.* The builders were Cavallero and Ventre. Alvin Sylva,

"Washington Street," *Chispa*, Vol. 18., No. 3, January-March 1979.

[15]ibid.

[16]Mr. Nevills' first wife was Esther Swaze. He married Ruth J. Nevills, then divorced her in 1887. They had one child, William. He then married Delia Frances Hagan, born in Cincinnati, raised in San Francisco. She was the niece of Judge Toohy. *Union Democrat,* June, 1897. According to Gaylord Staveley, there were four children born from Esther's marriage to Nevills: Eugene, Emerson, Maude, and Nellie Ettie. Letter, Gaylord Staveley, May 9, 1999.

[17]Kyle Wyatt, Railroads in Tuolumne County California: The Role and Importance to Certain Industries and Their Impact on County Economy, Development 1897-1917. Unpublished Master's thesis, University of the Pacific, May 1984.

[18]ibid.

[19]ibid.

[20]Dave Connery, "When the Railroad Came to Tuolumne," *Chispa,* Vol. 36, No. 3. January-March, 1997.

[21]ibid.

[22]ibid.

[23]*The Mother Lode Magnet*, July 24, 1897.

[24]*Chispa,* p. 1262.

[25]"The Hotel Nevills," *California Architecture and Building News*, August, 1898. Vol. 19, No. 8.

[26]ibid.

[27]"Great Enterprise," *Union Democrat* July, 1897.

[28]"A Great Transfer," *Union Democrat,* December 11, 1897.

[29]ibid.

[30]See Chapter on Rikert.

[31]Several reasons existed for Mrs. Rikert's problems. Because she was underfinanced, she depended on completing parts of the line in order to raise money for additional stocks. When delays and injunctions were levied against her railroad, she could not continue.

[32]*Chispa*, p. 1264.

[33]"An Accounting Wanted" *Union Democrat,* April 13,1901. Promises to Nevills included a large box factory which was later built in Tuolumne.

[34]*The Mother Lode Magnet,* July 14, 1899.

[35]*San Francisco Call*, October 3, 1898.

[36]*San Francisco Call,* March 20, 1898.

[37]ibid.

[38]ibid.

[39]ibid.

[40]*San Francisco Call,* April, 1898.

[41]ibid.

[42]*San Francisco Call,* April 23, 1898.

[43]*San Francisco Call,* May 14, 1898.

[44]*San Francisco Call,* May 15, 1898.

[45]*San Francisco Call,* May 18, 1898.

[46]*San Francisco Call,* May 21, 1898.

[47]*San Francisco Call,* June 4, 1898.

[48]*San Francisco Call,* June 25, 1898.

[49]*San Francisco Call,* October 16, 1898.

[50]*San Francisco Call,* October 18, 1898.

[51]*San Francisco Call,* October 26, 1898.

[52]*San Francisco Call,* November 16, 1898.

[53]ibid.

[54]*San Francisco Call,* November 19, 1898.

[55]*Mother Lode Magnet,* October 4, 1898.

[56]*San Francisco Call,* December 19, 1898.

[57]*San Francisco Call,* January 19, 1899.

[58]By the winter of 1903, a number of the rooms were unoccupied. It was reported by the *San Francisco Examiner* that the "mice and spiders are holding a carnival in Jamestown's palatial hotel." Sally Hamilton, "The Nevills Hotel," *Calaveras Tuolumne Telegram*, May 15, 1996. See "Revival of Old Time Freighting," *Mother Lode Magnet,* October 19,1901.

[59]*San Francisco Call*, November 30, 1898. Delia also took a much needed trip with friends to China and Japan. Perhaps a gift from a negligent husband? Clipping file, Genealogical Society, Sonora.

[60]*San Francisco Call,* May 9, 1901. In 1900, Delia narrowly escaped what her husband maintained was a case of poisoning. There was suspicion only, but no proof. *Mother Lode Magnet,* September 26, 1900.

[61]The Marshal asserted that Nevills grew violently angry over a difference as to the amount of taxes to be paid, and shook his fists in the marshal's face. *San Francisco Call,* January 19, 1901.

[62]"A Hearty Welcome," *Union Democrat,* September 28, 1901.

[63]ibid.

[64]*The Mother Lode Magnet,* March 25, 1903.

[65]ibid. April 15, 1903.

[66]In 1906, Nevills raised the $250,000 loan advanced by him by a friend, Charles F. Doe. But Ballard and Martin sued. *Mother Lode Magnet*, February 3.

[67]As late as April 26, Nevills was still suffering from bruises. *San Francisco Call,* April 26, 1906.

[68]*Tuolumne Independent,* February 3, 1906. Nevills was trying to raise $250,000 to pay a claim which the Union Trust Company held against him as trustees for the estate of the late Charles F. Doe. Nevills had borrowed this amount from Doe in 1904.

[69]The pledged securities consisted of 99,950 shares of the Guild Gold Mining Company; 99,950 shares of the Rawhide; 144,975 shares of the App mine; 1000 shares of the Paragon Vineyard; 92 shares of the La Favorita Vineyard. He also sold to T. W. Patterson of Fresno, the Columbia Mine on Moccasin Creek. *Tuolumne Independent*, February 10, 1906.

[70]Total production according to the 14th Report, State Mineralogist was six million dollars.

[71]"Thieves Get Fine Diamond," *San Francisco Call,* February 4, 1910.

[72]"Nevills Fears Not for Life," *San Francisco Call,* May 17, 1905.

[73]"Captain W. A. Nevills Dies in San Francisco," *Union Democrat*, July 13, 1912.

[74]Nevills Hotel fire 1915. On December 1915, the Sierra Railroad announced plans to erect a monument on the site in memory of Captain Nevills, but the tribute never materialized. Walter Bray, "The Sierra Railroad." *Chispa,* Vol. 22, No. 3. January-March, 1983. p. 751.

[75]It seemed that everyone Nevills once sued, now turned the tables on him. Unpaid attorneys, former partners, bankers, and others sued Nevills and plunged his estate into a quagmire of legal problems that continued well into the 1930's, long after his death. (Author).

[76]In spite of Nevills supposed worth of over $5,000,000 in 1900, the estate was deemed valueless. In 1916, Mrs. Nevills was sued when creditors attempted to recover old claims. However, Delia was living in an apartment in San Francisco and supporting herself. "Mrs. Nevills Is Sued for Fraud," *San Francisco Call,* February. 3, 1916.

[77]*The Mother Lode Magnet,* December 4,1901.

[78]"Nevills in Old Will Scorns Son," *San Francisco Call,* December 11, 1914. Billy, Nevills' son was left with $10 in Nevills 1905 Will. Apparently Nevills believed that his son was responsible for black-mailing him out of thousands of dollars and threatening his life. Billy died in 1941. Letter from Gaylord Staveley. June 11, 1999.

"All that glisters
is not gold."

— WILLIAM SHAKESPEARE
The Merchant of Venice

1947 DeSoto

Hollywood In Tuolumne County

The fantasy began early, before the turn of the century. It might even be said that the idea of moving pictures originated with a wager. Do all four hooves of a horse lift off the ground at the same time? Eadweard Muybridge, a photographer, was chosen to settle the bet.[1] In 1877, at former Governor Leland Stanford's farm in Palo Alto, California, Muybridge set up a battery of cameras side by side with a specially designed shutter mechanism.[2] As a horse ran across the path in front of the cameras, the cameras clicked. Muybridge viewed these images with a device known as the zoetrope and, voila, the result was a moving horse in action.[3] And, yes, all four hooves of the horse do indeed leave the ground at the same time. Muybridge approached the famous inventor, Thomas Edison, with the idea of using these moving pictures in conjunction with Edison's new phonograph. Imagine, pictures that speak!

Rapid experimentation followed. The result was Edison's kinetoscope, a machine that ran film with a continuous movement.[4] Edison applied for a patent in 1891, but thought so little of his invention that he failed to pay an additional $150 for rights that would have granted him an international copyright. That would prove to be a costly mistake.[5]

The kinetoscope sat idle in Edison's laboratory until 1894, when, on April 14, the first of several kinetoscope parlours opened in New York City.[6] For a penny one could see an object move: a man, a barking dog, a parade. These first "flickers" as they became known were often shown at amusement parks, shooting galleries, and arcades. In a sense, it was the beginning of film's association with outlandish advertising—the sensational, the greatest. They were all claims with which the film industry would forever be partnered.

When a vaudeville strike occurred in New York, the flickers were used as a theatrical fill-in to entertain audiences. As their popularity rose, audiences were moved to large funeral parlors where chairs were readily available to accommodate the people. The price of admission rose to a nickel and, for the first time, the flickering pictures were projected onto a screen. People could actually sit down and watch them in some degree of comfort.

Then the vaudeville strike ended. Surprisingly, people did not rush back immediately to the stage. What had seemed a fly-by-night fad hung around and, to the dismay of vaudevillians, spelled the end of one era and the beginning of another. The die was cast and movies have never looked back.

In 1903, a story line accompanied the flickering scenes. The film consisted of one entire reel and lasted a lengthy eight minutes. Moving pictures became motion pictures and *The Great Train Robbery* became a milestone in the history of film.[7] It was the first movie to give birth to the idea that a story could unfold before one's very eyes. Movies could moralize, teach, inspire and thrill us. Sometimes they would do so with great artistry, sometimes they would do so with profoundly bad taste. Nevertheless, cinema has been doing just that ever since.

Problems with protecting his invention plagued Edison. He had patented his new motion picture in 1897 and to safeguard his patent, he formed a trust which included several early film companies.[8] There were renegades, however—small producers who had been excluded from The Trust and were importing and acquiring bootleg equipment to make their own pictures. They tried to find obscure hideouts to shoot where they could escape the long arm of Edison's men. Like pirates, they fled New York to Florida, then to Cuba and, finally, to the ends of the earth, California. Here, they stood their ground and began to fight back. Very soon it became a losing battle for The Trust and the birth of the independent film studios began.[9]

Good weather made southern California an ideal place to film. The problem of setting up expensive lighting was eliminated. The bright California sun produced so much natural light that scenes could be filmed "a la natural." A variety of outdoor vistas made it possible to shoot any kind of story within a fifty-mile radius. Film companies could explore exotic Arabian melodramas in the Mojave Desert with natural sand dunes. In downtown Los Angeles, there was plenty of room for the antics of cars, trolleys, streetcars and the Keystone Cops. For a tropical paradise, one could film at the beaches of Malibu or Santa Monica or the many islands off the coast. For Westerns, there was the quiet San Fernando Valley and for snow-capped mountains, there was Mt. Baldy, Lake Arrowhead, Big Bear and Mt. San Jacinto. Every conceivable story line was possible, 365 days of the year.[10]

The good weather also brought Colonel William Selig to the West Coast in 1907. Driven out of Chicago by blizzards, snow and rain, he sent a company of players to Santa Monica to complete scenes for *The Count of Monte Cristo*, the first motion picture shot in the area.[11] A short time later, director Francis Boggs rented a vacant Chinese laundry at the corner of Eighth and Olive Streets in downtown Los Angeles. He built a forty foot square stage on an empty lot next door and filmed *The Heart of a Race Tout*. It was, the first movie to be made completely in California, released in 1909.[12]

Cecil B. DeMille, Jessie Lasky and Samuel Goldfish (later Goldwyn) persuaded Dustin Farnum, a popular actor of the day, to appear in their very first film. They planned to make the picture in Arizona, but headed instead to a small community west of Los Angeles.[13] With a population of less than 3,000 people, mostly farmers, Hollywood had a few barns available for rental. The group rented one half of a barn, while the owner kept his horses in the other half. Whenever the horses were watered, the water ran into DeMille's office and he was forced to wear galoshes or put his feet in a wastebasket. *The Squaw Man* was made on a budget of $15,000 and earned $225,000. Hollywood was off and running.

The Hollywood of the 1920's and early 1930's was simply one large movie set. Banks were regularly robbed, stores held up, streets roped off for auto accidents and even private homes were used for domestic dramas. Movie stars shopped in the same stores as everyone else, went to the same markets, lived nearby in the Hollywood Hills and were generally accessible to the public. But film makers sought more and more authenticity. As the industry grew, pioneers like D.W. Griffith experimented with camera angles, editing, music, authentic costumes and lighting techniques. Griffith, especially, was driven to make scenes as realistic as possible. He was notoriously cruel to his actors when it came to getting exactly the right expression. He would even go so far as to send scary telegrams to them the day of a shoot. Their mother had been killed or their son kidnapped or whatever Griffith thought would give him just the right look he wanted. Cameras were ready to roll to capture the first sign of terror or fear or panic.[14]

That quest for authenticity led filmdom to seek out more diverse areas where nature was pristine. Movie scouts for the major studio headed north. They discovered the Mother Lode. A small gold mining town nestled in the foothills of the Central Sierra Nevada provided ideal shooting for the burgeoning film companies. They found that Sonora had things you couldn't find in southern California, especially when Westerns were king. There were steam trains, small towns, a covered bridge and old buildings, which dated back to the Gold Rush. You could find exactly what the script called for.

When the early movie scouts arrived however, they saw that times were hard-pressed in the former Gold Rush communities. The heyday of gold mining was over. Lumber was the main industry and Sonora was recovering from World War I.

Unpaved streets lined in elm trees were still covered with leftover rock from the old Bonanza Gold Mine.[15] That was about to change.

In Sonora, filmed entertainment was first introduced by legitimate theater companies as a novelty feature and a diversion between acts of plays.[16] Three buildings in town accommodated theatrical productions. The most popular was the old Turn Verein Hall which faced Washington Street.[17] On Bradford Avenue, there was the Bradford Pavilion located east of the old county jail, which today houses the Tuolumne County Historical and Genealogical Society. The third, was the Opera House at the southern end of Washington Street.[18]

In 1901, electricity paved the way for the arrival of the motion picture. In August of that year, Stuart's Comic Players presented a musical show at the Turn Verein Hall that included a number of "Flickers." In 1903, progress continued when *Ali Baba and The Forty Thieves* came to town. There were illustrated songs and for 25¢ admission, one could view the new and revolutionary invention.[19]

In January 1904, Professor Bradshaw was heralded by the *Union Democrat* as offering a cinematic breakthrough that would "completely eclipse anything ever attempted in our city."[20] Among the films presented were *The Astronomer and the Moon, Robinson Crusoe* and *The Stolen Pie*.[21]

In 1905, the International Bioscope Company offered its bill of fare, with "less flickering than usually accompanies such pictures."[22] Later, the famous Vitagraph company arrived and featured Winette La Toura. The year ended with a full-length presentation of the famous fight between battling Nelson and Jimmy Britt for the lightweight championship of the world.

In 1906, just months after the April 18th earthquake in San Francisco, the Clark Bioscope Company offered its "miles of films" of the tragedy. During the next two years, various traveling companies presented motion pictures which were shown at Turn Verein Hall.

Then, in 1908, Sonora's first moving picture theater was

established by Emergy Girard and W. J. and F. J. Brenner of New York. It was apparent, even in the small town of Sonora, that moving pictures were the coming medium. A large comfortable theater was built on south Washington Street in 1917. It became known as the Sonora Theater.[23]

How well the audience received the new invention can be gleaned from the following quote from *The Banner*. "There is no place in Sonora equal to the moving picture show to give genuine and innocent pleasure to the people."[24] The following year *The Banner* wrote: "That the moving pictures continue to be the star attraction in this city is proven by the large audiences that attend each evening."[25]

In 1916, the first movie was made here, *The Half Breed*, with a cast that included Douglas Fairbanks. The film was based on a Bret Harte novel, *In the Carquinez Woods*. Wyatt Earp, heroic survivor of the famous shoot out at the OK Corral, made his appearance on the set.[26]

Hospitality shown to filmdom also began early. On July 4, 1919, the master, D.W. Griffith, appeared on stage at the Sonora Theater and made a very pleasing speech. He was presented with a gold nugget stick pin by Mr. Charles Segerstrom.[27] Tom Mix, one of the greatest movie legends of The West, often came to Sonora. On March 13, 1920, he was given a rousing reception at Jamestown after a card party given by the Native Daughters. *The Banner* noted that a fine buckskin was given to Mr. Mix and a gold nugget pin given to Mrs. Mix. A large banquet was served.[28] Another legend of The West, William S. Hart arrived in Sonora on October 10, 1919. He was filming *Sand* for Universal Studios.[29] To top it all off, Will Rogers, legend, icon, movie star, Ziegfeld Follies lead, and interpreter of American character, came to Sonora.[30]

In addition to the countryside with its lakes and streams and mountains, there was the famous Sierra Railroad. Built in 1897, its fifty-seven miles of track carried lumber products from high in the Sierras down to Oakdale in the valley below. In 1919, Universal Pictures arrived in Tuolumne County to film the final episodes of *The Red Glove*, a Perils-of-Pauline serial with a shoot-em-up and train robbery. As the Sierra's regular westbound passenger train left Sonora, the film company stopped it to shoot the train robbery. Permission had been requested in advance, and since there was no lengthy delay in the schedule, the railroad did not charge for it. However, the *Union Democrat* was prompted to note that it looked as if Tuolumne County would be a popular film location for awhile.[31] That would prove to be an understatement.

By the mid-1920's, a few of Sonora's businessmen began to realize that having motion picture companies in the county provided a big boost to the local economy. Begun at first as a gentleman's agreement, men like Irving Symons, one of the owners of Hales and Symons and Frank Davis, who owned a taxi service, joined forces to promote Sonora as a film location. They made sure that transportation and housing were provided for stars and extras in an orderly fashion. They also provided a service ensuring that the varieties of locations were made known to the film studios. The motto of Sonora was to serve hospitality and a warm welcome to the film community.[32]

Later, Frank Davis was succeeded by Henry Ruoff, a pharmacist who operated the location service from his Central Drugstore in downtown Sonora.[33] Ruoff had his friend Ernie Durham help him organize photo albums showing the county's diverse scenery.[34] They created a rate book that listed the cost of every possible element in a production from hotel rooms to horse rentals. By the late 1930's, Ernie Durham succeeded Ruoff as location contact and henceforth handled the job for over forty years.[35]

In 1937, this group decided its organization should be incorporated and known henceforth as the Sonora Motion Picture Association. Local businesses subscribed 5% of their gross sales, which financed the venture. Several other people offered their expertise in building supply, livestock, truck rentals, hotel, restaurants and other services. What began as a fledgling group developed into one of the oldest film organizations of its kind in California.[36]

Local people made as many as ten trips to Hollywood each year to meet with location managers from various film companies. For over fifty years the group continued to function and, in 1991, the Tuolumne County Visitor's Bureau became the officially-recognized California Film Commission liaison. In 1987, the Wild West Film Festival was launched. Each year it honors a particular actor or actress for his or her work.[37]

The county was responsible for launching the careers of many of filmdom's later-to-be legends: Henry Fonda, Janet Leigh, Marilyn Monroe and Grace Kelly. Over 400 films have been shot in Tuolumne County, spanning the silent era to the present.

And of course, there are stories. For example, there was the time when a mechanical part was desperately needed for the indispensable camera truck. Ernie Durham called everywhere to locate the part—the East Coast, Seattle, Los Angeles and San Francisco. The studio told Durham, "We don't care what you have to do to get the part, just get it! With the cost of shooting at $50,000 a day, the cost of finding the part is nothing."[38]

Jim Opie, Sr., operator of Opie's Garage told the studio he had found the part, but it was expensive, $75. "Do you still want it?" he asked. The studio tried to explain. "Look," they said, "If we can't get the part, we can't use the truck. If we can't use the truck, we can shoot around it for awhile, but it will cost a fortune to keep everyone waiting while the part arrives. We want that part now! Put it on an airplane, a chartered plane if necessary and fly it to Modesto. But get it!"[39] Then the weather closed in. Nothing was moving. So a taxi was hired and the part delivered to the set. Jim Opie, Sr. said he felt like a Hollywood Mogul ordering people around. But the shooting was right on schedule.

There was the story of Gary Cooper. It seems that the tall lanky "Coop" had a little too much to drink one night and at two a.m., lost his dentures in the toilet. Since he had to be ready for an early morning call the next day at five a.m., where could an extra set of teeth be located? Ernie Durham took "Coop" to the local funeral parlor where they looked over a basket of false teeth until they found a pair that fit. By six a.m. Cooper was on the set.[40]

Jeanette McDonald, sometimes known as the Iron Butterfly, was filming *Call of the Wild* in the 1930's. She insisted that she have silk sheets to sleep on each evening. The linen ones at the Sonora Inn simply would not do. Ernie Durham was dispatched to Turlock to pick up a set sent from Hollywood. When Ernie arrived back in Sonora, Ms. McDonald was pacing the lobby of the Sonora Inn, waiting for her sheets.[41]

But of all the stories one can find to write about, none can compare to the story of Ernie Durham's classic 1947 Desoto Chrysler. Ernie had been working with the movie industry in Sonora since the 1930's. A commercial photographer, he came to Sonora from Modesto in 1932 to photograph the mines and bring investors to the area. He got into motion pictures by taking photographs of movie sets whenever a production company came to town. Then, he began driving film stars around in 1935 when Will Rogers came to Sonora to film *The Country Gentleman*.[42]

In 1947, Ernie ordered from the Sonora Chrysler Corporation dealer, Ed Davis, a rare car: The DeSoto limousine, of which there were only 120 made between 1946 and 1948. There were lots of long wheelbase seven-passenger DeSotos made, but most were used as taxicabs. Few divided DeSoto limousines were built. In addition to the leather interior and divided window, Durham's limo shared its suspension with the eight-cylinder Chrysler and New Yorkers. It was a beautiful car, long and black, with a huge door to allow effortless entry and exit.[43]

This classic car was initiated on its maiden drive by Edward G. Robinson when *The Red House* was filmed in Tuolumne County in 1947. The famous bad guy and renown art collector loved the car. A tradition had begun.[44]

Another story involved eccentric billionaire Howard

Hughes. When *The Outlaw*, with vivacious Jane Russell was being shot, Durham was sent to San Francisco to pick up Hughes in the DeSoto. Finding him waiting at the prescribed place, he went to pick up his luggage and found two old weatherworn cardboard boxes tied up with rope sitting on the curb.[45]

Marilyn Monroe rode in the car when she made her first film, *Scudda Hoo, Scudda Hay*, a less than memorable film that would have faded into oblivion were it not for her subsequent legendary fame, established in such classics as *Gentlemen Prefer Blondes, The Seven Year Itch* and *Some Like It Hot*. Charlton Heston, Gregory Peck and Jean Simmons were driven in the DeSoto for the 1958 film *Big Country*. Barbara Stanwyck, Gary Cooper and Fred MacMurray were all chauffeured to the set in the car. Ronald Reagan rode in the car when making *Death Valley Days*. So too did Tony Curtis, Jack Lemmon and Natalie Wood, when filming *The Great Race*.[46]

One time, a transportation strike brought everything to a halt. Buses, trucks and airlines were not moving. This created a crisis for film crews on location. At the end of each day, it was mandatory that that day's shoot be sent to the lab to be processed and returned to the movie makers for the next day's filming. Ernie's 1947 DeSoto came to the rescue. At the end of each day, Durham would leave the Sierras bound for Hollywood with the day's filming in the back seat. In the wee hours of the morning, the processing would be finished and Durham would pick it up and leave for the Sierras. This went on every day for almost six weeks. And all of this driving was done over the old Grapevine route. It was so routine that the police along the way would wave at the DeSoto as it passed by them, twice each day.[47]

The television series, *The Little House on the Prairie*, was very popular in the Mother Lode. Residents especially liked Michael Landon. One day, he asked Ernie if he could take a ride in the DeSoto. For some reason, he had missed the opportunity, having been driven around in a Cadillac. He wanted to ride in the DeSoto. But, Ernie told him, "It's dirty." Michael asked

Ernie. "Where do you live?" Ernie told him "Ok, let's go to your house." Michael got out of the Cadillac and asked. "Where's the hose?" Landon washed the DeSoto down and said, "Now, I want a ride in that car tomorrow. You see," he explained to Ernie, "everyone from Dan Blocker to Lorne Green from *Bonanza* has ridden in that car, everyone except me. Now it's my turn." Landon got his wish.[48]

When Michael Landon became ill, Jim Opie, Sr. wrote him a letter. In it he explained that he was the last star to ride in the car and he wanted him to be the first when he got better. Unfortunately, Landon was unable to make the date.

The DeSoto turned its millionth mile in the early 60's. It had weathered seven engine rebuilds, one transmission replacement and one rear axle replacement. Jim Opie, Sr. did all of the restoring. One day, Jim got a call from Ernie Durham. "Come and pick up the car," Ernie told him matter-of-factly. "That's what he always did when it needed work," Opie recalled. Opie asked him, "What do you need done?" Ernie reached into his pocket and handed Jim the pink slip. He had been ill and he was worried about the fate of the old car. "It's yours," he told Jim. "I know you'll take care of it."[49]

Today, the beautiful black DeSoto resides in an honored place at Jim Opie, Sr.'s residence. "I wish the back seat of that car could talk," he said. "I wonder that our ears would burn."[50]

Footnotes

[1]Eadweard Muybridge, The Horse in Motion, (1878). English photographer, 1830-1904. Immigrated to the U.S. in 1852. In 1867, he accepted a commission to photograph surveys of the Pacific Coast. Along with J. D. Isaacs, Muybridge set up the now famous row of cameras with electrically operated shutters.

[2]Oscar Lewis, The Big Four, (1938). Leland Stanford, 1824-1893. Politician, one of the founders of the Central Pacific Railroad, successful merchant and Governor of California.

[3]Terry Burrows, Visual History of the Twentieth Century, (1999). Zoetrope: A device for giving an illusion of motion, consisting of a slitted drum that, when whirled, shows a succession of images placed opposite the slits within the drum as one moving image, 1865-70.

[4]Kinetoscope: An Edison invention where film passes behind a peephole for viewing by just one person. (Author).

[5]Edison held over 1,300 U.S. and foreign patents. However, Edison feared that a projected image would soon exhaust the novelty of moving pictures so he neglected working on the problems of projection. (Author).

[6]The first of these machines was eventually exported and from these, sprang the final development of motion pictures in England and Europe. (Author).

[7]In England, shortly after 1900, the Brighton School of film makers established themselves in the forefront of creative film making. However, the birth of the narrative film took place in 1903, when Edwin Porter, a director for Edison, presented *The Great Train Robbery.* That single reel contained all the seeds of modern editing techniques. (Author).

[8]Bruce Torrance, Hollywood, The First 100 Years, (1979), p. 71. Producers licensed by Edison formed the Motion Picture Patents Company or The Trust to safeguard their claims to film profits. The Trust included Edison's Vitagraph, Lubin, Selig, Essaney, Kalem, Pathe, and Milies.

[9]The original movie factories centered around New York. But as the disputes over patent rights flared, the tide moved to Santa Barbara, San Francisco and finally Hollywood, California. (Author).

[10]Los Angeles, the improbable city, had few natural resources. However, her one outstanding natural resource was the weather which proved to be a bonanza for the early film industry. (Author).

[11]Torrance, p. 68. With Selig, was cameraman-director Francis Boggs

and six actors and actresses who filmed on the beach at Santa Monica. They then moved to Colorado. However, the weather proved no more stable there than in Chicago and in 1909, the Selig Company returned to Los Angeles.

[12]ibid, p. 68.

[13]Torrance, p. 25. Hollywood, the film capital of the world began as the Rancho Los Feliz, a Spanish land grant of nearly 7,000 acres. It was in 1886, when Harvey Wilcox bought a 120 acre tract, that the small community was first platted. Daeida Wilcox named her Cahuenga Ranch "Hollywood" and in 1887, the legend was born.

[14]Torrance, p.73. D.W. Griffith's, Biograph Film Company moved from New York in 1908 and began making films on Sunset Boulevard. Here, his most spectacular and costly film, *Intolerance* was made in 1916.

[15]Janet Atkinson, Gold Rush Tales, (1997), p. 67.

[16]Carlo De Ferrari, "Tuolumne County's Movie Theatres," *Chispa*, Vol. 25, No. 3, p. 849.

[17]ibid.

[18]ibid.

[19]ibid.

[20]*Union Democrat*, January 1904.

[21]ibid.

[22]ibid.

[23]ibid.

[24]*The Banner,* November 4, 1910.

[25]*The Banner*, April 28, 1911.

[26]ibid.

[27]Larry Jensen, "Sierra on the Silver Screen," *Chispa,* Vol. 25.

[28]*The Banner,* July 4, 1919.

[29]*The Banner,* March 13, 1920.

[30]*Union Democrat,* October 10, 1919. Will Rogers filmed *The Country Gentleman* in Murphys in 1934. The Chamber of Commerce even got him to speak without pay!

[31]Jensen.

[32]Irving Symons, interview, August 10, 1998.

[33]Jensen.

[34]ibid.

[35]Jon G. Robinson, "Ernie Durham's million-mile '47 DeSoto was a Limo to the Stars." See also, *Old Cars News and Marketplace,* July 15, 1993, p. 22.

[36]Irving Symons interview.

[37]*Wild West Film Brochure*, September, 1992

[38]Interview with Jim Opie, Sr.

[39]ibid.

[40]ibid.

[41]ibid.

[42]Han Wingate, "Off Screen Kingpin," *Union Democrat,* September 23, 1988.

[43]Jon G. Robinson.

[44]ibid.

[45]ibid.

[46]ibid.

[47]Opie Interview.

[48]ibid.

[49]ibid.

[50]ibid.

*"Pictures are for entertainment,
messages should be delivered
by Western Union."*

— **SAM GOLDWYN**

Senator John Curtin

John Barry Curtin

The men and women who are our elected officials, today, seem a world apart in comparison to the rural, 19th century America into which John Curtin was born. But are they? The values in which that earlier world believed have not changed. I do see dramatic differences in technology. I see an agrarian society that has passed away like the dinosaurs. We live today in a global community, dictated by the economics of world markets. But in comparing the basic questions confronting legislators, the two worlds are surprisingly similar.

John Curtin was born in 1867 at Gold Springs, a small rural area in the Sierra Foothills.[1] Just two years before, the bloodiest war in our history had ended. When John was growing into manhood, Woodrow Wilson was completing his doctoral dissertation bemoaning the declining prestige of the Presidential office.[2] Organized labor was becoming a growing concern with strikes and picketing disrupting large cities.[3] There were obstacles of integrating Americans of African descent into the American mainstream which elicited heated debates.[4] Immigration resulting from the political turmoil in Europe created concern and fear among a predominately white, English speaking middle-class.[5] In the west, Indian wars were heating up.[6] The young nation, now a country joined from ocean to ocean, was on the brink of Imperialism.[7] American industry was creating a new class of wealthy men redefining the agrarian concepts which had defined an earlier American character.[8] And all the fundamental beliefs on which the American nation stood were being shaken to the core.[9] Fundamentally, the problems John faced were equal in significance to those we encounter today.

Tuolumne County seemed worlds away from many of these topical events. What concerned people was what was taking place in their own back yard. For Sonora and surrounding towns, that meant mining, agriculture and logging. Between 1900 and 1910, the population in the area had decreased from 11,166 to 9,979, while other counties witnessed triple digit growth.[10]

John's background was shaped by his Irish roots. His father was born in County Cork, Ireland in 1835. His family had fled the potato famine in 1846 and immigrated to America, arriving on the clipper ship, *The Sarah Perkins,* which had sailed to New York and then to Boston. He worked as a stagecoach driver, saved his money and paid for the passage of his mother, six sisters and two brothers. He married sixteen year-old Ann Cochran, also a native of Ireland.[11]

Soon thereafter, the news of the gold strike filtered into the Boston papers. Like thousands of other hopefuls, John's father set out for the gold fields in 1852. He entered the lumber business at Bodega Bay, above San Francisco, then went to Fiddletown, Drytown and Columbia, settling at Gold Springs.[12] He and a partner, Thomas Reed, accumulated capital of $18,000, but, unfortunately, they were enticed to loan money to a water ditch company which failed. In 1860, he entered the lucrative business of teaming and transporting freight.[13] A few years later, John was born.

Like other boys of his era, taking the time to acquire an education amounted to a luxury. He was needed to work on the ranch. However, John studied in his spare time. During the winter, he drove freight wagons between Oakdale and Sonora. He developed a love of the land, enhanced immeasurably the first time he saw the Yosemite Valley. The beautiful vistas were sheer magic. An area almost unheard of then, it fascinated the young boy and marked the beginning of a love affair which

Gold Springs, originally called Green Flat Diggins, on Parrots Ferry Road north of Columbia, dates back to 1852. The Miners and Businessman's Directory *of 1856 states that the camp then had a population of 500 citizens and boasted two stores, two boarding houses and a number of mechanic shops. The Bowling Alley Saloon was added two years later. The small boomtown never got very big because Columbia, a town of significant size in those days, was just over a half-mile away. This sketch depicting Gold Springs during the 1850s was drawn by artist Bruce Bomberger after conducting careful research of the area.*

would continue for the rest of his life. It was also to be the beginning of another quest which directed John's attention toward an injustice which he tried to remedy.

In 1864, President Lincoln had signed a law whereby Yosemite Valley and the Mariposa Big Tree Grove were granted to the State of California with the stipulation that "these premises shall be held for public use, resort and recreation...inalienable for all time."[14]

Fifteen years later, in 1879, John's parents purchased the 1,280 acre Cloudman ranch in western Tuolumne County where they raised cattle. They also leased land at Crane's Flat near The Yosemite Valley, where Curtin spent his summers. Curtin remembered it well. "I saw the Yosemite Valley first on the twelfth day of June, 1882, and if I live until June next, I will see it again."[15]

In 1890, Congress finally heeded the pleas of preservationist, John Muir and others and reserved and withdrew from settlement a large area of forested and mountainous land surrounding the Yosemite Valley Grant.[16] However, this divided authority inherent in an enclosed state park inevitably raised questions regarding the private property rights of those who resided there. For young John Curtin, the ensuing litigation would form a life long distrust of Government and shape the path he would take as a man.

John's father was already active in local politics. He served as a delegate to the Tuolumne County Democratic Convention.[17] So it would seem natural for the young son to follow in his father's footsteps. He apprenticed himself to a local attorney, E. A. Rodgers of Tuolumne County. In just a few months he had absorbed enough legal knowledge to pass a test administered by Rodgers which would enable him to practice law before the local bench. That same month he was elected District Attorney. While his formal education had ended, his political career was just beginning. He served two years as District Attorney and returned to private practice. In 1896, he was elected to the State Senate.[18] In 1897, he married Lucy Shaw and resided in a beautiful new home built on Columbia Way in Sonora, designed by Sonora's own architect, Clarence Ayers.[19]

During this same period, disturbing changes were occurring in Yosemite. Preservationists, like John Muir, deplored the destruction of the land when it was placed under private ownership, since the land was then typically developed. Muir maintained that this resulted in the loss of watershed, of timber and of the natural beauty of the place. His vocal stand was reflected in the creation of the Yosemite National Reserve.[20] The rules governing the new land, however, opened a Pandora's Box which inevitably pitted private property rights against those of the park and the Federal Government that administered it.

For three decades the land within the new Reserve had been

utilized by local people for hunting, fishing and stock raising.[21] Their rights, however, were about to be challenged. That conflict came with the arrival of the Fourth U.S. Cavalry, which was ordered to enforce the Reserve's rules and regulations. For cattlemen like the Curtins who owned patented lands lying within the park, the new laws meant that they were now forbidden to drive their stock without the permission of the military commander and the first acting park superintendent, Captain Abram E. Wood.[22] A confrontation was bound to erupt.

Soldiers began the practice of expelling the owners' herds of cattle on one side of the Reserve and then turning their flocks loose on the opposite side. It was a disaster. The first major rift occurred for John in 1893, when he requested to be allowed to drive his cattle through the park to his patented lands. His request was denied. Officials were concerned that the cattle might graze on Reserve land, so troops refused to let any ranchers cross the lands with their herds or graze their cattle on unfenced land adjacent to the federal reserve. John made a second request and this too was denied. Then he heard that troops patrolling the park had the authority to enter a man's home, set fire to it, take his cattle, remove them and even shoot them if necessary.[23] John felt this was fundamentally unjust and was contrary to everything he had learned about his government and the U.S. Constitution.

Sometime during this period, while herding his cattle to winter pasture, he was stopped by park officials and told to turn back. This infuriated Curtin. "If there is one right of American citizens that American blood was sacrificed for it was for full and free enjoyment of property rights."[24] The battle lines were drawn.

In 1894, Curtin was told by Captain G.H. Gale that some of his cattle had been picked up while in the park and driven from the Reserve. Captain Gale warned, "further disregard of the regulation will result in your property being put off the premises."[25] In 1895, still another altercation resulted and again Curtin was told "you have no right to have them [cattle] here."[26]

In July 1905, Curtin filed suit against Captain Benson, now Yosemite Park Superintendent. The case was transferred to the U.S. Circuit Court of the northern district of California.[27] The circuit court decided in favor of Captain Benson and Curtin immediately filed an appeal to the United States Supreme Court. In defending his stand, Curtin made one of the most powerful and emotional speeches ever heard in Washington D.C.

"I stand here, as a citizen, who is also a property owner, but under military law, I was not permitted to go to my own home. I was told," Curtin pleaded "that the Government has the right to confiscate my property and my only redress was in a court of law."[28]

John went on to describe another encounter that took place between a private citizen and the government in the park, which sent troops into a man's home. "They piled everything he owned together and set fire to it and the barn. But they were not finished. They then proceeded to take out every hoof of cattle and drive them over the Sierra Mountains, and those not strong enough, they shot. Do you think," John asked, "that I have a right to say that I don't want military rule in the Yosemite Valley?"[29]

John cited the government's harsh stand in enforcing fishing licenses. "One man," he explained, "walked with his hands tied behind him, forty miles because he did not have a license. Yet, there was not a single sign to inform a human being whether he was in the park or not. Is this the way you want people who visit Yosemite to be treated? We have had military rule long enough."[30] Quoting from legal precedents since the foundation of the Republic, the Senator from Tuolumne argued that "no bill should be passed that would force one man into court to protect his property rights."[31]

On November 20, 1911, the Supreme Court reversed their prior decision and found that, "the Department of the Interior had no right to make or enforce any rules respecting the use of private property within the State of California."[32]

The victory catapulted "Constitutional John" as he was now called, into a bid for Governorship of the State of California.

Curtin's record as a senator, was a distinguished one. He introduced a bill into the state constitution which would curtail the megalithic Southern Pacific, by a series of reforms. Unfortunately, the railroad proved too powerful. He would, however, continue to fight the railroad to equalize its financial obligation to the state.[33]

Senator Curtin introduced several bills to create an office for an Inspector of Mines. The bills failed, but they showed Curtin's concern for the working man.[34] In 1910, as a result of Curtin's work, a new tax system became the first amendment to the California Constitution. The intent of this amendment was implemented to end state dependence upon property tax and to assure that public utilities, including the Southern Pacific, long protected, contribute their fair share.

The climax of Curtin's political career came in 1914. He won the Democratic nomination for Governor. Hiram Johnson, a Progressive, had the backing of former President Theodore Roosevelt.[35] The campaign was, like most political forays, an arena of charges and counter-charges. It was made more confusing to the voters because of the new method of choosing candidates at open primary elections. It was a contest between Progressive Hiram Johnson, Republican John Fredericks, and Democrat J. Curtin.

Curtin was concerned with preserving the two-party system. Hiram Johnson believed that votes should represent all classes and all political affiliations.[36] Curtin did not kiss babies, but he gave demonstrations during the campaign of his ability to hitch a team of horses.[37]

Right from the start, however, Curtin was hampered by a lack of campaign funds. Also, Woodrow Wilson was noticeably silent, withholding his support for John until three days prior to the election.[38]

The election results were: Hiram Johnson, 460,495 votes. Fredericks, 271,990, and Curtin 116,121.[39]

After his unsuccessful bid for California's highest office, Curtin returned to Sonora. He continued to work on his ranch and to visit his beloved Yosemite.

He had good reason to be proud. His career was one marked with outstanding achievements. Perhaps his crowning legislative achievement was his authorship of Constitutional Amendment Number 1, by which the corporations of the State were required to pay for the upkeep of elementary schools. He also made sure that the public utilities paid their share of the cost of state government. He completed Highways 108 and 140 and opened Yosemite Valley to automobiles. Most of all, during a time of rampant corruption, he was called "the cleanest Democrat in the state."[40]

Curtin died at his Sonora ranch May 18, 1925. He was a man governed by ethical canons from which he never wavered. These are qualities that seem, unfortunately, all too rare today.[41]

Footnotes

[1]Representative Citizens of Northern California, Standard Genealogical Publishing Co., 1901.

[2]Woodrow Wilson, Congressional Government: A Study in American Politics, Boston, (1883).

[3]John Peter Altegeld, The Chicago Martyrs, San Francisco. (1899).

[4]Blair Lewis, The Prosperity of the South Dependent Upon Elevation of the Negro, Virginia, (1889).

[5]Josiah Strong, The Superiority of the Anglo-Saxon Race, Our Country, New York. (1885).

[6]Theodore Roosevelt, The Winning of the West, (1910).

[7]Henry Cabot Lodge, "Our Blundering Foreign Policy," Forum, 1895.

[8]Ida M. Tarbell, The History of the Standard Oil Company, New York, (1904).

[9]William Benton, *The Annals of America,* Vol. 11, 12, 1968.

[10]Allan Masri, *Constitutional John: The Life and Times of John Curtin*, Senior Thesis 1981, p. 4.

[11]Patrick Dowling, Genealogical File Museum, Clippings.

[12]John M. Curtin, Letter, Tuolumne County Museum Archives, "Curtin" File. Like William Murphy, a great many Irish had gathered in the Columbia area.

[13]Carlo De Ferrari, "Preserving the Mountain Heritage," *Chispa,* Vol. 29. No. 3, January-March 1990.

[14]J. B. Curtin, Speech in the Senate of California, 36th Session. January 25, 1905, p. 5.

[15]ibid.

[16]John Muir, Mountains of California, 2 Vols. Boston, (1917).

[17]Masri, p.11.

[18]ibid. "Although Curtin received no more than an elementary school education, he was reputed to be one of the best-read men in California." "Heart Attack Ends Life of Senator Curtin." *San Francisco Chronicle*, May 19, 1925.

[19]The house still stands today as beautiful as the day it was built. See Chapter on Clarence Ayers.

[20]Muir.

[21]De Ferrari.

[22]ibid.

[23]Curtin, speech.

[24]ibid.

[25]De Ferrari.

[26]ibid.

[27]ibid.

[28]Curtin, speech.

[29]ibid, p. 5.

[30]ibid.

[31]ibid, p. 35.

[32]De Ferrari.

[33]Franklin Hickborn, Story of the Session of the California Legislature of 1911, San Francisco, (1911), p. 41.

[34]State of California. Journal of the Senate, 33rd Session, Sacramento, 1899, p. 515

[35]Hickborn.

[36]ibid.

[37]Masri, *Constitutional John: The Life and Times of John Curtin.*

[38]Franklin Hickborn, "The Party, the Machine, and the Vote," *California Historical Society Quarterly* 39-1:21-24, March 1939, p. 24.

[39]Hickborn, p. 24.

[40]Senator Curtin represented Mariposa, Merced, Stanislaus and Tuolumne Counties in Sacramento in the 22nd, 34th, and 40th Sessions, 1899, 1901, 1903 and 1913. California State Library. California History Room.

[41]Henry Diamond, Land Use in America, (1996), p. 295. "The close of the 20th Century bears witness to the increasing tension between private property rights and Government regulation."

"History teaches us that men and nations behave wisely once they have exhausted all other alternatives."

— **ABBA EBAN**

Brubeck

Dave Brubeck

The roots of Dave Brubeck's childhood home lie along the historic Highway 49, just past Jackson and approximately five miles beyond Sutter Creek. This was not one of the important "gold towns" of the Mother Lode. Before deciding upon the name, Ione, the community went through a hosts of other titles. There were Bedbug, Ricky Ville, Freeze Out, Hardscrabble and Woosterville.[1]

In the year 2002, the town still seems caught in a 19th century time-warp. There are no major shopping centers and the population stands at 7,204. Dominating the town is an impressive landmark, the Preston Castle, a correctional institution which dates from the 1860's.[2] In a recent television Public Broadcasting program featuring Dave Brubeck, he nostalgically recalled waking up in his home in Ione and seeing the castle from his bedroom window.

It is hard to believe that a major jazz innovator such as Dave Brubeck had his origins here. I was to learn, however, that the career of Dave Brubeck is anything but conventional. He has been described as extremely individualistic, obstinate, stubborn, moral, and as naïve as a cub scout.[3] According to *Time Magazine*, "Brubeck is as untypical in the jazz field as a harp in a Dixieland combo."[4] All the facts of Brubeck's biography work against the logic of more stereotyped images of jazz life. Most jazz musicians, for example, flourish in the heart of large metropolitan cities. Jazz was born after all in New Orleans. Yet

Brubeck's musical development was totally divorced from any urban environment. A second observation about jazz musicians is that they find their own unique style in the ambiance of the nightclub scene, hearing and playing with other musicians. Brubeck's music, on the contrary, has strong classical roots. He flourished in an academic environment. His rise to fame also defies all the rules. Without the benefit of press agents or public relations campaigns, he soared to popularity on the strength of music that was not designed for mass public consumption.[5] Ted Giolia, in *West Coast Jazz Magazine*, noted that "No figure associated with the West Coast Jazz is better known than Brubeck and no West Coast musician has been more controversial than Dave Brubeck."[6]

Born in Concord, California, on December 6, 1920, Dave Brubeck moved from the Bay Area community with his family to a 45,000 acre ranch near Ione in 1932. His father, Howard Peter Brubeck, attended Polytechnic Business College in Oakland and went into business running a slaughter house and butcher shop.[7] In 1907, he married Elizabeth Ivey of Concord. They seemed to be complete opposites. She was cultured, intensely musical and sophisticated. Pete was a "rough and tough cowboy, a perfect example of the great American westerner."[8] He was also an expert roper, one of the best in the state, a skill he taught Dave.[9] His mother, "Bessie," longed to be a concert pianist. When Dave was in first grade, she went to England to study with Tobias Matthay and Dame Myra Hess. She also tried to complete her college degree, attending Berkeley and the University of Idaho. Events were to intervene. Dave was just twelve when his father was hired as a ranch manager for the H. Moffitt Rancho Arroyo Seco in Ione. In spite of the move, his mother continued to play. With five pianos in the home, she gave lessons and recitals in her studio. More importantly, she trained all her five sons to know and love music.[10] She was also adamant about the kind of music the children could listen to. No radio or phonograph playing was allowed. "Any music heard in her home should be created by the people within it."[11]

Upon graduation from high school, Dave opted for a career in Veterinary Science. He wanted to please his father who had given him four cows when he was eight and called Dave "his partner." "I was the last hope for the cattle business," Dave recalled. " I worked at it and enjoyed it."[12] Dave points out, however, that his father wanted his sons to be whatever they wanted to be. "He was enough of a man that he didn't need his sons to prove him."[13] Dave also protested his mother's music lessons. "Ma, you've got two musicians. I want to be a cattle-man."[14] Yet, Dave could not keep away from the ivory keys.

Entering the College of the Pacific in Stockton as a Pre-Med Veterinary student, Dave learned that his early upbringing on the piano and cello were simply too deeply ingrained. He had composed music by the age of four and he could play all the other students' piano lessons by ear. By five, he was improvising themes on his own.[15] At thirteen, he "began working with local dance bands, playing everything from hill-billy to two beat, to swing piano styles."[16]

In 1939, the Science Building and the Music Conservatory at the College were not that far apart. As the strains of music floated across the lawn to the science lab, Dave found it irresistible. He tried for a year to pursue his classes in science, but even his instructor could tell his mind was not on his work. One day, as Dave was trying to dissect a frog, his instructor said. "Dave, your heart is not with these formaldehyde frogs. Why don't you go across the lawn where you belong."[17] The die was cast and Dave never looked back.

The fact that he didn't read music, almost put his musical career at an end. Born cross-eyed, he wore glasses from the time he was in the cradle. He got around the problem early when he learned to compose music which his mother then wrote down for him. He could play almost anything he heard for the first time. Here, as elsewhere, Dave was destined to break the rules. In the music department at college, however, this inability to read music was justifiable reason to remove Dave from the school. Dr. Bodley told the faculty, "You're going to kick out one of the most talented kids in the Conservatory."[18] "If it weren't for him," Dave remembered. "I would never have gotten through school."[19] Everyone seemed to recognize Dave's talent.

One of the assignments in class, for example, was to harmonize a melody by Mozart. Eight or ten students produced trite versions. Then Dave sat down at the piano. "He rocked Mozart right out of the window."[20] How did he handle this problem of not being able to read music later? "I faked it good enough so they [bands] didn't know, and I didn't tell them."[21] While he never became a prolific music reader, he learned to write music and compose vocal works as well as complex scores for large groups of instruments.[22]

Dave lived in the era of swing. The music could be heard everywhere. Benny Goodman's *"Lets Dance"* was broadcast coast-to-coast in the 1930's. And, while Ione was not exactly the center of the musical universe, there were bands in Jackson, Angels Camp and Mokelumne Hill. This was an era when everyone wanted to dance and dance halls sprang up everywhere. He got gigs with professional musicians while still a teenager. It provided great experience and helped him to work his way through college. "Dave existed by playing piano at night and attending classes by day."[23] He began to spend every free hour "jamming" with other music students. He and his two roommates moved into a cellar apartment which they named, "The Bomb Shelter." It subsequently housed a continual jam session.[24] By his senior year in college, he had gained recognition for his advanced harmonies and individual style.

There was also a weekly campus radio show coordinated by a young and vivacious sophomore named Iola Whitlock.[25] She was an exceptional woman. When she graduated from Shasta High School, she walked away with more top honors than any other graduate. One of her short stories, *"The Tiger Kite,"* was included in the "Best Short Stories of 1946."[26] Named the "Most Outstanding High School Girl" by the Daughters of the

American Revolution and elected President of the honor society, Iola won accolades before she became a coed at the College of The Pacific.

Dave proposed to the young student under a doorway at the college. She sent her sorority sisters the following telegram: "Dave and I met in April. Engaged in May, romanced all summer. Been married in one day."[27]

Soon thereafter, Dave began studying music under the French composer Darius Milhaud, an instructor at Mills College since 1941. One of Dave's brothers was Milhaud's assistant for seven years and that may have provided the connection which first introduced Dave to Milhaud.[28] These lessons were, however, interrupted by the call of Uncle Sam and World War II. While stationed at Camp Haan and still in uniform, he managed to get a week-end pass to study with the famous Arnold Schoenberg in Los Angeles.[29] Dave recalled that things did not progress very well. The first lesson was just an introductory thing, as he described it. In the second lesson, he wrote something. Schoenberg wanted to have an explanation for every note. Dave explained, "because it sounds good."[30] That apparently was not good enough for Schoenberg. Dave asked him, "Why did he think he was the man who should determine the new music?" Schoenberg shouted back. "Because I know more than any man alive about music."[31]

Sent to Normandy, ninety days after D-Day, Dave was assigned to the front lines near Metz in France. This was the worst possible place to be. German forces were gearing up for a major assault. The casualty list for Americans was very high. Also, Dave had deep scruples about being in a position of taking a life. "I resolved never to have a cartridge in my gun."[32] Fate intervened. Minutes before being sent to the front, the area commander selected Dave to lead a band which he had organized.[33] After the end of World War II, Dave led his own band accompanying U.S. tours through France and Germany.

Upon his return from the war, Dave headed back to work with Darius Milhaud at Mills College. From 1946 to 1948, he worked with the noted music instructor, earning a master's degree.[34] He continued as a private student under the master's tutelage for another year. Milhaud was Dave Brubeck's "single most important influence."[35] Dave was at the crossroads when he began studying with Milhaud. "Stick with jazz," Milhaud told Dave just at the moment when his young protege was not at all sure he wanted to continue to play jazz. Milhaud was exploring the possibilities of utilizing American Jazz for symphonic use and he may have recognized in Brubeck's work a unique talent for achieving that goal.

Milhaud was also a master of polytonality, the technique of writing in two or more keys at once.[36] Dave may have picked up his initial interest in this on his ranch in Ione. Carl Nisei, from the Brubeck Institute at the University of the Pacific, related the following story: "On the ranch in Ione, Dave had to turn the well water on and he heard the plop plop of the horse and the water. The sound was different, an odd number of harmonic rhythms, hence his ability to hear sounds in more than one key."[37]

With Milhaud's instruction and his mother's classical training, Dave's innovative style began to take shape. Brubeck worked with block chords and carefully organized single-note lines, spiced with rhythmic variations that matched the melodic and harmonic divisions of his writing and playing. His ideas sprang from Johann Sebastian Bach, Art Tatum, Duke Ellington, Milhaud and his own fertile mind.[38] Dave would always defy conventional wisdom, never quite fitting into the predictable mold of what typically defined a jazz musician.

While Brubeck was at Mills, Jimmy Lyons, a disc-jockey on KNBC in San Francisco, heard a Brubeck 1948 concert. He liked what he heard and he asked the young musician to appear on his show. What began as a two-week date was extended to six months. Brubeck's career was launched.[39]

In 1950, Dave organized the Dave Brubeck Trio, the forerunner of the famous Brubeck Quartet which would make jazz history. When Dave appeared at the famous Black Hawk Jazz Club in San Francisco, he brought about a renaissance of jazz in that city which stood at the forefront of the Progressive Movement in jazz. No one else associated with West Coast Jazz is better known today than Dave Brubeck.

In 1952, he went east. In one of New York's basement dens, Brubeck's Quartet gave the east an earful.[40] "His harmonies are complex, built up to a pulsing climax. Brubeck often plays in two keys at once before he wrings his idea dry and the music subsides."[41] Dave explained, "When I play jazz, I am influenced by classical music; when I compose, I am influenced by jazz."[42]

In 1954, Dave made a clean sweep of both the *Metronome* All-Star Poll and the Downbeat Poll with his quartet, deposing George Shearing's quintet, defeating such jazz greats as *Louis Armstrong's All Stars, Garry Mulligan's Quartet* and *Benny Goodman's Sextet.* This formally established Dave Brubeck as the number one jazz combo in the United States."[43] Like the Pulitzer prize for literature, Dave won a tremendous vote of confidence when he was featured on the cover of *Time* magazine in 1954, the second jazz musician up to that time to be so honored.[44] In a matter of just five years, his fans had grown from a small West Coast clique to a coast-to-coast phenomena. He played Carnegie Hall, Los Angeles' Zardi's, Boston's Storyville and Manhattan's Basin Street.[45]

Dave's most outstanding contribution to jazz is his attempt to show that it is potentially as great as symphonic music. "Critics who place jazz geographically are like Puritans," Dave said. "The Puritans came here for religious freedom and ended up putting people in stocks."[46] George Avakian, eastern director of Columbia's popular album department and the man who convinced Brubeck to sign with Columbia Records said of Dave Brubeck. "He differs from everyone in the field. He's completely in a class by himself. I don't know of anyone quite like him."[47] Added to this enigma is the fact that Brubeck enjoys lasting popularity. Decades have passed since he was on the cover of *Time*, yet he continues to sell well and pack concert halls all over the world.

In February 2001, I attended the University of The Pacific's week long celebration and tribute to Dave Brubeck. When I walked into the Faye Spanos Concert Hall, a very youthful white-haired, eighty year-old musician was answering questions directed to him by members of the audience. A young man walked to the microphone and asked. "Why were you different, what were the things that shaped you?" Dave remained silent for a moment then responded, "You take what you are born with and you do your best."[48]

Dave's best has spawned awards from all over the world. President William Clinton awarded Dave the Presidential Medal of the Arts in 1995. In the spring of 1996, Dave was inducted into the International Jazz Hall of Fame and in 1999, the National Endowment for the Arts presented him with the Jazz Master's Award. In May 2000, the California Library Association recognized Dave's accomplishments by presenting him with their California Gold Medal Award. He has a star on the Hollywood Walk of Fame. He holds honorary doctorate degrees from six American Universities and one from the University of Duisburg in Germany. The French Government has cited him for his contribution to the arts. World tours have made him one of America's foremost goodwill ambassadors. He has performed before eight United States Presidents, nobility and Pope Paul II.[49] For a young musician who could not read music, Dave Brubeck has done rather well.

Footnotes

[1]Erwin G. Gudde, California Gold Camps, (1975), p. 331. The name Ione dates back to Greek mythology and is mentioned in *The Last Days of Pompeii.* Bulwer Lytton.

[2]John F. Lafferty, Preston School of Industry: A Centennial History 1894-1994, (1997). There are plans to restore the castle to its former grandeur. Tom Shone of Ione heads this project.

[3]Jimmy Lyons, "What's With Dave Brubeck," *Theme*, October 1953.

[4]"The Man on Cloud 7," *Time*, November 8, 1954, p. 70.

[5]Ted Gioia, "West Coast Jazz," *Modern Jazz in California 1945-1960.* University of California Press, p. 68.

[6]ibid, p. 66.
[7]*Amador Progress News*, January, 24, 1954.

[8]Fred Hall, It's About Time: The Dave Brubeck Story, University of Arkansas Press, p.6.

[9]ibid, p. 7. Dave's mother fought constantly to protect Dave's hands, and he was forbidden to practice some dangerous roping techniques.

[10]Conversation with Dr. Donald Walker at University of the Pacific. June 13, 2001. All six children followed musical careers. Howard became a composer and conductor. His work was performed in 1959 by the San Diego Symphony. Henry became a music instructor in Santa Barbara.

[11]Barry Ulanov, "Dave Brubeck," *Metronome*, March 1952, p. 17. According to Dr. Walker, Iola insisted that French be spoken at the dinner table. Conversation, June 13, 2001.

[12]Dave Brubeck, Archival Collection at University of The Pacific. "An Evening With Dave Brubeck," 1954.

[13]Hall, *It's All About Time*, p. 10

[14]"The Man on Cloud 7," *Time.*

[15]Barry Ulanov, *Metronome*, 1952.

[16]ibid.

[17]Dave Brubeck Concert, Friday, February 2, 2001

[18]Gioia, *West Coast Jazz*, p. 71.

[19]ibid, p. 71.

[20]ibid, p. 82.

[21]Hall, *It's all about Time*, p. 12.

[22]*Home Companion*, April 15, 1955.

[23]ibid.

[24]"Shasta High's Top Student Marries a Celebrity," *Record Searchlight*, May 1, 1956. Iola was well known for her work in debate, theater and radio. She was on the staff of the *Pacific Weekly* in Stockton.

[25]"Iola Whitlock Marries Dave Brubeck," *Pacific Weekly,* September 25, 1942. They were married in Carson City, Nevada.

[26]Dave Brubeck Collection, University of The Pacific

[27]Arnold Schoenberg taught at U.C.L.A. Schoenberg Hall bears his name.

[28]"Dave Brubeck," *Downbeat*, January 27, 1950.

[29]ibid.

[30]*Time*, November 8, 1954.

[31]"Dave Brubeck, What Makes Him Tick," *Downbeat*, August 8, 1957.

[32]Gioia, *West Coast Jazz*, p. 74. Mills College was a woman's college, but, for patriotic reasons, the college agreed to accept G.I.'s in certain fields of study.

[33]Hall*, It's About Time,* p. 99.

[34]Dave Brubeck Collection, University of The Pacific.

[35]Carl Nisei, interview, February 2001.

[36]Ulanov, *Metronome*, 1952.

[37]ibid.

[38]"Subconscious Pianist," *Time*, November 10, 1952.

[39]ibid.

[40]ibid.

[41]Ralph J. Gleason, "Dave Brubeck," *San Francisco Chronicle,* Vol. 17, No. 31. April 18, 1954.

[42]Louis Armstrong was the first jazz musician to be so honored.

[43]*Time*, November 1954.

[44]Dave Brubeck Collection, University of The Pacific.

[45]"Inside Dave Brubeck," *Record Whirl*, May 1955.

[46]Dave played his now legendary *"Take Five."* The Brubeck Festival, February 1-3, 2001.

[47]Brubeck Collection, University of The Pacific.

[48]ibid.

[49]ibid.

Business Directory

(Kindly Support Our Advertisers)

Columbia House
RESTAURANT
est. 1850
(209) 532-5134
Proprietors
Russ & Nancy Moreton
Main Street
Columbia State Park
P.O. Box 1297
Columbia, CA 95310

WRIGHT SISTERS
TaR
FLAT
ANTIQUES
Marianne Wright Levine
81 S. Washington Street
Sonora, CA 95370
STORE 209.533-2520
HOME 209.532-3857

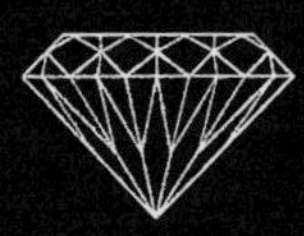

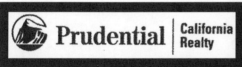

Biography

About the Author

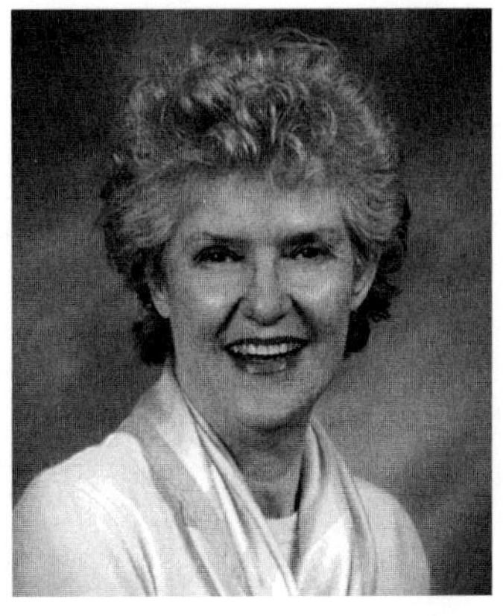

Janet I. Atkinson, native southern Californian, attended U.C.L.A. and Cal State Northridge with degrees in Art History and History. She wrote *Los Angeles County Historic Directory* in '88, followed by *Gold Rush Tales* in '97. Janet has written for the *Society of Architectural Historians*, *Los Angeles* magazine, *Elan* magazine, *Treasure, Chispa Historic Quarterly*, *Central Sierra Seasons* magazine and many more.

About the Artists

Wendell Dowling is a native southern Californian. "I never wanted to be anything but an artist for as long as I can remember." He attended Santa Paula High School, illustrated for countless engineering design firms, advertising agencies, books, magazines, airports and even comic strips. A free lance artist since 1974, his offices are at the Santa Paula Airport where he designed the first phase of the new Aviation Museum. His breathtaking murals grace the town of Santa Paula.

Chris Holman is a local artist and preservationist. She was born in Sonora and graduated from Chouinard's Art School in Los Angeles.

Mary Jane Reeb was born in San Francisco, and is a local Sonora photographer.

Please COPY THIS FORM and fill out and mail with your order.

ORDER FORM

- FOR -

MORE Colorful Men & Women of the Mother Lode

(Pre-order or until edition is sold out)

PRICE: $16.95 plus
$1.22 CA Sales Tax
plus Shipping & Handling charge of
$3.95 within the Continental US:

TOTAL PER BOOK: $22.12

PLEASE SEND MY BOOK(S) TO:

Name:______________________________

Address:______________________________

City________________State______Zip________

Send check or money order made out to:
Jan Irene Publications
P.O. Box 934
Sonora, CA 95370

For more information or questions,
call Jan Atkinson at (209) 532-2470 or
e-mail: janirene@mlode.com

Please COPY THIS FORM and fill out and mail with your order.